AF531307

Hospitality Marketing and Sales

HOSPITALITY MARKETING AND SALES

Ruchi Mehta

CENTRUM PRESS
NEW DELHI-110002 (INDIA)

CENTRUM PRESS

H.O.: 4360/4, Ansari Road, Daryaganj,
New Delhi-110002 (India)
Tel: 23278000, 23261597, 23255577, 23286875

B.O.: No. 1015, Ist Main Road, BSK IIIrd Stage,
IIIrd Phase, IIIrd Block, Bengaluru-560085 (INDIA)
Tel: 080-41723429

Email: centrumpress@gmail.com
Visit us at: www.centrumpress.com

Hospitality Marketing and Sales

First Edition, 2013

ISBN 978-93-81293-98-0

PRINTED IN INDIA

Printed at Balaji Offset, Delhi.

Contents

Preface

The best way to start selecting a niche market is to define who your best clients are. What industry are they in? How tightly can you define that market? What size is the company either in dollar sales or number of employees? What geographic region are they in? Next, look at your competitive advantages to analyse what you do best. What product or service do you provide that your competitors can't? What vertical market is not being serviced well by your competition?

Once these questions are answered you can search for prospects that match those criteria and then target your marketing to that niche market. You will be highlighting the competitive advantage that you identified in your sales pitch as well as your advertising. Please keep in mind that this doesn't mean that you won't accept business outside of that niche, it just means that you won't invest marketing dollars to solicit that business. By targeting your sales and advertising dollars your return on investment will be much greater.

These questions may appear obvious, and there is little doubt that you have identified what sets you apart in terms of your product, service, pricing, customer care, etc. However, if your marketing and communications materials do not immediately answer these questions, your prospect is left asking himself, why would I take a chance on a new supplier? Having said that, not all your ads have to communicate every conceivable benefit of your service offerings.

Remember, that some ads are meant only to introduce or strengthen a brand, while others are designed to develop a clear preference in the minds of prospects. What is does mean is that your overall communication strategy with your prospects has to clearly identify and then support your benefit claims. Once your prospect can clearly see that it's in her best interest to take a serious look at your product or service, you are now well into the sales cycle and on your way to winning a new client.

In order to grow your marketshare you need to be actively prospecting for new clients, yet sales reps often fail to conduct this important activity, and as their base of existing customers eventually shrinks over time, so does your company's revenue. Set a goal that you want to achieve each week for business development, including the number of brand new prospects to be called and appointments to be made. Schedule time for prospecting into your calendar every week. If you don't allot a specific time for this important task, it won't get done.

This book has over all covered a new ideal in this subject so it is useful for students.

—Author

1

Defining Hospitality

The world as we know it today exists as testimony to, and evidence of, the fact that people travel. Early patterns of travel were fundamentally directed by basic human needs (finding food and shelter), exchange (trade), relationships with natural phenomena (developing new settlements, escaping droughts or floods etc.) and as a result of conquest and conflict (occupation, expulsion, forced migration and re-settlement).

Such factors still exert considerable influence on a large proportion of the world's population today, with contemporary pilgrimage routes relatively easy to identify, frequently building on established trading relationships and patterns of diaspora and relocation.

From the late seventeenth and well into the twentieth century, motivations such as curiosity, education and social betterment took over as 'essential' travel evolved into discretionary leisure travel, gradually moving from a pursuit of the social elite of the developed world, to a widespread activity of the masses of the developed world, supported by a highly complex network of support structures and services.

It is all too easy to dismiss contemporary international tourism as a leisure activity somehow separate and below more 'worthy' social practices. As a leisure activity, tourism is carried out in 'leisure time', as a temporary discretionary activity, and as a form of 'reward' for, or counter to, daily work. However, the value of tourism cannot be solely judged in terms of the hedonistic recompense it brings to the individual. Nor can its value be solely expressed in relation to the economic benefits that it can undoubtedly generate. Tourism is centred on the fundamental principles of exchange between peoples and is both an expression and experience of culture. Tourism is cultural, and its practices and structures are very much an extension of the normative cultural framing from which it emerges. As such it has a vital part to play in helping us to understand ourselves, and the multilayered relationships between humanity and the material and non-material world we occupy.

Introduction: The Early Years

Travel In the Middle Ages

Travel in the Middle Ages was either on land or by water.

Rich people sometimes travelled in covered wagons. They must have been very uncomfortable as they did not have suspension and roads were bumpy and rutted. Others travelled on a box between two poles. Two horses, one in front and one behind carried it. They were trained to walk at the same pace.

On land the traveller had the choice of riding on an animal-packhorse, horse, ass or donkey, or of travelling in a carriage like the one above, if he was wealthy, or in a cart. The roads were poor and not surfaced as we know them. In the towns they may have been cobbled but in the country they were dirt tracks and in the rainy weather they were quagmires of dirt and mud. In winter, villages may have been cut off for weeks on end. But people had to travel and they made the best of the conditions. But travel was extremely slow.

There were inns for travellers in most towns and some of these inns still exist today. The rivers were forded or bridged and many of these bridges still stand today such as the fourteenth century bridge at Aylesford in Kent.

An alternative form of travel was by river. Barges and open boats could sail up many rivers and carry passengers to inland towns. But for travel over a long distance the only comfortable method of transport was by ship.

Travellers in the Middle Ages were not confined to their own country. The Knight, Squire, Shipman and the Wife of Bath in The Canterbury Tales had all travelled abroad. Merchants did not think twice about slipping across the Channel to the wool market in Calais or to Flanders. The soldiers of these times often fought on foreign soil, such as the soldiers who went on Crusades or the soldiers who fought at Agincourt or Crecy. It is not surprising therefore to find records of long journeys.

In the Middle Ages roads were no more than dirt tracks that turned to mud in winter. Men travelled on horseback (if they could afford a horse!). Ladies travelled in wagons covered in painted cloth. They looked pretty but they must have been very uncomfortable on bumpy roads as they had no springs. Worse, travel in the Middle Ages was very slow. A horseman could only travel 50 or 60 kilometres a day.

Some goods were carried by pack horses (horses with bags loaded on their sides) and peasants pulled along two-wheeled carts full of hay and straw.

However, whenever they could people travelled by water. It was faster and more comfortable than travelling by land. It was also much cheaper to send goods by water than by land. Some goods were taken by ship from one part of the English coast to another. This was known as the coastal trade. The main type of ship in the Middle Ages was called a cog. It had only one sail. Furthermore in the early Middle Ages ships did not have rudders. Instead they were steered by a huge oar on side of the ship. It was called the steer board. Today the right side of a ship is called the starboard. It was originally the 'steer board' side. (When you tied up a ship in port the steer board always faced outwards to sea otherwise it might be crushed between the ship and the quay. The left side of a ship always faced the quay so it was the 'port' side). The rudder was invented at the end of the 13th century.

In the Middle Ages people believed they would gain favour with God if they went on long journeys called pilgrimages to visit shrines. Geoffrey Chaucer (1340-1400) wrote the Canterbury Tales about a group of pilgrims who go to Canterbury to visit the burial place of Thomas Becket. They tell each other tales to pass the time.

Development in Road Transport in 17th to Early 19th Century

History

The first methods of road transport were horses, oxen or even humans carrying goods over dirt tracks that often followed game trails. As commerce increased, the tracks were often flattened or widened to accommodate the activities. Later, the travois, a frame used to drag loads, was developed. The wheel came still later, probably preceded by the use of logs as rollers.

With the advent of the Roman Empire, there was a need for armies to be able to travel quickly from one area to another, and the roads that existed were often muddy, which greatly delayed the movement of large masses of troops. To resolve this issue, the Romans built great roads. The Roman roads used deep roadbeds of crushed stone as an underlying layer to ensure that they kept dry, as the water would flow out from the crushed stone, instead of becoming mud in clay soils.

During the Industrial Revolution, and because of the increased commerce that came with it, improved roadways became imperative. The problem was rain combined with dirt roads created commerce-miring mud. John Loudon McAdam (1756-1836) designed the first modern highways. He developed an inexpensive paving material of soil and stone aggregate (known as macadam), and he embanked roads a few feet higher than the surrounding terrain to cause water to drain away from the surface. At the same time, Thomas Telford, made substantial advances in the engineering of new roads and the construction of bridges, particularly, the London to Holyhead road.

Various systems had been developed over centuries to reduce bogging and dust in cities, including cobblestones and wooden paving. Tar-bound macadam (tarmac) was applied to macadam roads towards the end of the 19th century in cities such as Paris. In the early 20th century tarmac and concrete paving were extended into the countryside.

Transportation

Transport on roads can be roughly grouped into two categories: transportation of goods and transportation of people. In many countries licencing requirements and safety regulations ensure a separation of the two industries.

The nature of road transportation of goods depends, apart from the degree of development of the local infrastructure, on the distance the goods are transported by road, the weight and volume of the individual shipment and the type of goods transported. For short distances and light, small shipments a van or pickup truck may be used. For large shipments even if less than a full truckload (Less than truckload) a truck is more appropriate. In some countries cargo is transported by road in horse-drawn carriages, donkey carts or other non-motorized mode. Delivery services) are sometimes considered a separate category from cargo transport. In many places fast food is transported on roads by various types of vehicles. For inner city delivery of small packages and documents bike couriers are quite common.

People (Passengers) are transported on roads either in individual cars or automobiles or in mass transit/public transport by bus/Coach (vehicle). Special modes of individual transport by road like rikshas or velotaxis may also be locally available.

Trucking and Hauling

Trucking companies (AE) or haulers/hauliers (BE) accept cargo for road transportation.

In Australia road trains replace rail transport for goods on routes throughout the centre of the country. B-doubles and semi-trailers are used in urban areas because of their smaller size. Low-loader or flat-bed trailers are used to haul containers, see containerization, in intermodal transport. Truck drivers operate either independently working directly for the client or through freight carriers or shipping agents. Some big companies operate their own internal trucking operations.

In the U.S. many truckers own their truck (rig), and are known as owner-operators. Some road transportation is done on regular routes or for only one consignee per run, while others transport goods from many different loading stations/shippers to various consignees. On some long runs only cargo for one lag of the route (to) is known when the cargo is loaded. Truckers may have to wait at the destination for the return cargo (from).

A Bill of Lading issued by the shipper provides the basic document for road freight. On cross-border transportation the trucker will present the cargo and documentation provided by the shipper to customs for inspection. This also applies to shipments that are transported out of a Free port. To avoid accidents caused by fatigue, truckers have to keep to strict rules for drivetime and required rest periods. Known in the U.S. as hours of service, and in the E.U. as drivers working hours. See e.g. "Hours of Work and Rest Periods (Road Transport) Convention, 1979" or. Tachographs record the times the vehicle is in motion and stopped. Some companies use two drivers per truck to ensure uninterrupted transportation; with one driver resting or sleeping in a bunk in the back of the cab while the other is driving.

For transport of hazardous materials truckers need a licence, which usually requires them to pass an exam. They have to make sure they affix proper labels for the respective hazard(s) to their vehicle. Liquid goods are transported by road in tank trucks (AE) or tanker lorries (BE) (also road-tankers) or special tankcontainers for intermodal transport. For unpackaged goods and liquids weigh stations confirm weight after loading and before delivery. For transportation of live animals special requirements have to be met in many countries to prevent cruelty to animals. For fresh and frozen goods refrigerator trucks or reefer (container)s are used.

Truck drivers often need special licenses to drive, known in the U.S. as a commercial driver's license. In the U.K. a Large Goods Vehicle license is required.

Modern Roads

Today roadways are principally asphalt or concrete. Both are based on McAdam's concept of stone aggregate in a binder, asphalt cement or Portland cement respectively. Asphalt is known as a flexible pavement, one which slowly will "flow" under the pounding of traffic. Concrete is a rigid pavement, which can take heavier loads but is more expensive and requires more carefully prepared subbase. So, generally, major roads are concrete and local roads are asphalt. Often concrete roads are covered with a thin layer of asphalt to create a wearing surface.

Modern pavements are designed for heavier vehicle loads and faster speeds, requiring thicker slabs and deeper subbase. Subbase is the layer or successive layers of stone, gravel and sand supporting the pavement. It is needed to spread out the slab load bearing on the underlying soil and to conduct away any water getting under the slabs. Water will undermine a pavement over time, so much of pavement and pavement joint design are meant to minimize the amount of water getting and staying under the slabs.

Shoulders are also an integral part of highway design. They

are multipurpose; they can provide a margin of side clearance, a refuge for incapacitated vehicles, an emergency lane, and parking space. They also serve a design purpose, and that is to prevent water from percolating into the soil near the main pavement's edge. Shoulder pavement is designed to a lower standard than the pavement in the travelled way and won't hold up as well to traffic. (Which is why driving on the shoulder is generally prohibited.)

Pavement technology is still evolving, albeit in not easily noticed increments. For instance, chemical additives in the pavement mix make the pavement more weather resistant, grooving and other surface treatments improve resistance to skidding and hydroplaning, and joint seals which were once tar are now made of low maintenance neoprene.

Traffic Control

Nearly all roadways are built with devices meant to control traffic. Most notable to the motorist are those meant to communicate directly with the driver. Broadly, these fall into three categories: signs, signals or pavement markings. They help the driver navigate; they assign the right-of-way at intersections; they indicate laws such as speed limits and parking regulations; they advise of potential hazards; they indicate passing and no passing zones; and otherwise deliver information and to assure traffic is orderly and safe.

200 years ago these devices were signs, nearly all informal. In the late 19th century signals began to appear in the biggest cities at a few highly congested intersections. They were manually operated, and consisted of semaphores, flags or paddles, or in some cases coloured electric lights, all modeled on railroad signals. In the 20th century signals were automated, at first with electromechanical devices and later with computers. Signals can be quite sophisticated: with vehicle sensors embedded in the pavement, the signal can control and choreograph the turning movements of heavy traffic in the most complex of intersections. In the 1920s traffic engineers learned how to coordinate signals along a thoroughfare to increase its speeds and volumes. In the 1980s, with computers, similar coordination of whole networks became possible.

In the 1920s pavement markings were introduced. Initially they were used to indicate the road's centerline. Soon after they were coded with information to aid motorists in passing safely. Later, with multi-lane roads they were used to define lanes. Other uses, such as indicating permitted turning movements and pedestrian crossings soon followed.

In the 20th century traffic control devices were standardized. Before then every locality decided on what its devices would look like and where they would be applied. This could be confusing, especially to traffic from outside the locality. In the United States standardization was first taken at the state level, and late in the century at the federal level. Each country has a Manual of Uniform Traffic Control Devices (MUTCD) and there are efforts to blend them into a worldwide standard.

Besides signals signs and markings, other forms of traffic control are designed and built into the roadway. For instance, curbs and rumble strips can be used to keep traffic in a given lane and median barriers can prevent left turns and even U-turns.

Pneumatic Tires

As the horse-drawn carriage was replaced by the car and lorry or truck, and speeds increased, the need for smoother roads and less vertical displacement became more apparent, and pneumatic tires were developed to decrease the apparent roughness. Wagon and carriage wheels, made of wood, had a tire in the form of an iron strip that kept the wheel from wearing out quickly. Pneumatic tires, which had a larger footprint than iron tires, also were less likely to get bogged down in the mud on unpaved roads.

Toll Roads in the United States

Early toll roads were usually built by private companies under a government franchise. They typically paralleled or replaced routes already with some volume of commerce, hoping the improved road would divert enough traffic to make the enterprise profitable. Plank roads were particularly attractive as they greatly reduced rolling resistance and mitigated the problem of getting mired in mud. Another improvement, better grading to lessen the steepness of the worst stretches, allowed draft animals to haul heavier loads.

A *toll road* in the United States is often called a *turnpike*. The term *turnpike* probably originated from the gate, often a simple pike, which blocked passage until the fare was paid at a *toll house* (or *toll booth* in current terminology). When the toll was paid the pike, which was mounted on a swivel, was turned to allow the vehicle to pass. Tolls were usually based on the type of cargo being transported, not the type of vehicle. The practice of selecting routes so as to avoid tolls is called shunpiking. This may be simply to avoid the expense, as a form of economic protest (or boycott), or simply to seek a road less travelled as a bucolic interlude.

History, Funding through Tolls

Companies were formed to build, improve, and maintain a particular section of roadway, and tolls were collected from users to finance the enterprise. The enterprise was usually named to indicate the locale of its roadway, often including the name of one of both of the termini. The word *turnpike* came into common use in the names of these roadways and companies, and is essentially used interchangeably with *toll road* in current terminology.

In the United States, toll roads began with the Lancaster Turnpike in the 1790s, within Pennsylvania, connecting Philadelphia and Lancaster.

In New York State, the Great Western Turnpike was started in Albany in 1799 and eventually extended, by several alternate routes, to near what is now Syracuse, New York.

Toll roads peaked in the mid 19th century, and by the turn of the twentieth century most toll roads were taken over by state highway departments. The demise of this early toll road era was due to the rise of canals and railroads, which were more efficient (and thus cheaper) in moving freight over long distances. Roads wouldn't again be competitive with rails and barges until the first half of the 20th century when the internal combustion engine replaces draft animals as the source of motive power.

With the development, mass production, and popular embrace of the automobile, faster and higher capacity roads were needed. In the 1920s limited access highways appeared. Their main characteristics were dual roadways with access points limited to (but not always) grade-separated interchanges. Their dual roadways allowed high volumes of traffic, the need for no or few traffic lights along with relatively gentle grades and curves allowed higher speeds.The first limited access highways were *Parkways*, so called because of their often park-like landscaping and, in the metropolitan New York City area, they connected the region's system of parks. When the German Autobahns built in the 1930s introduced higher design standards and speeds, road planners and road-builders in the United States started developing and building toll roads to similar high standards. The Pennsylvania Turnpike, which largely followed the path of a partially-built railroad, was the first, opening in 1940.

After 1940 with the Pennsylvania Turnpike, toll roads saw a resurgence, this time to fund limited access highways. In the late 1940s and early 1950s, after World War II interrupted the evolution of the highway, the US resumed building toll roads. They were to still higher standards and one road, the New York State Thruway, had standards that became the prototype for the U.S. Interstate Highway System. Several other major toll-roads which connected with the Pennsylvania Turnpike were established before the creation of the Interstate Highway System. These were the Indiana Toll Road, Ohio Turnpike, and New Jersey Turnpike.

US Interstate Highway System

In the United States, beginning in 1956, Dwight D. Eisenhower National System of Interstate and Defence Highways, commonly called the Interstate Highway System was built. It uses 12 foot (3.65m) lanes, wide medians, a maximum of 4% grade, and full access control, though many sections don't meet these standards due to older construction or constraints. This system created a continental-sized network meant to connect every population centre of 50,000 people or more.

By 1956, most limited access highways in the eastern United States were toll roads. In that year, the federal Interstate highway program was established, funding non-toll roads with 90% federal dollars and 10% state match, giving little incentive for states to expand their turnpike system. Funding rules initially restricted collections of tolls on newly funded roadways, bridges, and tunnels. In some situations, expansion or rebuilding of a toll facility using Interstate Highway Program funding resulted in the removal of existing tolls. This occurred in Virginia on Interstate 64 at the Hampton Roads Bridge-Tunnel when a second parallel roadway to the regional 1958 bridge-tunnel was completed in 1976.

Since the completion of the initial portion of the interstate highway system, regulations were changed, and portions of toll facilities have been added to the system. Some states are again looking at toll financing for new roads and maintenance, to supplement limited federal funding. In some areas, new road projects have been completed with public-private partnerships funded by tolls, such as the Pocahontas Parkway (I-895) near Richmond, Virginia.

The Grand Tour

The Grand Tour was the traditional travel of Europe undertaken by mainly upper-class European young men of means. The custom flourished from about 1660 until the advent of large-scale rail transit in the 1840s, and was associated with a standard itinerary. The tradition continued after rail and steamship travel made the journey less of a burden, and American and other overseas youth joined in. It served as an education rite of passage. Primarily associated with Britain (particularly the British nobility and wealthy gentry), similar trips were made by wealthy young men of Protestant Northern European nations on the Continent.

The New York Times described the Grand Tour in this way: Three hundred years ago, wealthy young Englishmen began taking a post-Oxbridge trek through France and Italy in search of art, culture and the roots of Western civilization. With nearly unlimited funds, aristocratic connections and months (or years) to roam, they commissioned paintings, perfected their language skills and mingled with the upper crust of the Continent.

The primary value of the Grand Tour, it was believed, lay in the exposure both to the cultural legacy of classical antiquity and the Renaissance, and to the aristocratic and fashionable society of the European continent. In addition, it provided the only opportunity to view specific works of art, and possibly the only chance to hear certain music. A grand tour could last from several months to several years. It was commonly undertaken in the company of a knowledgeable guide or tutor. The Grand Tour had more than superficial cultural importance; as E.P. Thompson stated, "ruling-class control in the 18th century was located primarily in a cultural hegemony, and only secondarily in an expression of economic or physical (military) power."

History

Essentially, the Grand Tour was a scholar's pilgrimage to Rome, which was home to the Colosseum, considered one of the Wonders of the World, and Saint Peter's tomb. Catholic Grand tourists might be interested to visit the pilgrimage sites St. Thomas' body at Canterbury, and the *Shrine of the Three Kings at Cologne Cathedral,* along the way. These places were not only religious centres, but had been at various times magnets for artists, who won commissions for altarpieces or Royal portraits. Since medieval times, a tour to such places was considered essential for budding young artists to understand proper painting and sculpture techniques. The advent of the printing press and the spread of woodcuts and engravings from the 15th century onwards, had done much to popularize such trips, and following the artists themselves, the elite considered travel to such centres (outside of warzones of course) as necessary rites of passage.

In Britain, Thomas Coryat's travel book *Coryat's Crudities* (1611), published during the Twelve Years' Truce, was an early influence on the Grand Tour. Larger numbers of tourists began their tours after the Peace of Münster in 1648. According to the *Oxford English Dictionary,* the first recorded use of the term (perhaps its introduction to English) was by Richard Lassels, an expatriate Roman Catholic priest, in his book *An Italian Voyage,* which was published posthumously in Paris in 1670 and then in London. Lassels' introduction listed four areas in which travel furnished "an accomplished, consummate Traveller": the intellectual, the social, the ethical (by the opportunity of drawing moral instruction from all the traveller saw), and the political.

The idea of travelling for the sake of curiosity and learning was a developing idea in the 17th century. With John Locke's *Essay Concerning Human Understanding* (1690) it was argued, and widely accepted, that knowledge comes entirely from the external senses, that what one knows comes from the physical stimuli to which one has been exposed, thus, one could "use up" the environment, taking from it all it offers, requiring a change of place. Travel, therefore, was necessary for one to develop the mind and expand knowledge of the world. As a young man at the outset of his account of a repeat Grand Tour the historian Edward Gibbon remarked that "According to the law of custom, and perhaps of reason, foreign travel completes the education of an English gentleman." Consciously adapted for intellectual self-improvement, Gibbon was "revisiting the Continent on a larger and more liberal plan"; most Grand Tourists did not pause more than briefly in libraries.

The typical 18th century sentiment was that of the studious observer travelling through foreign lands reporting his findings on human nature for those unfortunate to have stayed home. Recounting one's observations to society at large to increase its welfare was considered an obligation; the Grand Tour flourished in this mindset.

The Grand Tour not only provided a liberal education but allowed those who could afford it the opportunity to buy things otherwise unavailable at home, and it thus increased participants' prestige and standing. Grand Tourists would return with crates of art, books, pictures, sculpture, and items of culture, which would be displayed in libraries, cabinets, gardens, and drawing rooms, as well as the galleries built purposively for their display; The Grand Tour became a symbol of wealth and freedom. Artists who especially thrived on Grand Tourists included Pompeo Batoni the portraitist, and the vedutisti such as Canaletto, Pannini and Guardi. The less well-off could return with an album of Piranesi etchings.

The "perhaps" in Gibbon's opening remark cast an ironic shadow over his resounding statement. Critics of the Grand Tour derided its lack of adventure. "The tour of Europe is a paltry thing", said one 18th century critic, "a tame, uniform, unvaried prospect". The Grand Tour was said to reinforce the old preconceptions and prejudices about national characteristics, as Jean Gailhard's *Compleat Gentleman* (1678) observes: "French courteous. Spanish lordly. Italian amorous. German clownish." The deep suspicion with which Tour was viewed at home in England, where it was feared that the very experiences that completed the British gentleman might well undo him, were epitomised in the sarcastic nativist view of the ostentatiously "well-travelled" maccaroni of the 1760s and 70s.

After the arrival of steam-powered transportation, around 1825, the Grand Tour custom continued, but it was of a qualitative difference—cheaper to undertake, safer, easier, open to anyone. During much of the 19th century, most educated young men of privilege undertook the Grand Tour. Germany and Switzerland came to be included in a more broadly defined circuit. Later, it became fashionable for young women as well; a trip to Italy, with a spinster aunt chaperon, was part of the upper-class woman's education, as in E.M. Forster's novel *A Room with a View*.

Travel Itinerary

The most common itinerary of the Grand Tour shifted across generation in the cities it embraced, but the tourist usually began in Dover, England and crossed the English Channel to Ostend, in Belgium, Calais, or Le Havre in France. From there the tourist, usually accompanied by a tutor (known colloquially as a "bear-leader") and if wealthy enough a league of servants, could rent or acquire a coach (which could be resold in any city or disassembled and packed across the Alps, as in Giacomo Casanova's travels, who resold it on completion), or opt to make the trip by boat as far as the alps, either travelling over the Seine to Paris, or the Rhine to Basel.

Upon hiring a French-speaking guide, the tourist and his entourage would travel to Paris. There the traveller might undertake lessons in French, dancing, fencing, and riding. The appeal of Paris lay in the sophisticated language and manners of French high society, including courtly behaviour and fashion. Ostensibly this served the purpose of preparing the young man for a leadership position at home, often in government or diplomacy. From Paris he would typically go to urban Switzerland for a while, often to Geneva (the cradle of the Protestant Reformation) or Lausanne. ("Alpinism," or mountaineering, was a development of the 19th century.) From there the traveller would endure a difficult crossing over the Alps into northern Italy (such as at St. Bernard Pass), which included dismantling the carriage and luggage. If wealthy enough, he might be carried over the hard terrain by servants.

Once in Italy the tourist would visit Turin (and, less often, Milan), then might spend a few months in Florence, where there was a considerable Anglo-Italian society accessible to travelling Englishmen "of quality" and where the *Tribuna* of the Uffizi gallery brought together in one space the monuments of High Renaissance paintings and Roman sculptures that would inspire picture galleries dressed with antiquities at home, with side trips to Pisa, then move on to Padua, Bologna, and Venice. The British idea of Venice as the "locus of decadent Italianate allure" made it an epitome and cultural setpiece of the Grand Tour.

From Venice the traveller went to Rome to study the ruins of ancient Rome. Some travellers also visited Naples to study music, and (after the mid-18th century) to appreciate the recently-discovered archaeological sites of Herculaneum and Pompeii and perhaps for the adventurous thrilling ascent of Mount Vesuvius. Later in the period the more adventurous, especially if provided with a yacht, might attempt Sicily (the site of Greek ruins) or even Greece itself. But Naples or later Paestum further south was the usual terminus. From here the traveller traversed the Alps heading north through to the German-speaking parts of Europe. The traveller might stop first in Innsbruck before visiting Berlin, Dresden, Vienna and Potsdam, with perhaps some study time at the universities in Munich or Heidelberg. From then travellers visited Holland and Flanders (with more gallery-going and art appreciation) before returning across the Channel to England.

Authorisation to Travel

Other Political Hindrance to Travel

Travel outside the boundaries of one's Country had always been subject to restrictions, as we have seen from some of the constraints imposed by the state under the Roman Empire. Few PEOPLE travelled any GREAT DISTANCE, and those that did so were generally involved with affairs of state. Monarchs were suspicious of intrigues and alliances with foreign states, and vetted SUCH TRAVEL carefully, issuing letters of authority to members of court, ostensibly to facilitate TRAVEL but equally to ensure that they were aware of the movements of their subjects.

Passports have their ORIGIN in the medieval testimoniale, a letter from an ecclesiastical superior given to a pilgrim to avoid the latter's possible arrest on charges of vagrancy. Later, papers of authority to TRAVEL were MORE widely issued by the state, particularly DURING periods of warfare with neighbouring European countries. However, when Belgium sought to require visitors to present passports for inspection in 1882, there was widespread indignation in the British press. The introduction of compulsory passports as a permanent requirement in Britain is of relatively recent ORIGIN, dating only from 1916, as a result of controls DURING the WORLD War I. The institution of a formal immigration service in the UK is ALSO a twentieth-CENTURY phenomenon, being established under the Aliens Act 1905.

We should not underestimate the importance of a common currency, and the difficulties and expense incurred when changing currencies while travelling ABROAD. As we have seen, under the Roman Empire the universal acceptance of Roman coinage proved to be a GREAT facilitator for TRAVEL, in contrast to the WEALTH of currencies even within individual countries in the MIDDLE Ages.

Fynes Moryson, an academic who travelled extensively on the Continent, was to write in 1589 of finding over twenty different coinages in Germany, five in the Low Countries and as many as eight in Switzerland. Moneychangers cheated the visitor and were sometimes difficult to find. At a TIME when the European Union is planning the introduction of the Euro as a common currency throughout the Union's membership, it is worth our while considering the benefits that could accrue to tourists and the boost which this could give to tourism in the twenty-FIRST CENTURY.

The social, political, economical and cultural upheavals in the last two centuries are due to two components: one regards the "revolution" which took place in the ideas' ground, the other one regarding the technical development and innovation. This contributed to the appearance of industrial revolution and division of labour, which rise the productivity's degree, rising the leisure time for employees. As such, countries touched by these two revolutions become more civilized and their people enjoyed a better living standard. As soon as this happened in different countries, their citizens become more and more attracted by different activities regarding the spending of their leisure time.

Tourism became a mass phenomenon. It is noteworthy to be mentioned that the transportation and communication sectors are very responsive to technical developments and innovations; they are absorbed very quickly by those two sectors and this contribute to big social, economical and political upheavals.

"In many instances the great social and political upheavals throughout history have been preceded by major advances in the technology of transportation and communications" 1954, quoted in Gilpin, 1989, p. 56). As it is a human activity with social and economical implications, tourism is touched by the transportation and communication's improvement. Today, countries which want to enter efficiently the globalization (or regionalization) processes must develop two elements: one regards the integration of their networks with networks in other countries (or if it is possible, the creation of a international "hub" in/from that country's territory); the other one aspect regards the opening needed for receiving new ideas, new people, or put in very few words, being receptive to another people's culture for the rising of human treasury's knowledge. Here it is timely to look at Geneva's previous example. International tourism could fully serve these aims.

Tourist activity has implications on many levels:

- it has a monetary dimension (it generates revenues at destination's place);
- it has a dimension regarding the transfer of ideas—as people travel with their ideas "in their heads and souls";
- it permits cultural interaction between the tourist's (culture) and the receiver's (culture);
- this could start a process of mutual understanding between the nations to whom they belong to;
- as the people from different states understand each other (due to their contacts), the states to whom they belong to will start "rapprochement" to each other, element which in the long run will contribute to the rising of political interdependence between this countries, for the benefits of their citizens, their economy and their society, without culture playing a great role in this "game". This could be a very brave step on the way to political unification of those—until then—two separate political entities. This could be regarded as an Enlightenment characteristic, which has the vocation of universality and in this way, tourism—beside scientific cooperation and trade—could bring in the people's vision the idea of the one humanity which can surpass its specific cultural condition, through the acknowledgement of their allegiance to one global family.

The Development of the Spas

No one know exactly where the word spa comes from, but there are two main theories. One is that spa is an acronym for the Latin phrase, "salus per aquae," or "health through water."

Others believe the origin of the word "spa" comes from the Belgian town of Spa, known since Roman times for its baths. They speculate that the town was so prominent that the very word spa became synonymous in the English language with a place to be restored and pampered.

Modern spas have their roots in ancient towns famed for the healing powers of their mineral waters and hot springs. Travellers would come to "take the waters" and restore their health.

The practice of bathing in hot springs and mineral waters dates at least to the Babylonians and Greeks, and knowing people, probably much sooner!

In the 19th century, Europe's great spas were destinations for the wealthy, who went there to "take the waters." Water treatments are still considered the heart of the spa experience in Europe. Today massages and facials are by far the most popular spa treatments in America. The term spa is associated with water treatment which is also known as balneotherapy. Spa towns or spa resorts (including hot springs resorts) typically offer thermal or mineral water for drinking and bathing. They also offer various health treatments. The belief in the curative powers of mineral waters goes back to prehistoric times. Such practices have been popular world-wide, but are especially wide-spread in Europe and Japan. Day spas are also quite popular, and offer various personal care treatments.

History

The practice of travelling to hot or cold springs in hopes of effecting a cure of some ailment dates back to pre-historic times. Archaeological investigations near hot springs in France and Czech Republic revealed Bronze Age weapons and offerings. In Great Britain, ancient legend credited early Celtic kings with the discovery of the hot springs at Bath, England.

Many people around the world believed that bathing in a particular spring, well, or river resulted in physical and spiritual purification. Forms of ritual purification existed among the native Americans, Persians, Babylonians, Egyptians, Greeks, and Romans. Today, ritual purification through water can be found in the religious ceremonies of Jews, Muslims, Christians, Buddhists, and Hindus. These ceremonies reflect the ancient belief in the healing and purifying properties of water. Complex bathing rituals were also practiced in ancient Egypt, in pre-historic cities of the Indus Valley, and in Aegean civilizations. Most often these ancient people did little building construction around the water, and what they did construct was very temporary in nature.

Bathing in Greek and Roman Times

Some of the earliest descriptions of western bathing practices came from Greece. The Greeks began bathing regimens that formed the foundation for modern spa procedures. These Aegean people utilized small bathtubs, wash basins, and foot baths for personal cleanliness. The earliest such findings are the baths in the palace complex at Knossos, Crete, and the luxurious alabaster bathtubs excavated in Akrotiri, Santorini; both date from the mid-2nd millennium BC. They established public baths and showers within their gymnasium complexes for relaxation and personal hygiene. Greek mythology specified that certain natural springs or tidal pools were blessed by the gods to cure disease. Around these sacred pools, Greeks established bathing facilities for those desiring healing. Supplicants left offerings to the gods for healing at these sites and bathed themselves in hopes of a cure. The Spartans developed a primitive vapor bath. At Serangeum, an early Greek *balneum* (bathhouse, loosely translated), bathing chambers were cut into the hillside from which the hot springs issued. A series of niches cut into the rock above the chambers held bathers' clothing. One of the bathing chambers had a decorative mosaic floor depicting a driver and chariot pulled by four horses, a woman followed by two dogs, and a dolphin below. Thus, the early Greeks used the natural features, but expanded them and added their own amenities, such as decorations and shelves. During later Greek civilization, bathhouses were often built in conjunction with athletic fields.

The Romans emulated many of the Greek bathing practices. Romans surpassed the Greeks in the size and complexity of their baths. This came about by many factors: the larger size and population of Roman cities, the availability of running water following the building of aqueducts, and the invention of cement, which made building large edifices easier, safer, and cheaper. As in Greece, the Roman bath became a focal centre for social and recreational activity. As the Roman Empire expanded, the idea of the public bath spread to all parts of the Mediterranean and into regions of Europe and North Africa. With the construction of the aqueducts, the Romans had enough water not only for domestic, agricultural, and industrial uses, but also for their leisurely pursuits. The aqueducts provided water that was later heated for use in the baths. Today, the extent of the Roman bath is revealed at ruins and in archaeological excavations in Europe, Africa, and the Middle East. The Romans also developed baths in their colonies, taking advantage of the natural hot springs occurring in Europe to construct baths at Aix and Vichy in France, Bath and Buxton in England, Aachen and Wiesbaden in Germany, Baden, Austria, and Aquincum in Hungary, among other locations. These baths became centres for recreational and social activities in Roman communities. Libraries, lecture halls, gymnasiums, and formal gardens became part of some bath complexes. In addition, the Romans used the hot thermal waters to relieve their suffering from rheumatism, arthritis, and overindulgence in food and drink. The decline of the Roman Empire in the west, beginning in A.D. 337 after the death of Emperor Constantine, resulted in Roman legions abandoning their outlying provinces and leaving the baths to be taken over by the local population or destroyed.

Thus, the Romans elevated bathing to a fine art, and their bathhouses physically reflected these advancements. The Roman bath, for instance, included a far more complex ritual than a simple immersion or sweating procedure. The various parts of the bathing ritual — undressing, bathing, sweating, receiving a massage, and resting — required separated rooms which the Romans built to accommodate those functions. The segregation of the sexes and the additions of diversions not directly related to bathing also had direct impacts on the shape and form of bathhouses. The elaborate Roman bathing ritual and its resultant architecture served as precedents for later European and American bathing facilities. Formal garden spaces and opulent architectural arrangement equal to those of the Romans reappeared in Europe by the end of the eighteenth century. Major American spas followed suit a century later.

Bathing in Medieval Times

With the decline of the Roman Empire, the public baths often became places of licentious behaviour, and such use was responsible for the spread rather than the cure of diseases. A general belief developed among the European populace was that frequent bathing promoted disease and sickness. Medieval church authorities encouraged this belief and made every effort to close down public baths.

Ecclesiastical officials believed that public bathing created an environment open to immorality and disease. Roman Catholic Church officials even banned public bathing in an unsuccessful effort to halt syphilis epidemics from sweeping Europe. Overall, this period represented a time of decline for public bathing.

People continued to seek out a few select hot and cold springs, believed to be holy wells, to cure various ailments. In an age of religious fervour, the benefits of the water were attributed to God or one of the saints. In 1326 Collin le Loup, an ironmaster from Liege, Belgium, discovered the chalybeate springs of Spa, Belgium. Around these springs, a famous health resort eventually grew and the term "spa" came to refer to any health resort located near natural springs. During this period, individual springs became associated with the specific ailment that they could allegedly benefit.

Bathing procedures during this period varied greatly. By the 16th century, physicians at Karlsbad, Bohemia, prescribed that the mineral water be taken internally as well as externally. Patients periodically bathed in warm water for up to 10 or 11 hours while drinking glasses of mineral water. The first bath session occurred in the morning, the second in the afternoon. This treatment lasted several days until skin pustules formed and broke resulting in the draining of "poisons" considered to be the source of the disease. Then followed another series of shorter, hotter baths to wash the infection away and close the eruptions.

In the English coastal town of Scarborough in 1626, a Mrs. Elizabeth Farrow discovered a stream of acidic water running from one of the cliffs to the south of the town. This was deemed to have beneficial health properties and gave birth to Scarborough Spa. Dr. Wittie's book about the spa waters published in 1660 attracted a flood of visitors to the town. Sea bathing was added to the cure, and Scarborough became Britain's first seaside resort. The first rolling bathing machines for bathers are recorded on the sands in 1735.

Bathing in the 18th Century

In the 17th century most upper-class Europeans washed their clothes with water often and washed only their faces (with linen), feeling that bathing the entire body was a lower-class activity; but the upper-class slowly began changing their attitudes toward bathing as a way to restore health later in that century. The wealthy flocked to health resorts to drink and bathe in the waters. In 1702 Queen Anne of England travelled to Bath, the former Roman development, to bathe. A short time later, Richard (Beau) Nash came to Bath. By the force of his personality, Nash became the arbiter of good taste and manners in England. He along with financier Ralph Allen and architect John Wood transformed Bath from a country spa into the social capital of England. Bath set the tone for other spas in Europe to follow. Ostensibly, the wealthy and famous arrived there on a seasonal basis to bathe in and drink the water; however, they also came to display their opulence. Social activities at Bath included dances, concerts, playing cards, lectures, and promenading down the street.

A typical day at Bath might be an early morning communal bath followed by a private breakfast party. Afterwards, one either drank water at the Pump Room (a building constructed over the thermal water source) or attended a fashion show. Physicians encouraged health resort patrons to bathe in and drink the waters with equal vigor. The next several hours of the day could be spent in shopping, visiting the lending library, attending concerts, or stopping at one of the coffeehouses. At 4:00 P.M., the rich and famous dressed up in their finery and promenaded down the streets. Next came dinner, more promenading, and an evening of dancing or gambling.

Similar activities occurred in health resorts throughout Europe. The spas became stages on which Europeans paraded with great pageantry. These resorts became infamous as places full of gossip and scandals. The various social and economic classes selected specific seasons during the year's course, staying from one to several months, to vacation at each resort. One season aristocrats occupied the resorts; at other times, prosperous farmers or retired military men took the baths. The wealthy and the criminals that preyed on them moved from one spa to the next as the fashionable season for that resort changed.

During the 18th century a revival in the medical uses of spring water took place among some Italian, German, and English physicians. This revival changed the way of taking a spa treatment. For example, in Karlsbad the accepted method of drinking the mineral water required sending large barrels to individual boardinghouses where the patients drank physician-prescribed dosages in the solitude of their rooms. Dr. David Beecher in 1777 recommended that the patients come to the fountainhead for the water and that each patient should first do some prescribed exercises. This innovation increased the medicinal benefits obtained and gradually physical activity became part of the European bathing regimen. In 1797 in England Dr. James Currier published *The Effects of Water, Cold and Warm, as a Remedy in Fever and other Diseases*. This book stimulated additional interest in water cures and advocated the external and internal use of water as part of the curing process.

Bathing in the 19th and 20th Centuries

In the 19th century, bathing became a more accepted practice as physicians realized some of the benefits that cleanliness could provide. A cholera epidemic in Liverpool, England in 1842 resulted in a sanitation renaissance — more people bathed and washed their clothes. That same year a house in Cincinnati, Ohio, received the first indoor bathtub in the United States. Bathing, however, was still not a universal custom. Only one year later — in 1843 — bathing between November 1 and March 15 was outlawed in Philadelphia, Pennsylvania, as a health measure, and in 1845 bathing was banned in Boston, Massachusetts, unless under the direct orders of a physician. The situation improved, however, and by 1867 in Philadelphia most houses of the well-to-do had tubs and indoor plumbing. In England, hot showers were installed in barracks and schools by the 1880s. The taboos against bathing disappeared with advancements in medical science; the worldwide medical community was even promoting the benefits of bathing. In addition, the Victorian taste for the exotic lent itself perfectly to seeking out the curative powers of thermal water.

In most instances the formal architectural development of European spas took place in the 18th and 19th centuries. The architecture of Bath, England, developed along Georgian and Neoclassical lines, generally following Palladian structures. The most important architectural form that emerged was the "crescent" — a semi-elliptical street plan used in many areas of England. The architecture of Karlsbad, Marienbad, Franzenbad, and Baden-Baden was primarily Neoclassical, but the literature seems to indicate that large bathhouses were not constructed until well into the 19th century. The emphasis on drinking the waters rather than bathing in them led to the development of separate structures known as *Trinkhallen* (drinking halls) where those taking the cure spent hours drinking water from the springs.

By the mid-19th century the situation had changed dramatically. Visitors to the European spas began to stress bathing in addition to drinking the waters. Besides fountains, pavilions, and Trinkhallen, bathhouses on the scale of the Roman baths were revived. Photographs of a 19th century spa complex taken in the 1930s, detailing the earlier architecture, show a heavy use of mosaic floors, marble walls, classical statuary, arched openings, domed ceilings, segmental arches, triangular pediments, Corinthian columns, and all the other trappings of a Neoclassical revival. The buildings were usually separated by function — with the Trinkhalle, the bathhouse, the inhalatorium (for inhaling the vapors), and the *Kurhaus* or *Conversationhaus* that was the centre of social activity. Baden-Baden featured golf courses and tennis courts, "superb roads to motor over, and drives along quaint lanes where wild deer are as common as cows to us, and almost as unafraid."

The European spa, then, started with structures to house the drinking function — from simple fountains to pavilions to elaborate Trinkhallen. The enormous bathhouses came later in the 19th century as a renewed preference for an elaborate bathing ritual to cure ills and improve health came into vogue. European architects looked back to Roman civilizations and carefully studied its fine architectural precedents. The Europeans copied the same formality, symmetry, division of rooms by function, and opulent interior design in their bathhouses. They emulated the fountains and formal garden spaces in their resorts, and they also added new diversions. The tour books always mentioned the roomy, woodsy offerings in the vicinity and the faster-paced evening diversions. By the beginning of the 19th century the European bathing regimen consisted of numerous accumulated traditions. The bathing routine included soaking in hot water, drinking the water, steaming in a vapor room, and relaxing in a cooling room. In addition doctors ordered that patients be douched with hot or cold water and given a select diet to promote a cure. Authors began writing guidebooks to the health resorts of Europe explaining the medical benefits and social amenities of each. Rich Europeans and Americans travelled to these resorts to take in cultural activities and the baths.

Each European spa began offering similar cures while maintaining a certain amount of individuality. The 19th century bathing regimen at Karlsbad can serve as a general portrayal of European bathing practices during this century. Visitors arose at 6:00 AM to drink the water and be serenaded by a band. Next came a light breakfast, bath, and lunch. The doctors at Karlsbad usually limited patients to certain foods for each meal. In the afternoon visitors went sight-seeing or attended concerts. Nightly theatrical performances followed the evening meal. This ended around 9:00 PM with the patients returning to their boardinghouses to sleep until six the next morning. This regimen continued for as long as a month and then the patients returned home until the next year. Other 19th century European spa regimens followed similar schedules.

At the beginning of the 20th century, European spas combined a strict diet and exercise regimen with a complex bathing procedure to achieve benefits for the patients. One example will suffice to illustrate the change in bathing procedures. Patients at Baden-Baden, which specialized in treating rheumatoid arthritis, were directed to see a doctor before taking the baths. Once this occurred the bathers proceeded to the main bathhouse where they paid for their baths and stored their valuables before being assigned a booth for undressing. The bathhouse supplied bathers with towels, sheets, and slippers.

The Baden-Baden bathing procedure began with a warm shower. The bathers next entered a room of circulating, 140-degree hot air for 20 minutes, spent another ten minutes in a room with 150-degree temperature, partook of a 154-degree vapor bath, then showered and received a soap massage. After the massage, the bathers swam in a pool heated approximately to body temperature. After the swim, the bathers rested for 15 to 20 minutes in the warm "Sprudel" room pool. This shallow pool's bottom contained an 8-inch (200 mm) layer of sand through with naturally carbonated water bubbled up. This was followed by a series of gradually cooler showers and pools. After that, the attendants rubbed down the bathers with warm towels and then wrapped them in sheets and covered them with blankets to rest for 20 minutes. This ended the bathing portion of the treatment.

The rest of the cure consisted of a prescribed diet, exercise, and water-drinking program. The European spas provided various other diversions for guests after the bath, including gambling, horse racing, fishing, hunting, tennis, skating, dancing, golf, and horseback riding. Sight-seeing and theatrical performances served as further incentives for people to go to the spa. Some European governments even recognized the medical benefits of spa therapy and paid a portion of the patient's expenses. A number of these spas catered to those suffering from obesity and overindulgence in addition to various other medical complaints. In recent years, elegance and style of earlier centuries may have diminished, but people still come to the natural hot springs for relaxation and health.

Spas in Colonial America

Some European colonists brought with them knowledge of the hot water therapy for medicinal purposes, and others learned the benefits of hot springs from the Native Americans. Europeans gradually obtained many of the hot and cold springs from the various Indian tribes. They then developed the spring to suit European tastes. By the 1760s British colonists were travelling to hot and cold springs in Connecticut, Pennsylvania, New York, and Virginia in search of water cures. Among the more frequently visited of these springs were Bath, Yellow, and Bristol Springs in Pennsylvania; Saratoga Springs, Kinderhook, and Ballston Springs in New York; and Warm Springs, Hot Springs, and White Sulphur Springs, West Virginia (now in West Virginia) in Virginia.

Colonial doctors gradually began to recommend hot springs for ailments. Dr. Benjamin Rush, American patriot and physician, praised the springs of Bristol, Pennsylvania, in 1773. Dr. Samuel Tenney in 1783 and Dr. Valentine Seaman in 1792 examined the water of Saratoga Springs in New York and wrote of possible medicinal uses of the springs. Hotels were constructed to accommodate visitors to the various springs. Entrepreneurs opened taverns where the travellers could lodge, eat, and drink. Thus began the health resort industry in the United States.

Bathing in 19th and 20th Century America

After the American Revolution, the spa industry continued to gain popularity. By the mid 1850s hot and cold spring resorts existed in 20 states. Many of these resorts contained similar architectural features. Most health resorts had a large, two-story central building near or at the springs, with smaller structures surrounding it. The main building provided the guests with facilities for dining, and possibly, dancing on the first floor, and the second story consisted of sleeping rooms. The outlying structures were individual guest cabins, and other auxiliary buildings formed a semicircle or U-shape around the large building.

These resorts offered swimming, fishing, hunting, and horseback riding as well as facilities for bathing. The Virginia resorts, particularly White Sulphur Springs, proved popular before and after the Civil War. After the Civil War, spa vacations became very popular as returning soldiers bathed to heal wounds and the American economy allowed more leisure time. Saratoga Springs in New York became one of the main centres for this type of activity. Bathing in and drinking the warm, carbonated spring water only served as a prelude to the more interesting social activities of gambling, promenading, horse racing, and dancing.

Saratoga Springs in New York had extensive architectural development by the 1830s – a time when the buildings of Hot Springs, Arkansas, were small log and frame structures without particularly distinctive detailing – just basic envelopes to keep occupants from the weather. By 1815 Saratoga had large, four-story, Greek revival hotels. The availability of train and steamship service to that destination by 1832 meant larger numbers of more sophisticated clients. With the exception of specialized baths provided in boardinghouses or small bathhouses connected with the hotels, Saratoga's development during the 19th century was based on leisure pursuits other than baths. Although Saratoga and other spas in New York centred their developments around the healthful mineral waters, their real drawing card was the complex social life – that included pursuits from gambling on racehorses to seeing the latest Paris fashions. Going to the mountains for the summer was a major exodus undertaken by urban dwellers who could afford it, and Saratoga became a hub of summer activity. Private development there featured enormous hotels with great ballrooms, opera houses, stores, and clubhouses. In 1865 the Union Hotel had its own esplanade, with fountain and formal landscaping, and two small bathhouses. Yet, during the 19th century the bathhouses were auxiliary structures and not the central features of the resort.

During the last half of the 19th century western entrepreneurs developed natural hot and cold springs into resorts — from the Mississippi River to the West Coast. Many of these spas offered individual tub baths, vapor baths, douche sprays, needle showers, and pool bathing to their guests. The various railroads that spanned the country promoted these resorts to encourage train travel. Hot Springs, Arkansas, became a major resort for people from the large metropolitan areas of St. Louis and Chicago.

The popularity of the spas continued into the 20th century. Some medical critics, however, charged that the thermal waters in such renowned resorts as Hot Springs, Virginia, and Saratoga Springs, New York, were no more beneficial to health than ordinary heated water. The various spa owners countered these arguments by developing better hydrotherapy for their patients. At the Saratoga spa, treatments for heart and circulatory disorders, rheumatic conditions, nervous disorders, metabolic diseases, and skin diseases were developed. In 1910 the New York state government began purchasing the principal springs to protect them from exploitation. When Franklin Delano Roosevelt was governor of New York, he pushed for a European type of spa development at Saratoga. The architects for the new complex spent two years studying the technical aspects of bathing in Europe. Completed in 1933, the development had three bathhouses — Lincoln, Washington, and Roosevelt — a drinking hall, the Hall of Springs, and a building housing the Simon Baruch Research Institute. Four additional buildings composed the recreation area and housed arcades and a swimming pool decorated with blue faience terra-cotta tile. Saratoga spa's Neoclassical buildings were laid out in a grand manner, with formal perpendicular axes, solid brick construction, and stone and concrete Roman-revival detailing. The spa was surrounded by a 1,200-acre (4.9 km^2) natural park that had 18 miles (29 km) of bridle paths, "with measured walks at scientifically calculated gradients through its groves and vales, with spouting springs adding unexpected touches to its vistas, with the tumbling waters of Geyser Brook flowing beneath bridges of the fine roads. Full advantage has been taken of the natural beauty of the park, but no formal landscaping". Promotional literature again advertised the attractions directly outside the spa: shopping, horse races, and historic sites associated with revolutionary war history. New York Governor Herbert Lehman opened the new facilities to the public in July 1935.

Other leading spas in the country during this period were French Lick, Indiana; Hot Springs and White Sulphur Springs, West Virginia; Hot Springs, Arkansas; and Warm Springs, Georgia. French Lick specialized in treating obesity and constipation through a combination of bathing and drinking the water and exercising. Hot Springs, Virginia, specialized in digestive ailments and heart diseases, and White Sulphur Springs, Virginia, treated these ailments and skin diseases. Both resorts offered baths where the water would wash continuously over the patients as they lay in a shallow pool. Warm Springs, Georgia, gained a reputation for treating infantile paralysis by a procedure of baths and exercise. President Franklin D. Roosevelt, who earlier supported Saratoga, became a frequent visitor and promoter of this spa.

Spa Treatment

A body treatment, spa treatment, or cosmetic treatment is non-medical procedure to help the health of the body. It is often performed at a resort, destination spa, day spa, beauty salon or school.

Typical treatments include:

- facials – facial cleansing with a variety of products
- massage
- waxing – the removal of body hair with hot wax
- body wraps-wrapping the body in hot linens, plastic sheets and blankets, or mud wraps, often in combination with herbal compounds.
- aromatherapy
- skin exfoliation – including chemical peels and microdermabrasion
- nail care such as manicures and pedicures
- bathing or soaking in any of the following:

  - o hot spring
    - * Onsen (Japanese Hot Springs)
    - * Thermae (Roman Hot Springs)
  - o hot tub
  - o mud bath
  - o peat pulp bath
  - o sauna
  - o steam bath
- nutrition and weight guidance
- personal training
- yoga and meditation

Recent Trends

By the late 1930s more than 2,000 hot-or cold-springs health resorts were operating in the United States. This number had diminished greatly by the 1950s and continued to decline in the following two decades. In recent past, spas in the U.S. emphasized dietary, exercise, or recreational programs more than traditional bathing activities.

Up until recently, the public bathing industry in the U.S. remained stagnant. Nevertheless, in Europe, therapeutic baths have always been very popular, and remain so today. The same is true in Japan, where the traditional hot springs baths, known as *onsen*, always attracted plenty of visitors.

But also in the U.S., with the increasing focus on health and wiliness, such treatments are again becoming popular.

Resort or Place of Treatment

- A destination spa, a resort for personal care treatments.
- A day spa, a form of beauty salon.
- A spa town, a town visited for the supposed healing properties of the water.

Medication or Equipment

- A foot spa.
- A hot tub, in United States usage.
- A soda fountain, in United States usage.

- Spa (mineral water), from the sources in Spa.
- Spas usually offer mud baths for general health, or to address a variety of medical conditions. This is also known as 'fangotherapy'. A variety of medicinal clays and peats is used.

International Spa Association Definitions

Spa-places devoted to overall well-being through a variety of professional services that encourage the renewal of mind, body and spirit.

Types of Spa

- Club spa-A facility whose primary purpose is fitness and which offers a variety of professionally administered spa services on a day-use basis.
- Cruise ship spa – A spa aboard a cruise ship providing professionally administered spa services, fitness and wiliness components and spa cuisine menu choices.
- Day spa – A spa offering a variety of professionally administered spa services to clients on a day-use basis.
- Dental spa – A facility under the supervision of a licensed dentist that combines traditional dental treatment with the services of a spa.
- Destination spa-A destination spa is a facility with the primary purpose of guiding individual spa-goers to develop healthy habits. Historically a seven-day stay, this lifestyle transformation can be accomplished by providing a comprehensive program that includes spa services, physical fitness activities, willness education, healthful cuisine and special interest programming.
- Medical spa-A facility that operates under the full-time, on-site supervision of a licensed health care professional whose primary purpose is to provide comprehensive medical and wiliness care in an environment that integrates spa services, as well as traditional, complimentary and/or alternative therapies and treatments. The facility operates within the scope of practice of its staff, which can include both aesthetic/cosmetic and prevention/wiliness procedures and services. These spas typically use balneotherapy, employing a variety of peloids.

"Balneotherapy treatments can have different purposes. In a spa setting, they can be used to treat conditions such as arthritis and backache, build up muscles after injury or illness or to stimulate the immune system, and they can be enjoyed as a relief from day-to-day stress."

- Mineral springs spa-A spa offering an on-site source of natural mineral, thermal or seawater used in hydrotherapy treatments.
- Resort/hotel spa-A spa owned by and located within a resort or hotel providing professionally administered spa services, fitness and wiliness components and spa cuisine menu choices.

The Rise of the Seaside Resorts

History of the Seaside Resort

The coast has always been a recreational environment, although until the mid-nineteenth century, such recreation was a luxury only for the wealthy. Even in Roman times, the town of Baiae, by the Tyrrhenian Sea in Italy, was a resort for those who were sufficiently prosperous. During the early nineteenth century, the Prince Regent popularized Brighton, on the south coast of England, as a fashionable alternative to the wealthy spa towns such as Cheltenham. Later, Queen Victoria's long-standing patronage of the Isle of Wight and Ramsgate in Kent ensured the seaside residence was a highly fashionable possession for those wealthy enough to afford more than one home. Nowadays, many beach resorts are available as far afield as Goa in India. It was in the mid-nineteenth century that it became popular for people from less privileged classes to take holidays at seaside resorts. Improvements in transport brought about by the industrial revolution enabled people to take vacations away from home, and led to the growth of coastal towns as seaside resorts.

British Seaside Resorts

The popularization of the seaside resort during this period was nowhere more pronounced than in Blackpool. Blackpool catered for workers from across industrial Northern England, who packed its beaches and promenade. Other northern towns shared in the success of this new concept, especially from trade during Wakes weeks. The concept spread rapidly to other British coastal towns including several on the coast of North Wales and notably Rhyl, and Llandudno, the largest resort in Wales and known as "The Queen of the Welsh Resorts", a title first implied as early as 1864.

Some resorts, especially those more southerly such as Bournemouth and Brighton, were built as new towns or extended by local landowners to appeal to wealthier vacationers. The south coast has many seaside towns, the most being in Sussex which has the title 'Sussex by the Sea.'

From the last quarter of the twentieth century, the popularity of the British seaside resort has declined for the same reason that it first flourished: advancements in transport. The greater accessibility of foreign holiday destinations, through package holidays and, more recently, European low-cost airlines, affords people the freedom to holiday abroad. Despite the loyalty of returning holiday-makers, resorts such as Blackpool have struggled to compete against the favourable weather of Southern European alternatives. Now, many symbols of the traditional British resort (holiday camps, end-of-the-pier shows and saucy postcards) are regarded by some as drab and outdated; the skies are imagined to be overcast (although British summers from the late 1980s onwards have often been warmer and sunnier than at any other time in living memory) and the beach windswept. This is not always true; for example Broadstairs in Kent has retained much of its old world charm with Punch and Judy and donkey rides and still remains popular being only one hour from the M25.

Many seaside towns have turned to other entertainment industries, and some of them have a good deal of nightlife. The cinemas and theatres often remain to become host to a number of pubs, bars, restaurants and nightclubs. Most of their entertainment facilities cater to local people and the beaches still remain popular during the summer months. Although international tourism turned people away from British seaside towns, it also brought in foreign travel and as a result, many seaside towns offer foreign language schools, the students of which often return to vacation and sometimes to settle.

A lot of people can also afford more time off and 'second holidays' and short breaks which still attract a lot of people to

British seaside towns and a lot of young people and students are able to take short holidays and to discover the town's nightlife. A lot of seaside towns boast large shopping centres which also attract people from a wide area and a lot of day trippers still come to the coastal towns but on a more local scale than during the 19th century.

A lot of coastal towns are also popular retirement hotspots and many older people take short breaks in the autumn months.

In contrast, the fortunes of Brighton, which has neither holiday camps nor end-of-the-pier shows, have grown considerably, and, because of this, the resort is repeatedly held up as the model of a modern resort. However, unlike the *Golden Miles* of other British resorts, the sea is not Brighton's primary attraction: rather it is a backdrop against which is set an attitude of broad-minded cosmopolitan hedonism. The resulting sense of uniqueness has, coupled with the city's proximity to London, led to Brighton's restoration as a fashionable resort and the dwelling-place of the affluent.

Other English coastal towns have successfully sought to project a sense of their unique character. In particular, Southwold on the Suffolk coast is an active yet peaceful retirement haven with an emphasis on calmness, quiet countryside and jazz. Weymouth, Dorset offers itself as 'the gateway to the Jurassic Coast', Britain's only natural World Heritage Site. Newquay in Cornwall offers itself as the 'surfing capital of Britain', hosting international surfing events on its shores.

Torbay in South Devon is known is also known as the English Riviera. Consisting of the towns of Torquay, Paignton with its pier and Brixham, the bay has 20 beaches and coves along its 22-mile (35 km) coastline, ranging from small secluded coves to the larger promenade style seafronts of Torquay's Torre Abbey Sands and Paignton Sands. Northern Ireland has a number of seaside resorts, such as Portrush, situated on the north coast, with its two beaches and a world-famous golf course. Royal Portrush Golf Club. Other Northern Irish seaside resorts are Newcastle, located on the east coast at the foot of the Mourne Mountains, Portstewart, and Bangor. Bangor Marina is one of the largest in Ireland and the marina has on occasion been awarded the "Blue Flag" for attention to environmental issues.

Irish Seaside Resorts

Irish Riviera

The "Irish Riviera" features the seaside resorts of Youghal, Ardmore, Dungarvan, Cobh and Ballycotton, all set close to the south coast of Ireland. Youghal has been a favoured holiday destination for over 100 years, situated on the banks of the Blackwater river as it reaches the sea. Youghal is well known for its beaches, having been, until 2008, the only town in the Republic of Ireland with two beaches awarded EU Blue Flag status. Dungarvan is a seaside market town beneath the mountains in the centre of the Irish south coast. Kinsale is often described as a food lover's and yachting town, with a diverse range of restaurants, as well as a large and active creative community with numerous art galleries and record and book shops.

County Clare

Lahinch is a seaside resort, popular because of its long beach, golf links, promenade, and Seaworld (a leisure complex). Lahinch is also popular with surfers. Ballyvaughan is a village and small port on the southern shores of Galway Bay.

American Seaside Resorts

American seaside resorts developed along the New England coast in the late 19th century with the Mid-Atlantic region developing slightly later. Southern seaside resorts did not develop until the 1890s. In Florida, the community of Cocoanut (now Coconut) Grove began development as a resort town in the 1880s with the building of the Bayview House which closed in 1902. Visitors to the greater Miami area then flocked to Camp Biscayne (in Coconut Grove), the Royal Palm Hotel and other resort hotels in Miami, and in smaller numbers to the keys, particularly to Long Key where the Long Key Fishing Camp was particularly active in the 1910s.

Some examples of well known and sought after American seaside resort towns are:

- Carlsbad, California
- Corona Del Mar, California
- Coronado, California

- Dana Point, California
- Laguna Beach, California
- Montecito, California
- Newport Beach, California
- Pebble Beach, California
- Miami Beach, Florida
- Palm Beach, Florida
- Saint Augustine, Florida
- Ocean City, Maryland
- Provincetown, Massachusetts
- Atlantic City, New Jersey
- Cape May, New Jersey
- Fire Island, New York
- The Hamptons, New York
- Myrtle Beach, South Carolina
- South Padre Island, Texas
- Virginia Beach, Virginia

Conditions Favouring the Expansion of Travel in 19th Century

Age of Steam

When trains got started in the early 19th century, people thought that moving 20 m.p.h. might cause insanity. On the other hand, it is not speed but an enraging motionlessness — the stalled freeway, or the runway where you sit for an hour or two awaiting takeoff — that causes derangement today. We are spoiled. It has been a while since we sat back in a plane or a car and told ourselves, "Life has not many things better than this."

The objective profit and loss have suffered too. Airlines explore the temptations. Amtrak staggers ahead, feckless and insolvent, through train wrecks and slowdowns. It is time to make very large changes — to rearrange the mix of the three basic modes of mass transportation: air, rail and highway.

The answer to the nation's transportation problems clearly lies neither in an expansion of aviation nor in putting more cars on additional highways. My choice would be the oldest mode of the three: rail. It is not a sentimental or nostalgic choice. The aviation industry, like the vast infrastructure for cars, is dangerously overbuilt. In recent years aviation has sucked regional boosters into ill-conceived drives for more airports and more flights, even short ones – all at immense expense.

Airplanes are indispensable for long trips over oceans, over a continent or half a continent. But air travel makes no sense over short distances. In any case, the evolution of cell phones and e-mail and the Internet and videoconferencing means that people need to travel less on business, not more. When ideas and images fly so magically, then our clumsy, inconvenient bodies need not do so – or not so much. Comparisons have been loaded to denigrate trains in favour of cars and air travel. It is true the rehabilitation of the nation's railroads would cost billions. But the arithmetic on costs and energy efficiency argues, in the long term, in favour of boldly creative, high-speed regional rail systems that would take the environmental and traffic pressures off highways and airports.

Trains are two to eight times as fuel efficient as planes. As things stand, passenger trains receive only 4% as much in federal subsidies as the $13 billion given annually to the airline industry. Highways receive $33 billion in federal funds. Both airlines and highways have dedicated sources of federal funding: gasoline and ticket taxes. Rail systems should receive equivalent sources of income.

A halfhearted, partly realized plan will only validate the criticisms and doom the new railroads. What is needed is leadership of the kind that Charles de Gaulle demonstrated in backing France's immensely successful high-speed rail, and vision on the scale of President Eisenhower's push for the interstate highway system. The 21st century paradox is that it is not railroads that are old-fashioned and retrograde but rather those essentially inefficient flying machines.

Early Tourism in North America

Tourism in the United States is a large industry that serves millions of international and domestic tourists yearly. Tourists visit the US to see natural wonders, cities, historic landmarks and entertainment venues. Americans seek similar attractions, as well as recreation and vacation areas. Tourism in the United States grew rapidly in the form of urban tourism during the late nineteenth and early twentieth centuries. By the 1850s, tourism in the United States was well-established both as a cultural activity and as an industry. New York, Chicago, Washington, D.C. and San Francisco, all major US cities, attracted a large number of tourists by the 1890s. By 1915, city touring had marked significant shifts in the way Americans perceived, organized and moved around in urban environments. Democratization of travel occurred during the early twentieth century when the automobile revolutionized travel. Similarly air travel revolutionized travel during 1945–1969, contributing greatly to tourism in the United States. By 2007 the number of international tourists had climbed to over 56 million people who spent $122.7 billion dollars, setting an all time record.

The travel and tourism industry in the United States was among the first commercial casualties of the September 11, 2001 attacks, a series of terrorist attacks on the US. Terrorists used four commercial airliners as weapons of destruction, all of which were destroyed in the attacks with 3,000 casualties. In the US, tourism is either the first, second or third largest employer in 29 states, employing 7.3 million in 2004, to take care of 1.19 billion trips tourists took in the US in 2005. As of 2007, there are 2,462 registered National Historic Landmarks (NHL) recognized by the United States government. As of 2008, the most visited tourist attraction in the US is Times Square in Manhattan, New York City which attracts approximately 35 million visitors yearly.

History

19th Century: The rise of urban tourism in the United States during the late nineteenth and early twentieth centuries represented a major cultural transformation concerning urban space, leisure antural activity and as an industry. Although travel agents and package tours did not exist until the 1870s and 1880s, entrepreneurs of various sorts from hotel keepers and agents for railroad lines to artists and writers recognized the profit to be gained from the prospering tourism industry. The rise of locomotive steam-powered trains during the 1800s enabled tourists to travel more easily and quickly. In the United States 2,800 miles (4,500 km) of track had been completed by 1840, by 1860 all major eastern US cities were linked by rail, and by 1869 the first trans-American railroad link was completed. Yosemite Park was developed as a tourist attraction in the late 1850s and early 1860s for an audience who wanted a national icon and place to symbolize exotic wonder of its region. Photography played an important role for the first time in the development of tourist attractions, making it possible to distribute hundreds of images showing various places of interest.

New York, Chicago, Washington, D.C. and San Francisco, all major US cities, attracted a large number of tourists by the 1890s. New York's population grew from 300,000 in 1840 to 800,000 in 1850. Chicago experienced a dramatic increase from 4,000 residents in 1840 to 300,000 by 1870. Dictionaries first published the word 'tourist' sometime in 1800, when it referred to those going to Europe or making a round trip of natural wonders in New York and New England. The absence of urban tourism during the nineteenth century was in part because American cities lacked the architecture and art which attracted thousands to Europe. American cities tended to offend the sensitive with ugliness and commercialism rather than inspire awe or aesthetic pleasure. Some tourists were fascinated by the rapid growth of the new urban areas: "It is an absorbing thing to watch the process of world-making; both the formation of the natural and the conventional world," wrote English writer Harriet Martineau in 1837.

As American cities developed, new institutions to accommodate and care for the insane, disabled and criminal were constructed. The Hatford, Connecticut American School for the Deaf opened in 1817, Ossining, New York state prison in 1825, the Connecticut State Penitentiary at Wethersfield in 1827, Mount Auburn Cemetery in 1831, the Perkins School for the Blind in 1832, and the Worcester State Hospital in 1833. These institutions attracted the curiosity of American and foreign visitors. The English writer and actress Fanny Kemble was an admirer of the American prison system who was also concerned that nature was being destroyed in favour of new developments. Guidebooks published in the 1830s, 40s and 50s described new prisons, asylums and institutions for the deaf and blind, and urged tourists to visit these sights. Accounts of these visits written by Charles Dickens, Harriet Martineau, Lydia Sigourney and Caroline Gilman were published in magazines and travel books. Sigourney's *Scenes in My Native Land* (1845) included descriptions of her tour of Niagara Falls and other places of scenic interest with accounts of her visits to prisons and asylums. Many visited these institutions because nothing like them had existed before. The buildings which housed them were themselves monumental, often placed on hilltops as a symbol of accomplishment.

Early Tourism

By 1915, city touring had marked significant shifts in the way Americans perceived, organized and moved around in urban environments. Urban tourism became a profitable industry in 1915 as the number of tour agencies, railroad passenger departments, guidebook publishers and travel writers grew at a fast pace. The expense of pleasure tours meant that only the minority of Americans between 1850 and 1915 could experience the luxury of tourism. Many Americans travelled to find work, but few found time for enjoyment of the urban environment. As transportation networks improved, the length of commuting decreased, and income rose. A growing number of Americans were able to afford short vacations by 1915. Still, mass tourism was not possible until after World War II.

During the nineteenth century, tourism of any form had been available only to the upper and middle classes. This changed during the early twentieth century through the democratization of travel. In 1895, popular publications printed articles showing the car was cheaper to operate than the horse. The development of automobiles in the early 1900s included the introduction of the Ford Model T in 1908. In 1900, 8,000 cars were registered in the US, which increased to 619,000 by 1911. By the time of the Model T's introduction in 1908, there were 44 US households per car. Early cars were a luxury for the wealthy, but after Ford began to dramatically drop prices after 1913, more were able to afford one.

The development of hotels with leisure complexes had become a popular development during the 1930s in the United States. The range of "club" type holidays available appealed to a broad segment of the holiday market. As more families travelled independently by car, hotels failed to cater to their needs. Kemmons Wilson opened the first motel as a new form of accommodation in Memphis, Tennessee in 1952.

Although thousands of tourists visited Florida during the early 1900s, it was not until after World War II that the tourist industry quickly became Florida's largest source of income. Florida's white sandy beaches, hot summer temperatures and wide range of activities such as swimming, fishing, boating and hiking all attracted tourists to the state. During the 1930s, architects designed Art Deco style buildings in Miami Beach. Visitors are still attracted to the Art Deco district of Miami, Florida. Theme parks were soon built across Florida. One of the largest resorts in the world, the Walt Disney World Resort, was opened in Orlando, Florida in 1971. In its first year, the 28,000-acre (110 km^2) park added $14 billion to Orlando's economy.

Late 20th Century

The revolution of air travel between 1945 and 1969 contributed greatly to tourism in the United States. In that quarter century, commercial aviation evolved from 28-passenger airliners flying at less than 200 mph (320 km/h) to 150-passenger jetliners cruising continents at 600 mph (970 km/h). During this time, air travel in the US evolved from a novelty into a routine for business travellers and vacationers alike. Rapid developments in aviation technology, economic prosperity in the United States and the demand for air travel all contributed to the early beginnings of commercial aviation in the US. During the first four decades of the twentieth century, long-haul journeys between large American cities were accomplished using trains. By the 1950s, air travel was part of every-day life for many Americans. The tourism industry in the US experienced exponential growth as tourists could travel almost anywhere with a fast, reliable and routine system. For some, a vacation in Hawaii was now a more frequent pleasure. Air travel changed everything from family vacations to Major League Baseball, as had steam-powered trains in the nineteenth and early twentieth centuries. By the end of the twentieth century, tourism had significantly grown throughout the world. The World Tourism Organisation (WTO, 1998) recorded that, in 1950, arrivals of tourists from abroad, excluding same-day visits, numbered about 25.2 million. By 1997, the figure was 612.8 million. In 1950 receipts from international movements were US$2.1 billion, in 1997 they were $443.7 billion.

21st Century

The travel and tourism industry in the United States was among the first commercial casualties of the September 11, 2001 attacks, a series of terrorist attacks on the US. Terrorists used four commercial airliners as weapons of destruction, all of which were destroyed in the attacks with 3,000 casualties. In the first full week after flights resumed, passenger numbers fell by nearly 45 percent, from 9 million in the week before September 11 to 5 million. Hotels and travel agencies received cancellations across the world. The hotel industry suffered an estimated $700 million loss in revenue during the four days following the attacks. The situation recovered over the following months as the Federal Reserve kept the financial system afloat. The U.S. Congress issued a $5 billion grant to the nation's airlines and $10 billion in loan guarantees to keep them flying. In the US, tourism is either the first, second or third largest employer in 29 states, employing 7.3 million in 2004, to take care of 1.19 billion trips tourists took in the US in 2005. The US outbound holiday market is sensitive in the short term, but possibly one of the most surprising results from the September 11, 2001 attacks was that by February 2002 it had bounced back for overseas travel, especially to destinations like New Zealand. This quick revival was generally quicker than many commentators had predicted only five months earlier. The United States economy began to slow significantly in 2007, mostly because of a real-estate slump, gas prices and related financial problems. Many economists believe that the economy entered a recession at the end of 2007 or early in 2008. Some state budgets for tourism marketing have decreased, such as Connecticut which is facing soaring gas prices.

Landmarks

As of 2007, there are 2,462 registered National Historic Landmarks (NHL) recognized by the United States government. The majority of these are located in New York, California, Massachusetts and Pennsylvania. Each major US city has thousands of landmarks. For example, New York City has 23,000 landmarks designated by the Landmarks Preservation Commission. These landmarks include various individual buildings, interiors, historic districts, and scenic sites which define the culture and character of New dork City.

Natural Wonders

The Grand Canyon is one of the most well known landmarks in the US. Other landmarks include Mount Rushmore, the Apalachians, the Rocky Mountains, and Stone Mountain.

Sport

Since the 1960s, sport has become an international affair, attracting a considerable amount of media attention, revenue, participants and political interest. Estimates of the US sports industry's size vary from $213 billion to $410 billion. In 1997, 25% of tourism receipts in the United States were related to sports tourism; this would have valued the market at approximately $350 billion annually. The nature of the sport's media relationship has been distinctly shaped by the emergence of American capitalism since the 1830s. Sports in the United States have attracted tourists for many decades. The 1997 New York City Marathon attracted 12,000 visitors from outside the US of 28,000 participants.

Other Late-ninteenth-century Development

At the end of the nineteenth century, however, there began to be signs that a rapidly developing tourism industry, treated as a part of the economy, might threaten nature and culture. In 1913, Prof. Jan Gwalbert Pawlikowski, a lawyer, alpinist and one of the most active nature protectors, wrote in his prophetic work *Culture and Nature:* "Some people, moved by the beauty of nature, wanted to share their impressions with others and started to facilitate access to it by building roads, trails and shelters. A docile public understood that nature must be beautiful, for the spirit of the epoch demanded it.... Seriously, modern man needs some comfort, so shelters were replaced by hotels which the catering and alcoholic beverage business eagerly supported. Would this not be in the interest of a superior level of excellence, since the public's love of nature would contribute to the national wealth? So, the trails were equipped with railings and guide-posts, narrow paths were turned into roads and, eventually, engineering skill achieved a miracle: in the manner of Herostratus, it violated mountains by building railways up to their summits."

Unfortunately, subsequent development confirmed the accuracy of this diagnosis, and not only in mountain regions. The next decades were dominated by economic and consumer interests that disregarded the consequent environmental devastation. A certain disillusionment came about by the end of the 1960s, a period that can be recognized as a turning-point for the awakening of ecological consciousness on a global scale. People started to look for ways of reconciling economic development with ecological security, a quest which, in a theoretical sense, has been crowned with the World Conservation Strategy.

In terms of tourism, this change in emphasis was possible because, alongside the vast commercial tourist industry, there had continued a strong trend of traditional nature tourism, based on the knowledge, joy and satisfaction resulting from contacts with nature, historical monuments and people of different cultures-a form of tourism where physical effort is not viewed as a nuisance but as a source of satisfaction, that wonderful feeling that occurs on the top of a mountain after long hours of climbing. Tourist adventures can be experienced either alone or with companions. In the latter case, there is an additional humanistic aspect: the consciousness of a close rel The 20th century saw a massive increase in the amount of leisure time and disposable income that the British population had. This was reflected in their sudden demand for more leisure opportunities. The public wanted bigger, better and more extreme leisure activities. Sports developed into national pastimes, as it became cheaper for people to travel around the country following football teams and rugby games. The 20th century was also the time of great technological change. It saw cinemas, music, computers, game consoles and the internet play an even greater role in the lifestyles of both the young and the old. Not only were there now new forms of leisure, but the development of aeroplanes and the increase in holiday parks also meant that more people than ever before could afford to go on holiday, both in Great Britain and abroad.

2

Marketing for Youth Customer

Under a democratic dispensation South Africa has become a favourable destination for foreign students, especially from African countries, to further their academic qualifications. This trend has given prominence to a market segment in the tourism industry, namely, educational tourism. Given the relative underdevelopment of technology in most African countries, opportunities for scholars to enter a worldwide web of learning (e-learning) is at present not a possibility.

Temporary migration for study purpose to another country remains the only way in which Africans can obtain specialized education. Though the main travel motive of student tourists is education, international students have time to travel during university breaks and in this event they visit tourist spots in the host country making a contribution to the growing tourism market. Little is however known about the non-educationally related time spent in a foreign country, moreover, their leisure, recreational and tourist activities. This paper will shed some light on the concept educational tourism and hopefully contribute to the emerging body of literature on this tourism market segment. After a statistical overview of foreign students in South Africa, will we use data collected in a survey among foreign students at the University of the Western Cape in Cape Town to deliberate the potential for this market segment.

Internationally, educational tourism has been recognized as an important market segment in the tourism industry and is indeed not a new concept. Although definitions of educational tourism abounds, the best way to conceptualise the market segment is to look at the broad range of activities. These include the classic education-like school trip and study tours (referred to as a model for benign tourism by some scholars), sabbatical and exchange programmes, under and postgraduate study programmes, short courses, and language courses where tourism and English is considered a powerful combination.

Expatriates working at overseas universities are also known to arrange compulsory fieldtrips for students during their summer vacations. Interwoven with cultural tourism are educational tourists now visiting Buenos Aires to learn to tango, foreigners are being enticed to visit Cape Town for a photographic week "during which they snap the city's most beautiful people *au naturel* in picturesque natural landscapes, taking cooking lessons in France, and learn about the Gorillas in the misty mountains of Rwanda. Eco-tourism or enviro-education is an added overlapping aspect of this market segment.

Educational travel providers are in most cases religious organizations, non-profit organizations, private institutions, private and public sectors, educational institutions such as universities, and private language schools. Despite the seemingly, abundant educational tourism activities, do numerous authors acknowledge the absence of qualitative and quantitative research done on this topic.

What is clear though is that educational tourism is becoming a major potential growth market as the international student population expands annually. Current figures estimate for example a total of 540 000 foreign students in the USA whereas in Western Australia, 20,000 overseas students contributed to an estimated $ 430,000 in domestic spending and other tourism related activities. Another study in Australia estimated the annual expenditure by international students in 1997 as 3.337 billion Australian dollars, almost three times higher than the 1992 figures.

Globalisation has directly contributed to an increase in special interest tourism (such as educational tourism) as boundaries, work opportunities and a new international division of labour emerges. In this regard an IAU statement tabled at the UNESCO World Conference on Higher Education in 1998 emphasized that "higher education and research are among the primary forces that create the conditions of globalization. Through scientific discovery and their contributions to technological progress in communications, information and transportation, universities have been key actors in bringing about globalization in trade and production of goods and services. Through education and training they also prepare the individuals who can best take advantage of these new conditions"

In Australia for example a concerted effort by the national government through the Australian Tourist Commission (ATC) resulted in the signing of an international educational memorandum of understanding to promote Australian international education. The ATC states that there are many opportunities to develop this segment such as strategic partnerships and industry involvement (such as airways). National prestige is seemingly a major recruitment strategy adopted by Australia. Autonomous universities are however in competition to attract foreign students and according to Knight and de Wit recruitment can be divided into four categories: "(a) academic grounds related to the institution's prestige; (b) economic and financial motives; (c) cultural, social, political, and diplomatic considerations; and finally, (d) fear of being outperformed by a competitor or of simply appearing outmoded". It is therefore likely to expect that in the next decade the number of international students may double and hence there is 'great promise for the consumption of tourism products'.

Educational tourism in South Africa Visser recently published a comprehensive review of tourism related research in South Africa between 1973 and 2003. The report however makes no reference to studies covering educational tourism as a market segment. So too, has a study on migration patterns of students from Lesotho to South Africa in *Africa Insight,* not made a direct link between tourism and foreign students. The International Educational Association for South Africa (IEASA) was established in 1997 in view of the need for South African institutions of higher learning "to respond to the unprecedented interest from the international community in the tertiary education sector in this country".

The Association argued, for the country "to remain competitive within the global economic and political environment, it is imperative for higher education in this country to provide opportunities for local staff and students to obtain a global perspective to their study and research activities, and to promote the country's tertiary education sector amongst the international academic community". South Africa is thus not only in the educational production side of tourism but also exporting its own students.

Lubbe gave the example of an agreement signed between the government and Cuba to train medical students. IEASA also pointed out that South Africa offers quality education at a lower cost, and that, especially African students do not have to leave the continent. Educational tourism is also said to result in the mobility of professionals, multilateral networks and the kind of international feel, which is helpful in combating xenophobia and racial tensions.

It does not matter from which point of view this tendency is debated, education has become an export commodity. During 2002 a total of 6 459 916 foreign travellers entered South Africa of which 0.6% (94 015) indicated entry for study purpose. A breakdown according world region of origin, clearly shows that most educational tourists are from Africa constituting more than three quarters of educational tourists. There is, however, no huge discrepancy between other regions with Europe and Asia and North America producing the majority educational tourists. Mashinini and Mashinini made reference to the SADC Protocol on Higher Education and Training that stresses the importance of developing human resources that would facilitate "free mobility of human capital. They further argue that South Africa will bear the brunt of this protocol. A closer look at the tourists coming from Africa reflects a spatial nucleus coming from the SADC region: Botswana (38 471), Swaziland (8 530), Lesotho (7 565), Zimbabwe (66 44), Namibia (5 841), Mozambique (5 076), Angola (2 786) and Zambia (1 536). With the exception of a few countries are students from all over Africa studying in the country.

Agreements between certain South African universities and African countries have become a distinct feature of the tertiary educational sector after 1994. For example, agreements between the Botswana Government and the unbundled Vista University saw a great number of students enrolling at various Vista campuses in the country in the early 2000s.

The above figures from Statistics South Africa in relation to an official estimate of 47,000 international students studying in

South Africa in 2004 made by the International Education Association of South Africa (IEASA) reflects a general inconsistency in using numbers to illustrate accurately a market segment such as tourism education..

Data was also collected from the Department of Education on the number of all foreign students registered at South African tertiary institutions. The dramatic increase in intake over a three year period, especially at South Africa's universities.

Majority of the foreign students are from SADC countries followed by over 7000 from all other continents and lastly over 6000 from other parts in Africa. The percentage of foreigners as registered students at tertiary institutions increased by 2% between the 2000-2003 period. The intake of students from the North Americas doubled over this period whilst the intake from Botswana increased by more than 6000 students.

Although the University of South Africa (UNISA) has the greatest number of foreign students is it the University of Cape Town where the percentage of foreign students in relation to local students is the highest. The University of Port Elizabeth has shown the greatest decline in foreign student intake whilst the University of the North-West experienced the biggest growth, probably attributed to an intake of students from neighbouring Botswana.

It was not possible to determine the specific courses students are enrolled for but the percentage of foreign students studying towards a post-graduate degree. It is the traditionally well-off former advantaged institutions such as UCT, University of Pretoria, University of the Witwatersrand, and Free State that attract a high percentage of postgraduate students. The University of the Western Cape also attracted a high percentage of foreign students. It is to this institution where the remaining focus of this paper will shift.

Case Study: University of the Western Cape

Against the background of the above the remaining sections of this paper will focus on findings from a case study survey conducted among foreign students based at one of the universities in Cape Town. The survey focused on a broad range of issues that included an investigation into the potential economic contribution of international students, why they have chosen this institution in particular, how much they spent on travel related activities, and on living expenses. In addition tourist travelling patterns and means of getting information about tourist places were also investigated. A total of forty questionnaires were distributed to international students via a snowball sampling technique. An attempt was made to get representation of students staying on and off campus. The questionnaire was divided into four sections: demographic information, UWC as study destination, student spending patterns, social cultural and recreational aspects, and organisational matters.

Foreign Student Numbers

The international student population at the University of the Western Cape increased dramatically over the past five years. Student enrolments increased from 162 in 1998 to 1169 in 2004. This reflects a percentage growth of 621% over a 6 year period.

The region of origin for international students is summarised in. Majority of the students are from Africa, but the greatest percentage growth has been from elsewhere in the world (877%). Most students are from Botswana, Namibia and Zambia and Lesotho.

There has been a dramatic increase in students from China in 2004, making up 10% of the total foreign student population.

Student Characteristics

The students taking part in the survey represents twenty different nationalities. Majority of respondents are full time enrolled (95%) and are mostly from African countries (65%). An interesting observation is the age category of the students. Most of the respondents are in the age groups of 36-40 (27.5%), and 25-30 (27.5%). A mere 23% are younger than 25. The market segment in this case caters thus mainly for people who left school and probably worked for a number of years saving up money to sponsor their own studies (25% in this survey are self sponsored). Having had working experience and admittedly being more mature than school leavers, foreign students are viewed in a study in the USA to be of a high academic quality, and that they are easily absorbed into research and tutorship positions. Government sponsored students accounted for 30%.

Accommodation is arguably one of the most important components in the tourism industry. It is maintained that the "success of tourism destinations is largely dependant upon the appropriate development of the accommodation sector". In developing countries, national data on the actual economic contribution of tourism accommodation, for example the revenue it earns, number of employment created, expenditure of tourists are unknown, and highly speculative. Accommodation is a broad concept and the categorization of tourist accommodation varies at different scales of investigation.

Considered as part of the tourism hospitality sector, accommodation can be grouped into six types, namely, a paying, rented, static/permanent, serviced, primary purpose, holiday/ business establishment. Basically four options of accommodation are evident from the survey where 45% indicated that they reside on campus, 45% live in rental houses, and a minority live in an International hostel, with friends and family.

The University of the Western Cape is a choice destination because of course availability (42%) in a specific field, for example dentistry. Another reason for studying at UWC is the fact that the university fees are affordable in comparison to other universities in the country (this accounted for 18% response rate). To a lesser extent relatives and friends also influenced the choice of the university as a study destination (15%). Apart from these, some students came to UWC as a result of inter-institutional exchange agreements and collaboration (12%).

Most (83%) of the respondents did not have any problem interacting with the local students. This finding is indicative of the nature of educational tourism, namely to learn about new cultural lifestyles. Asked to rank their attitude towards South Africans, the majority indicated that their attitudes were fair (65%) this is followed by those who said that their attitudes were good (12%). Only (5%) of the respondents had a bad/very bad attitude towards South Africans.

Travel Patterns

A number of questions related to travelling patterns focused on the variety of trips undertaken, where tourism information was accessed, where they travel during holidays, and reasons for and not exploring the country. The survey found that 20% of African students do not travel at all. Day trips outside Cape Town are fairly popular (38%), while almost half of the respondents indicated having gone on a weekend trips outside Cape Town at least once during a year. Only 35% indicated having gone on a week trip outside Cape Town. Of this, African students are in the minority.

The reasons why international students travelled outside Cape Town are visiting friends and relatives, adventure, and simply to escape the daily routine of being a student. Of the places visited Durban, Johannesburg and Port Elizabeth were ranked best followed by Pretoria. Majority of the students indicated that they mainly visit places in Cape Town during the vacations however.

Students who do not travel, indicated financial reasons as the biggest obstacle. Other major problems include a lack of personal transport, lack of safety and security, hostility towards foreigners, and to a lesser extent some students indicated that most of the time, they are too busy with studies to have time to travel.

It is apparent that mainly students from Europe, America and Asia make use of tourism information centres whereas students originating from other African countries acquired information mainly from friends and family members in South Africa. Other information sources such as television, internet and newspapers accounted for 9.4 %. Most respondents preferred to organise their trips in groups (52.5 %) and mainly do so due to lack of own transport. Female respondents prefer to travel in groups for safety reasons (47.5 %), and a minority organise theirs individually (4.9%).

Most of the students go home during the end of the year university holiday (55%). Majority of these are married (refer to age categories above) and the one's not committed stay to explore the country further. The likelihood of repeat visits to the tourist spots was determined, and respondents were asked if they would return to these after they have gone home (i.e. once they finished their studies). Majority of the respondents indicated that they would like to return to those tourist spots and more especially would like to come back with their family members (95%). It is evident from the above findings that foreign students are indeed a potential lucrative tourism market.

Economic Impact

The *Sunday Business Times* reported that education is becoming a profitable business for institutions and the country as a whole. According to the article, South African institutions are tapping into a growing market where the total revenue generated from higher education in 2003 amounted to R 21.5 billion. About R 1.4 billion of this was generated by international students. International students are said to spent between R2500-R4000 a month on goods and services. When their relatives also visit they spent between R 5000 and R 12,00028.

Our survey estimated that three quarters of the respondents consider South Africa an affordable (i.t.o cost of living and tuition fees) destination, especially if compared to Europe or America. Those that indicated that South Africa is not affordable stated that foreigners are at a disadvantage in terms of exchange rate to the Dollars from their currencies.

A cross tabulation between considering the country affordable and world region of origin showed that all respondents from Europe, America, and Asia indicated that South Africa is affordable. A mere 27% African respondents stated the country is not affordable. Affordability also translates into purchasing patterns. With the exception of major capital expenses such as a motor car, have most Africans spent more money than students from other regions on electrical appliances. Asian and European students mostly invested in a car, primarily to travel and resell again when they return to their country.

African students spent the least on travelling and tourism related activities in comparison to the other students. More Africans however spent more than R3001 per month on living expenses (excluding accommodation) as do American and Asian students. European students spent most money on a monthly basis while Americans on average spent most on travelling. Regional differentiation is of significance to tourism planners especially when identifying new niche markets such as package tours for target groups.

The average amount spent on accommodation per month is R727,00. If the sample is considered representative of the UWC foreign student body then the following amounts spent per year is brought into the Western Cape economy: R19 million per year on living expenses; R24 million per year on travelling and tourism related activities; and R10 million on accommodation. Just over R50 million is therefore estimated to be spent by foreign students at UWC per year. Given the fact that the province is blessed with four major universities (UCT, Univ. of Stellenbosch, UWC, and Pentech and Cape Tech combined) with an estimated 4000 foreign students an annual injection of R200 million can be considered a substantial boost into the economy. (The figure may be higher if other educational institutions such as the language and vocational colleges are also taken into consideration).

Conclusion

A national estimation of a total revenue generated in higher education for 2003 amounted to 21.5 billion Rand, of which 1.4 billion generated by international students. Although it may seem only a fraction of the total capital generated in the tourism industry, are ramifications of foreign students as tourists not given any thought in local debates around tourism development.

With an increasing trend in international students to the country (and to the University of the Western Cape in particular) is there a huge potential to develop this lucrative market segment further. Not only does this market contribute positively to the domestic economy of South Africa, it also contributes to creating a socio-cultural awareness among locals, a so-called 'cosmopolitan feel'. Presence of foreign students is also said to fight against xenophobia and aiding exchange of academic ideas and removing the borders between nations by the establishment of multilateral networks. It facilitates cultural appreciation by other people from different backgrounds.

The following five general recommendations are based on the findings from the survey:

(1) Universities and other higher institutions of learning should increase their marketing efforts to this market segment in order to exploit its potentiality to the fullest.

(2) South African institutions should position themselves in order to increase the number of international students. And, for those who are already having big numbers of international students, they should strive to maintain them.

(3) Tourism marketers should work hand in hand with higher educational institutions in order to exploit this market segment exhaustively. On the same note, they should see to it that they provide a positive image of the country and the institutions of learning.

(4) Tourism marketers should also think of targeting this market segment on a serious note, by maybe, offering some incentives to international students.

(5) University managements should recognise the contribution of this market segment, and take active steps to ensure that foreign students are indeed looked after as visitors, and not simply as a students. Annual surveys among students to identify areas of concern, problems, and so on is a useful method to keep track of the needs and expectations of foreign students as tourists.

Exploring Nature Based and Cultural Educational Tourism

As the new millennium unfolds, we are becoming increasingly aware of the finite, interconnected and precious nature of our planet home. Likewise, tourism is becoming an increasingly popular expression of this awareness. Tourism not only provides an escape from the everyday working life of many, but it also represents the everyday working life of many more. With advances in transportation and information technology, ever more remote areas of the earth are coming within reach of the traveller. In fact, tourism is now the world's largest industry, with nature tourism the fastest growing segment. In response to this increasing appreciation of nature experiences, a new travel ethic has arisen which is now called ecotourism.

This term has become increasingly popular in both conservation and travel circles. Most tourism in natural areas today is not ecotourism and is not therefore, sustainable. Ecotourism can be distinguished from nature tourism by its emphasis on conservation, education, traveller responsibility and active community participation. Specifically, ecotourism is not only the act of a foreigner visiting a foreign land, but also the participation of and effects on the local populations of touristed areas. These facilities and programs become part of the local culture, and it is up to the planning of tourism to make sure that they stay within the original framework of the culture.

With the definition of traditional tourism in mind, ecotourism can be discussed as a different entity based on the involvement of local populations in all aspects of tourism. Indigenous populations are the most knowledgeable about the area, and they "possess the practical and ancestral knowledge of the natural features of the area".

Maintaining the important bond between its education and its environment is important to the survival of an ecotourism program. This is especially important now, in a time when ecotourism is part of the development strategy of nearly every developing country.

In the second section, it provides a brief description of how and why ecotourism has evolved and what it means. The broadly accepted definition of ecotourism is presented along with definitions of other terms related to ecotourism. In the third section, we suggested a model of the various players involved in ecotourism management and development.

In the fourth section, we argued naturalist guide of the role and how it could be cultivated to develop ecotourism. Finally, I make an assertion volunteer tourism that could be another form of alternative eco-tourism for the theoretical development of EATOF member's countries.

Literature Review

The Definition of Ecotourism

There are various definitions of ecotourism, most of which have to do with combining the travel industry with an ideal that emphasizes conservation and preservation of the wilderness in which people spend their vacations. The Ecotourism Society defines ecotourism as "responsible travel which conserves environments and sustains the well-being of local people,".

Ecotourism is a relatively new concept, and it is still often misunderstood or misused. Some people have abused the term to attract conservation conscious travellers to what, in reality, are simply nature tourism programs which may cause negative environmental and social impacts. While the term was first heard in the 1980s, the first broadly accepted definition, and one which continues to be a valid "nutshell" definition was established by The International Ecotourism Society in 1990: *Responsible travel to natural areas that conserves the environment and improves the well-being of local people.* As awareness and experience of the activity has grown, so has our need for a more comprehensive and detailed definition. Martha Honey (1999) has proposed an excellent, more detailed version: Ecotourism is travel to fragile, pristine and usually protected areas that strives to be low impact and usually small scale. It helps educate the traveller; provides funds for conservation; directly benefits the economic development and political empowerment of local communities; and fosters respect for different cultures and for human rights.

However, consensus exists among organizations involved with ecotourism including The Nature Conservancy around the definition adopted in 1996 by the World Conservation Union (IUCN) which describes ecotourism as:

Environmentally responsible travel and visitation to natural areas, in order to enjoy and appreciate nature and any accompanying cultural features, both past and present that promote conservation, have a low visitor impact and provide for beneficially active socio-economic involvement of local peoples.

The Nature Conservancy has adopted the concept of ecotourism as the type of tourism that it recommends its partners use in most protected area management, especially for national parks and other areas with fairly strict conservation objectives. For The Nature Conservancy, ecotourism represents an excellent means for benefiting both local people and the protected area in question. It is an ideal component of a sustainable development strategy where natural resources can be utilized as tourism attractions without causing harm to the natural area. An important tool for protected area management and development, ecotourism must be implemented in a flexible manner. However, the following elements are crucial to the ultimate success of an ecotourism initiative. Ecotourism must:

- have a low impact upon a protected area's natural resources;
- involve stakeholders (individuals, communities, ecotourists, tour operators and government institutions) in the planning, development, implementation and monitoring phases;
- respect local cultures and traditions;
- generate sustainable and equitable income for local communities and for as many other stakeholders as possible, including private tour operators;

- generate income for protected area conservation;
- educate all stakeholders about their role in conservation.

Evolution of Ecotourism

Ecotourism is a concept that evolved over the last 20 years as the conservation community, people living in and around protected areas, and the travel industry witnessed a boom in nature tourism and realized their mutual interests in directing its growth. Ecotourism has brought the promise of achieving conservation goals, improving the well-being of local communities and generating new business promising a rare win-win situation. Relations among conservationists, communities and tourism practitioners have not always been smooth and collaborative.

However, the concept and practice of ecotourism brings these different actors together. Ecotourism has emerged as a platform to establish partnerships and to jointly guide the path of tourists seeking to experience and learn about natural areas and diverse cultures.

Conservationists and Ecotourism

Specific circumstances on all sides motivated this new interest in ecotourism. On the conservation side, protected area managers were in the midst of redefining conservation strategies. For practical reasons, they were learning to combine conservation activities with economic development as it became obvious that traditional conservation approaches of strict protectionism were no longer adequate and new ways of accomplishing goals were needed.

For years, conservationists established and managed protected areas through minimal collaboration with the people living in or near these areas. Circumstances in many countries, particularly in developing regions, have changed dramatically in recent years and have affected approaches to conservation.

Local Stakeholders and Ecotourism

Over the past two decades, many developing countries have experienced large population increases with declining or stagnant economic conditions. These countries have frequently been pressured into exploiting their natural resource base in an unsustainable fashion in order to meet immediate economic needs and to pay interest on foreign debt. This combination leads more people to compete for fewer natural resources. Outside protected areas, the natural resources that many people have depended upon for sustenance and many businesses have relied upon for profit making have disappeared. For most countries, protected areas have become the last significant pieces of land that still retain important reserves of plant and animal diversity, water, clean air and other ecological services. Meanwhile, protected areas have become increasingly attractive to farmers, miners, loggers and others trying to make a living. The economic development pressures on these areas have intensified on local, national and global scales. Thus, ecotourism has become very important for potentially reconciling conservation and economic considerations. Because of this competition for resources, conservationists realized that local people and economic circumstances must be incorporated into conservation strategies. In most cases, local people need financial incentives to use and manage natural resources sustainably. Existing economic and political conditions often limit their options and increase their reliance on natural areas.

Conservation work often means creating alternatives to current economic practices so that multiple-use zones around protected areas can be maintained and threats to protected areas minimized. In looking for alternative economic activities, conservationists have become more creative and are exploring many options. Ecotourism is one such alternative. The rationale behind ecotourism is that local tourism businesses would not destroy natural resources but would instead support their protection. Ecotourism would offer a viable strategy to simultaneously make money and conserve resources. Ecotourism could be considered a "sustainable" activity, one that does not diminish natural resources being used while at the same time generating income.

Related Terms

As a popular word, ecotourism has been used loosely. But if implemented fully, it is a critically important conservation strategy for achieving sustainable development.

There are a variety of related terms that are frequently linked, and sometimes confused with ecotourism, including the following:

- Nature tourism is simply tourism based on visitation to natural areas. Nature tourism is closely related to ecotourism but does not necessarily involve conservation or sustainability. This is the type of tourism that currently exists in most natural areas before a plan is established and conservation measures are in place. As different elements of ecotourism are integrated into a nature tourism program, its effect on the environment may change.

- Sustainable nature tourism is very close to ecotourism but does not meet all the criteria of true ecotourism. For example, a cable car carrying visitors through the rainforest canopy may generate benefits for conservation and educate visitors, but because it represents a high degree of mechanization and consequently creates a barrier between the visitor and the natural environment, it would be inappropriate to describe as an ecotourism initiative. In altered and heavily-visited areas, sustainable nature tourism may be an appropriate activity. For example, larger "eco" resort development would not be considered low impact if it required significant clearing of native vegetation but may contribute to conservation financially and provide conservation education.

The line between sustainable nature tourism and ecotourism is subtle but very important. A project must meet all of the necessary criteria listed above before it can accurately be defined as ecotourism. Projects that fall short on any of the criteria do not truly benefit conservation or the people involved over the long term.

- Cultural, ethno or cultural heritage tourism concentrates on local traditions and people as the main attractions. This kind of tourism can be divided into two types: The first and conventional type is where tourists experience culture through museums and formalized presentations of music and dance in theatres, hotels or occasionally in communities themselves. In many instances, this has lead to the "commodification" of culture as it becomes adapted for tourist consumption, often resulting in degradation of the hosts" cultural traditions. The second type is more anthropological and contains a strong visitor motivation for learning from indigenous culture rather than simply viewing an isolated manifestation of it. For example, there is growing interest in learning how indigenous people use natural resources. It is important that cultural tourism be managed on terms defined by host communities and that indicators of the cultural impact of tourism be monitored to ensure visitation does not erode the cultural resource.

- Green/Sustainable tourism refers to travel operations that use natural resources judiciously. Green or sustainable tourism can be considered the "greening" of the tourism industry. Examples include the airline industry becoming more energy efficient, the cruise line industry recycling its waste or large hotel chains adopting environmental regulations. Large hotels have discovered that by advising guests to reduce water consumption or recommending that they not expect their towels to be washed every day, the hotels not only gain a "greener" image which is increasingly important to consumers, but they also reduce operating costs. Thus, green tourism is clearly an attractive proposition to the conventional tourism industry. In reality, reducing the hotel's water consumption by 15%, although desirable and relatively easy to achieve at most large hotels, is not enough to convert the hotel into a sustainable operation. Sweeting et al. (1999) review this issue comprehensively and make recommendations for reducing conventional tourism's impact on the environment.

While greening the existing conventional mass tourism industry will produce some benefits, new developments in natural areas, including beaches, need to address energy consumption, waste management and environmental interpretation in the design phase and not as an afterthought if they are to be truly sustainable.

Large hotels washing towels only every other day may not be enough to protect the water table in an arid area. Not building the hotel in the first place in an area where water resources are scarce may be the best option.

Developing a sustainable or green tourism industry in all its dimensions is as worthy a cause as working to maintain protected areas through tourism. In fact, some would argue that promoting sustainability of the broader tourism would be a better conservation mission than focusing on protected areas alone. However, for the present purposes the focus will be on ecotourism development. It may be easiest to think of ecotourism which works to protect natural areas through tourism and sustainable tourism which works to make the whole tourism industry more environmentally friendly as two valuable, but distinct, missions.

Key Considerations for Successful Ecotourism

These days, most conservationists recognize that working with communities is fundamental to achieving protected area goals and conservation strategies, including ecotourism. There are a number of basic principles that should be considered in planning for community involvement in ecotourism activities. Ecotourism organized at the local community level can rarely be successful without assistance or cooperation from tourism operators. Links to the market, language skills and poor communications are three major aspects which limit communities ability to "go it alone" in ecotourism. Protected area managers must play a role in guiding ecotourism implementation outside of the protected area, but in many cases that role may have to be a "second-hand" one. NGOs are generally perceived as neutral parties and thus more acceptable as providers of technical assistance to local communities. In some cases, the NGOs may be the protected area managers. Training, for example in basic accounting and guiding, is a key need for communities to effectively participate in ecotourism. This is a role that NGOs are best placed to provide.

For ecotourism to promote conservation, local people must clearly benefit and understand that the benefits they receive are linked to the continued existence of the protected area. There must be a close working relationship between the protected area administration and the surrounding communities.

Unfortunately, the limited benefits provided by many tourism projects frequently are not recognized by local residents as connected to the protected area.

A huge range of players with varying interests and goals participates in ecotourism. Some play more prominent roles than others, but almost all are represented in the development and management of ecotourism sites.

A key to the success of ecotourism is the formation of strong partnerships so that the multiple goals of conservation and equitable development can be met. Partnerships may be difficult because of the number of players involved and their different needs, but forging relationships is essential. The key players can be classified as community organizations and individuals, private sector tourism industry members and a variety of government officials and non-governmental organizations. Their effective interaction creates effective ecotourism.

Core Decision Makers

Local Government. Officials

Many government departments should participate in ecotourism planning, development and management. These departments include tourism, natural resources, wildlife and protected areas, education, community development, finances and transportation. Ecotourism involves officials primarily from the national level, although regional and local levels also contribute to the process.

Government officials have several significant functions in ecotourism. They provide leadership. They coordinate and articulate national goals for ecotourism.

As part of their overall tourism plans, they provide vision for this industry. They may even propose a national ecotourism plan; in Australia, the government created a National Ecotourism Strategy and then committed AUS$10 million for its development and implementation.

Government officials at the national level may also establish specific policies for protected areas. For example, government officials decide about visitor use fee systems at protected areas, and their policies outline what systems are established and how revenues will be distributed.

They may also delineate private sector practices, e.g., tour operators may be required to use local tour guides in certain areas or developers'' property ownership rights may be regulated. Government policies direct ecotourism activities and may easily advance or hinder their growth.

Additionally, government officials are responsible for most basic infrastructure outside protected areas ranging from airline facilities in big cities to secondary roads leading to remote sites.

The government generally takes the lead in all major transportation systems and issues. It may also provide other services important to ecotourism such as health clinics in rural areas.

Finally, government officials promote ecotourism. Sometimes the promotion is part of a national tourism campaign. At other times, advertisements for specific nature sites are created or perhaps a flagship species is identified and promoted. National government participation gives prominence to ecotourism destinations.

Local Communities.

People who live in or near protected areas are not a homogeneous group. Indeed, even within one small community there will be a diversity of people with a range of views and experiences.

But we can make a few generalizations about local residents and their relationship to ecotourism. First, some rural communities that once featured quiet living are finding themselves in the middle of an international trend. Nature tourists are invading their homelands, but they are generally just passing through the neighbourhood, not coming to meet residents. Residents have mixed reactions to this intrusion. Some want nothing to do with tourists; they want privacy and do not welcome the changes that tourism brings. Others are intrigued by tourism and are taking steps to develop it. Tourism may be particularly alluring if other employment options are limited or if residents feel tourism may help protect their precious resources.

Many communities in developing countries are hosting visitors and creating ecotourism programs. Sometimes their motivation is to protect their surrounding natural resources. For others, they may see ecotourism in a more economic perspective, as a means to gain income. Many communities have organized their own ecotourism programs.

Whatever their initial reaction to tourism, local residents are often unprepared for its demands. Those who do not want tourism have no means to stop it. They often cannot compete with the powerful tourism industry or the fiercely independent travellers who want to discover new areas. Those who are interested in pursuing tourism may not be familiar with its costs and benefits.

Many have little experience in tourism business enterprises and are not connected to international tourism markets. The interests and concerns of local residents regarding tourism development need special attention.

Tourism touches all the other groups involved professionally, in a mostly economic sense. For members of communities, it also touches their personal lives by affecting their lifestyles, traditions and cultures, as well as their livelihood and their long standing ways of organizing themselves socially and politically. In addition, most of the other players enter into tourism voluntarily, whereas in many cases communities must deal with tourism impacts whether or not they choose to. Local residents play an important role in ecotourism for two main reasons.

First, it is their homelands and work places that are attracting nature travellers. Equity and practicality require that they be active decision-makers in ecotourism planning and management.

Second, local residents are key players in conserving natural resources both within and outside of neighbouring protected areas. Their relationship to and uses of natural resources will determine the success of conservation strategies for protected areas. In addition, local or traditional knowledge is often a key component of visitors' experience and education.

Tourism Industry

The tourism industry is massive. It involves a huge variety of people including: tour operators and travel agents who assemble trips; airline and cruise ship employees; minivan drivers; staff of big hotels and small family lodges; handicraft makers; restaurant owners; tour guides; and all the other people who independently offer goods and services to tourists. The complexity of this sector indicates how challenging it can be for protected area staff and local communities to learn about and form partnerships with the tourism industry.

Consumers are in contact with many members of the tourism industry throughout their journeys. For an international trip, the traveller often first contacts a travel agent, tour operator or airline. The agent will generally contact an outbound tour operator based in the tourist's country of origin, who in turn will contact an in bound tour operator based in the destination country. The in bound tour operator is best placed to make local travel arrangements such as transportation, accommodations, and guide services.

Once the traveller is at the destination, many local entrepreneurs will also become part of this scenario. One element that binds all businesses within the tourism industry is the pursuit of financial profit. There may be additional motivations for some businesses, particularly those involved in ecotourism, but tourism companies exist only when they are profitable. Members of the tourism industry are valuable to ecotourism for many reasons.

First, they understand travel trends. They know how consumers act and what they want. Second, the tourism industry can influence travellers by encouraging good behaviour and limiting negative impacts in protected areas. Third, the tourism industry plays a key role in promoting ecotourism. Its members know how to reach travellers through publications, the Internet, the media and other means of promotion, thus providing a link between ecotourism destinations and consumers.

Non-governmental Organizations

Non-governmental organizations are valuable players because they provide a forum for discussion and influence regarding ecotourism. They offer a means of communication with great numbers of interested individuals. These organizations can serve as vehicles for bringing together all the elements of ecotourism. NGOs can play many different roles in ecotourism implementation: directly, as program managers or site administrators; and indirectly, as trainers, advisors, business partners with ecotourism companies or communities and, in exceptional circumstances, as providers of ecotourism services.

There are several different types of non-governmental organizations. Among them are for-profit tourism associations consisting of private tour operators, airlines and hoteliers; ecotourism associations such as those in Belize, Costa Rica, Ecuador, etc., that bring together groups from all the sectors involved; and other trade organizations that handle travel issues.

These NGOs often have members who meet regularly and communicate industry concerns through publications such as newsletters. Members are often asked to subscribe to certain principles or "codes of ethics." These associations and organizations are effective at keeping the industry informed about current trends and events. Another set of non-governmental organizations involved with ecotourism includes the private, non-profit groups that focus on conservation and development or may be dedicated specifically to ecotourism. Their focus may be local, national or international. Frequently, these organizations serve as facilitators between protected areas, communities and all the other players in ecotourism, sometimes providing financial and technical assistance or directly managing ecotourism sites. Some of these NGOs have constituencies that enjoy nature and would be interested in ecotourism education and promotion.

NGOs play an important role in advancing ecotourism implementation through their positive interaction with local communities, the private sector tourism industry, government-administered protected areas and others. The particular role adopted by an NGO depends upon the set of circumstances within which it operates, e.g., its mission and purpose, the degree of openness to NGO collaboration and the interest of the tourism industry. Opportunistic situations also arise which affect an NGO''s role, such as donation of a tract of land for ecotourism purposes or development of a friendly relationship with a community leader.

Supporting Players

Funders

Many different groups can fund the development of ecotourism through loans or grants: financial institutions, including investment corporations; bilateral and multilateral donor agencies; private investors; venture capital funds such as the Ecoenterprise Investment Fund; NGOs; and private banks. These contributions are often critical for protected areas that pursue ecotourism. Typically there are studies to carry out, facilities to build, infrastructure to create and people to train. With protected area budgets so limited, outside funding is necessary.

Financial institutions do not generally participate in planning for ecotourism or in decisions about what is appropriate for a particular protected area. In this regard, they may be considered a second-tier player in ecotourism, but they are important nonetheless. For anyone that wants to develop ecotourism, access to funds is often the biggest obstacle confronted.

Academics

Academics at universities is another group that plays a secondary, though valuable, role in the planning and daily functions of ecotourism. It is a group that helps to frame the issues of ecotourism and raise questions to ensure that ecotourism meets its stated goals. Researchers and academics facilitate learning by asking such questions as: Who exactly is benefiting from ecotourism? How do we measure benefits? How does ecotourism contribute to our existing knowledge about conservation? What are the links between ecotourism and tourism? Academics can focus on the big picture and help us understand how ecotourism interacts with other concepts and global trends.

In addition to helping shape the hypotheses, academics conduct research. In coordination with NGOs, governments and local communities, they may:

- Educate and create naturalist guides.;
- produce data about tourism patterns;
- inventory flora and fauna;
- document tourism impacts and share results to develop a good base of information;
- provide material to guide us in our discussions and conclusions about ecotourism;
- facilitate the sharing of this information and conceptual thinking through conferences, publications, the Internet, etc.

Travellers

Travellers have a unique position as players in ecotourism. They are the most vital participants in the industry and provide motivation for everyone else's activities, but few participate in formal meetings about ecotourism. Nevertheless, the choices they make when they select a tourism destination, choose a tour operator or travel agent and, ultimately, the kind of tour in which they wish to participate, have a tremendous impact upon the eventual success or failure of ecotourism projects.

Ecotourism, then, is a multifaceted, multi-disciplinary, multi-actor activity requiring communication and collaboration among a diverse range of actors with different needs and interests.

Consequently, achieving ecotourism is a challenging process though ultimately enormously rewarding for all involved.

Creating Naturalist Guides

Naturalist guides play a central role in the implementation of the ecotourism concept. They are the principal providers of the educational element to the ecotourism activity, and their capacity and commitment ensures that the negative impacts of tourism are minimized. At the same time, guiding is an obvious economic opportunity for people from local communities. These and other important benefits underline the importance of a protected area establishing and implementing a naturalist guide training and licensing program.

The use of tour guides in protected areas is not a new phenomenon. Guides have been a part of nature tourism in many places for many years. These tour guides usually were employed by private tour operators and had little or no relationship to the protected area they worked in even though they didn't have any background knowledge about the importance of environment. Over the years, this situation began to change as protected area managers realized the potential for using guides to increase contact with visitors and for accomplishing other ecotourism objectives as well.

The Roles of Naturalist Guides

Naturalist guides truly play a multifaceted role. They have responsibilities to their tour operator employers, to their clients the visitors, and to the protected areas and communities where they work. Tour operators count on guides to provide experience enriching interpretation of natural and cultural attractions to add value to the tourists' itinerary. They also require guides to manage logistical aspects of trips in the field, such as coordinating with accommodation, food and transport service providers. Guides are responsible for the tourists'' safety and in general represent their tour operator employer in the field.

Tourists look to the naturalist guide for information, interpretation and insight about the places they are visiting; for help preparing for a visit through formal briefings and informal talks; and generally to be a friendly, knowledgeable intermediary with unfamiliar places and people. Protected area authorities look to the guides as extensions of the park ranger staff, to educate the visitors, to protect the natural and cultural resources of the area visited, to participate in monitoring programs and generally to support the conservation objectives of an area. In addition to these roles, a naturalist guide should seek to inspire visitors to become supporters of conservation.

Nature Interpreters

Environmental interpretation is a subset of communication that focuses on how best to explain environmental and ecological concepts to the general public. One of the central tenets of ecotourism is to educate the visitor. Naturalist guides, who spend a considerable amount of time with visitors, are in a perfect position to educate through skilled interpretation. Many local residents have a detailed knowledge of the plant and animal life as well as of other natural and cultural attractions. They can also relate first-hand experiences with wildlife, medicinal plants and other local phenomena.

Conservationists

As the main contacts that visitors may have with an ecotourism site, guides serve as important role models both to visitors and their own communities. Their attitude and behaviour send an important message to others about the ecotourism concept. Does the guide pick up pieces of trash along the hiking trail? Does the guide actively support and cooperate with site managers by reporting illegal activities? Does the guide adapt ecotourism to his/her own home and community situation? Some tour guides make a point of discussing the importance of conserving the incredible diversity found at a site, what the major threats to it are and what visitors might do to help conserve it.

Park Rangers

Unfortunately, not all visitors to ecotourism sites know how to behave appropriately in sensitive natural and cultural settings. It is the guides' responsibility to ensure that visitors are aware of all applicable rules and regulations as well as other relevant ethical considerations. In a polite but firm manner, they must make sure that visitors comply with whatever restrictions there may be. This is perhaps the most difficult role that guides have because their major responsibility is to help provide visitors with an enjoyable experience. As members of the private sector, it can, in rare situations, create a conflict of interest between the guides' conservation obligations and their obligation to the visitor and, in some cases, their employer. For example, a tour operator might promise clients a close encounter with a whale, but a guide may judge that at a given moment the whales seen in the distance are nursing young and should not be approached. The guide's obligations to an employer and to a park authority might be divergent at this point. Guides need special training in how best to deal with these situations. They also must be vested with the authority to report and deal with infractions of rules and regulations.

Monitors of Tourism Impact

Since guides visit the ecotourism site/protected area on a frequent basis, they are in a unique position to notice certain kinds of impact, such as trail erosion, increasing rareness of a particular bird species, etc. They are also in an excellent position to carry out formal monitoring observations for the site's managers. In many places, guides take the time to carry out observations of the number of nesting birds or of the regeneration of a plant species in a designated quadrant. This can be of valuable assistance to a site's managers when they are short-handed or simply do not have trained personnel to carry out these tasks.

Liaison with Local Communities

When guides are from local communities, they can serve an important role in improving communication between the site's administration and local people. This is particularly important when there may be some misunderstanding between the two different "communities," which there frequently is. Naturalist guides should establish government financed organizations to further conservation objectives.

In order for a naturalist guide system to work well in an ecotourism site situation, several conditions must be met.

Control and Licensing

The site must have effective control over the use of guides and the conditions under which guides will operate within the site. This implies that managers either own the site or that there is legislation or some other legal mandate for exercising this control.

Most effective guide systems have a licensing mechanism. The site's administration, or some higher authority acting at the administration's request, will issue a license to guide visitors within the site if the guide complies with relevant rules and regulations. The site's administration reserves the right to suspend or revoke the license if a guide's behaviour is inappropriate. Licenses are usually extended to those individuals who pass a training course or a test. The site's administration reserves the right to set other criteria for attending a training course, such as: being a member of a local community, being of a minimum age, the absence of a police record and having a minimum level of education. It is important to avoid flooding the market with too many licensed guides as this would force down wage levels as many compete for an insufficient number of jobs. However, it is necessary to have a sufficient number of guides to satisfy demand; a rough guide would be to license about 25% more guides than will be working each season.

In spite of the control that the site's administration must exercise over the guides' activities, the relationship between them should be more than one of employer and employee. Both the site administration and the guide have much to offer each other, and they should actively carry out their respective roles in order to benefit from each other's work. Unfortunately, it is not uncommon for one side or the other to lose sight of their mutually supportive roles and for the relationship to become non-productive. Constant and positive feedback is the best way to avoid this situation. Involving tour operators and guides in the ecotourism program planning process from the beginning is also crucial.

Training

Naturalist guides need training in order to fulfil the many roles they are charged with. The primary themes for a training course curriculum are listed below.

- Natural history of the site and surrounding areas. What are the major species, plant and animal communities and ecosystems? How do they interact with one another? What is their conservation status?
- Cultural attractions. What are the historical, archaeological and traditional cultural activities that can be found in the

site and surrounding areas? What is the relationship between natural and cultural attractions?

- Site conservation priorities and activities.

Guides should be able to explain to visitors what the site's management is doing to further the conservation of the natural and cultural resources found in the site as well as how the site relates to other protected areas and the surrounding communities.

- Rules and regulations. Guides need to be aware of all the rules and regulations governing public use of the site and its facilities. In particular, they need to be aware of what ecotourism is and how it is applied at this site.
- Group management. All guides need to learn how to best manage a group of visitors that can have widely varying attention spans and reasons for being there. Maintaining everyone's attention and keeping the group together can sometimes be a major chore. Experienced guides are sometimes the best people to teach this part of the course.
- Interpretive/communication techniques. There are very special techniques for communicating ideas to a group of disparate people. Learning the techniques comes easily for some guides; for others, a significant amount of time will need to be spent. Training should not be a one-time event for guides. Good guides should be continually refreshing and updating their knowledge, and the site's administration should consider carrying out periodic courses for this purpose. Courses should be developed with, and at least partly financed by, the tourism industry. In addition to specialists in each of the themes outlined, tour operators should be instructors in courses, as should older, respected members of the local community.

Young men often dominate the competition for places in guide training courses, but it is important to ensure that women participate too. They make good guides, and at least 50% of tourists are women! Rare (formerly the RARE Centre for Tropical Conservation), with the support of The Nature Conservancy, has developed a comprehensive guide training manual that is highly recommended.

Guide Availability

Ecotourism encourages the inclusion of local people in as many circumstances as possible. While it may be useful to utilize local people as naturalist guides, managers should realize that residents may not be "natural" naturalist guides. Their interests or educational levels may be obstacles to reaching the level of expertise required of guides at a site. Significant training may be needed before they can function effectively.

Work Availability

Work availability is a very sensitive issue in many situations. Naturalist guides have the potential to earn significantly more money than other members of their community. For this reason, when a site initiates a naturalist guide system, there are sometimes many more candidates than available work. Managers must be careful not to create high expectations among guide candidates, especially if visitor numbers are not sufficient to guarantee work for everyone.

If some candidates for a training course are selected over others who appear to have similar qualifications, conflicts may arise. Site managers may do several things to minimize these problems:

- Ensure that specific criteria are used to select guide candidates and that the criteria are strictly followed. Limit training course size to a specific number of people and accept candidates on a first come, first serve basis.
- Initiate policies that encourage or mandate the use of local guides in the ecotourism site or in specific locations or zones within the site. This may cause conflicts with other, non-local guides.
- Encourage the creation of a naturalist guides association that will help to organize guides and their response to a limited number of guiding opportunities, e.g., a system of rotation. This is also an excellent way to minimize cutthroat competition and to standardize prices. The site could mandate that guides charge only a certain amount for a given service, but the mandate would be better received and complied with if the guides were allowed to determine their own price structure.

Language Skills

Local guides can face a language barrier since most ecotourists are from another country, usually one where a different language is spoken. Local guides can be very ingenious at communicating with visitors whose language they do not speak. However, they cannot express themselves at the level that a high quality naturalist guide would need to communicate effectively, expressing complex ideas and concepts.

It is not uncommon for organized tours to arrive at an ecotourism site with a guide who works with the tour company and comes from the capital city, or even another country. Sometimes these guides are very knowledgeable about the site, but many are not. However, local community members should be given priority for positions as naturalist guides.

In the case of areas that are ancestral lands of local communities, hiring a trained local naturalist guide should be obligatory. If tour operators require higher level scientific interpretation, they may choose to hire a university educated non-local guide to also accompany their clients. Training courses for local guides will likely emphasize different themes than courses for university-educated naturalists. If the situation is developed appropriately, guides from both categories can learn a lot from each other. Regardless, all guides should take and pass the training course and be licensed. It should be mandatory to train and provide licenses to local guides.

Conclusion

The environment is one of the primary concerns of ecotourism, which often involves travel to relatively undisturbed areas. As the tourism product is often dependent upon nature, negative impacts upon that resource should be minimized. As Cater [1994] notes, even the most conscientious tourist will have some degree of impact on the environment and so ecotourism should therefore attempt to minimize that impact. Many studies of tourism attempt to identify an environmental carrying capacity but a major difficulty of this technique is that it "implies the existence of fixed and determinable limits to development and that if one stays below those threshold levels no changes or deterioration will occur". Great importance is attached to the need for local participation in ecotourism. According to Wallace and Pierce [1996], ecotourism is a type of tourism that "maximizes the early and long-term participation of local people in the decision making process that determines the kind and amount of tourism that should occur". There are important reasons for local involvement other than a moral obligation to incorporate the people tourism will affect. The degree of control the local population has over tourism in their locality is generally perceived as being a significant element of sustainability. As was noted earlier, ecotourism is required to provide direct economic benefits to the local community and minimize negative environmental and socio-cultural impacts. The most likely way these objectives can be achieved is if the local community are actively participating in and empowered through ecotourism.

The final principle to which ecotourism should adhere is that of education. Ecotourism should involve education among all parties – local communities, government, non-governmental organizations, industry and tourists before, during and after the trip. Guides should therefore have been taught conservation issues and the tourists should be told about local conservation efforts and why they are deemed important. Tourists should be made aware of the damaging potential of their stay and should be properly informed on "ecotourism etiquette" and how to behave to reduce any negative impacts they might have.

A pool of trained and licensed naturalist guides can be a tremendous asset to protected area conservation. Creating a naturalist guide program should be a high priority for all sites with an ecotourism program.

Proposal

The annual "yellow dust" spring storms, which originate in China's Gobi Desert before sweeping south to envelop the Korean peninsula and parts of Japan, are blamed for scores of deaths and billions of dollars in damage every year in South Korea. The dust picks up heavy metals and carcinogens such as dioxin as it passes over Chinese industrial regions, before hitting North and South Korea and Japan.

The state-sponsored Korea Environment Institute said the dust kills up to 165 South Koreans a year, mostly the elderly or those with respiratory ailments, and makes as many as 1.8 million ill so that volunteer tourism could be an another form of alternative eco-tourism for the theoretical development of EATOF members countries. Accepting that a person is rarely forced to go on vacation, we can then infer that tourism as an activity is voluntary. An exploration of volunteer tourism consists of the principles it adheres to, its goals, and the characteristics that define eco tourism.

The motivations of volunteer tourism can broadly be stated as volunteer-minded and vacation-minded. Push and pull factors also look at the motivations of participants.

One of the example of volunteer tourism is to dispatch a voluntary team consisting of some EATOF youngsters and citizen to plant trees in desert areas in China and Mongolia to reduce damages from desertification and yellow dust. It can provide people of EATOF countries with opportunities to realize the importance of voluntarism and environmental movement.

The tourism strengthen partnership of cooperation on combating desertification and yellow dust. In cooperation with the all EATOF member, the Green forest is going to be established a long green belt, namely the Great Green Wall in Kubuqi desert in Inner Mongolia, China to fight desertification and yellow dust storm.

Through various programs such as tree planting, environmental education and cultural exchange, the Green Forest will provide young people and citizen with opportunities to realize the importance of voluntarism and environmental movement.

Goals

The volunteer tourism aims to arouse public awareness on the issues of desertification and yellow dust storms, to promote participation of the young generation in environmental activities, and to contribute to the establishment of ingenuous friendship among youths all over the world.

Vision

1. To combat desertification and yellow dust storms by constructing.
2. Organize Green Corps in cooperation with the all EATOF members.
3. Make a brighter future for the next generation.

Travel Agencies Selling the Nature Versus Sustainable Tourism Development

The growth in alternative forms of tourism has occurred simultaneously with an increased recognition of the need to implement the concept of sustainable development. Eco-tourism has been widely assumed to be inherently sustainable, although few attempts have been made to verify this assumption. Eco-tourism incorporates environmental and cultural conservation objectives, and emphasizes economic benefits to local communities.

Hence, eco-tourism would appear to be, and is increasingly presented as, a tool for sustainable development. However, it also has the potential to be more environmentally damaging than mass tourism since it typically occurs in fragile environments and opens up previously undiscovered destinations to the mass market.

By the late 1980s, a shift in the tourism industry's marketing strategy occurred alongside the emergence of the global environmental movement. In the decade of "green consumerism", critical consumers were soon leading the demand for "environmentally sound" holidays. Tour operators and travel companies began to promote themselves and their products as "environmentally friendly", and a number of companies published ethical and environmental codes of conduct and guidelines for travellers as well as guidelines for self-regulation. Tour companies also started to promote eco-tourism holidays to all corners of the world, to coincide with the inclusion of the environment on the mainstream political agenda. At the same time the tourist hunting industry has expanded dramatically.

Literature Survey

Sustainable Development

In the 1987 Brundtland Report of the World Commission on Environment and Development, sustainable development is defined as the " development that meets the needs of the present without compromising the ability of future generations to meet their own needs" (World Commission on Environment and Development, 1987:43). To meet the needs of the present, the new development has to provide ground on which the basic necessities of all humans and the opportunities for a better life can be satisfied.

Sustainable development is being discussed for the last two decades, mostly among academicians. The core elements of these discussions are:

- The idea that the needs of present and future generations must be considered;
- The need to ensure that renewable and non-renewable resources are conserved, not exhausted;
- The requirement that access to and use of natural resources must take fair account of the needs of all people;
- A recognition that issue of environment and sustainable development must be treated in an integrated manner.

Sustainable Tourism Development

The tourism and recreation industry is at a crossroads in its development. Now as one of the world's largest industries, it is increasingly confronted with arguments about its sustainability and compatibility with environmental protection and community development. Consideration of tourism, the environment, and concepts of sustainability should consider four key challenges: (1) a better understanding of how tourists value and use natural environments; (2) enhancement of the communities dependent on tourism as an industry; (3) identification of the social and environmental impact of tourism; and (4) implementation of systems to manage these impacts.

The tourism and recreation industry is confronted with serious and difficult choices about its future. The decisions made now will for decades affect the lifestyles and economic opportunity of residents in tourism destination areas. Many of these decisions are irreversible because once communities lose the character that makes them distinctive and attractive to nonresidents, they have lost their ability to vie for tourist-based income in an increasingly global and competitive market place.

Owen (1993) characterizes sustainable tourism development as:

- Tourism should be one part of a balanced economy.
- The use of tourism environments must allow for long-term preservation and for use of those environments.
- Tourism should respect the character of an area.

- Tourism must provide long-term economic benefits.
- Tourism should be sensitive to the needs of the host population.

Butler suggests the following working definition of sustainable development in the context of tourism: "tourism which is developed and maintained in an area (community, environment) in such a manner and at such a scale that it remains viable over an indefinite period and does not degrade or alter the environment (human and physical) in which it exists to such a degree that it prohibits the successful development and well being of other activities and processes".

The growth in alternative forms of tourism has occurred simultaneously with increased recognition of the need to implement the concept of sustainable development. As with "eco-tourism", "sustainable development" is another environmental catch phrase with no single definition. On the face of it, no other economic activity would appear to lend itself to sustainable development better than tourism. Alternative forms of tourism that incorporate environmental and cultural conservation objectives with an emphasis on economic benefits to local communities would appear to be a panacea for sustainable development. Because damage to the environment threatens the resource base on which alternative forms of tourism depend, it would be logical to expect all involved in tourism to ensure the protection of these resources. All forms of tourism consume resources such as land and energy. However, when practiced against the standards of its definition, the small scale and dispersed nature of eco-tourism, combined with connotations of sound environmental management, means that it has the potential to consume far less basic resources than other forms of tourism or other developments.

A recent article in the UK Youth Hostel Association's magazine, Triangle, takes up this theme:

> *"Spending your holiday in one of the latest artificial all-weather tropical pleasure domes or in intensely developed but properly managed holiday resorts like Benidorm and Torremolinos can be more environmentally friendly than indulging in trips to remote or fragile areas where tourism is more likely to be environmentally and culturally damaging and puts*

little or nothing back into managing and protecting the environment".

Quoted in the same article, the popular conservationist David Bellamy comments "Eco-tourism is already a dirty word. Hill walking, jungle trekking and all the rest are just as potentially harmful as conventional resort holidays, if not more so. Most of the tourism industry is simply sponging off clean water, fresh air, the natural and cultural environment and is putting nothing back in. But there are praiseworthy exceptions, which not only do not damage the environment, but also actually help to restore it. This is real eco-tourism.".

In addition to the potential damage caused locally to tourist destinations, the air transport of tourists to remote areas of the globe seriously undermines the concept of sustainability of the industry as a whole. For example, air travel contributes 2-3 percent of global emissions of fossil fuel derived carbon dioxide, the principal greenhouse gas, as well as nitrogen oxides, which contribute to low-level ozone formation. Paradoxically, nitrogen oxides released at high altitudes also contribute to the thinning of the protective ozone layer over the earth.

Not all of the impacts of tourism are necessarily negative. If development and change are bound to occur in a particular site from some activity or other, tourism may be a far less damaging alternative than many other more polluting industries. The Overseas Development Association (ODA) Manual of Environment Appraisal (1996) provides a checklist to help develop management strategies to minimize negative impacts and maximize positive benefits. Therefore, alternative or other forms of tourism are not necessarily a panacea for sustainable development, unless well planned and well regulated. In most countries, there usually is no coordination between programs that promote and market tourism and those that manage environment and culture. On the other hand, agencies dealing with the promotion of tourism are not involved with the evaluation of its effects or with advance planning and management of the adverse impacts of tourism through avoidance, mitigation, and compensation strategies.

Eco-tourism

The term "eco-tourism" is often assumed largely to alternative tourism that involves international travel by people from rich developed countries to developing countries, as a means of providing much needed foreign exchange for hard-pressed national economies, and earnings for poor rural people. The notion of these interrelated conservation and economic benefits has led to much confusion surrounding the variety of terms currently in use that appear to have similar meanings and aims. These include "alternative tourism", "sustainable tourism", "soft tourism", "special interest tourism", "green tourism", and "eco-tourism". Some of these terms frequently appear to be used interchangeably, while others may be defined in a variety of ways.

In reality, eco-tourism has become widely adopted as a generic term to describe tourism that has, as its primary purpose, an interaction with nature, and that incorporates a desire to minimize negative impacts. Implicit in the term is the assumption that local communities should benefit from tourism and will help to conserve nature in the process. In this study, the term "Eco-tourism" will be used to generalize all the other terms, and if a specific section of eco-tourism like wildlife tourism or alternative tourism is explained, then those terms will be used specifically. The terms "eco-tourists" and "eco-tours" will be used in this study to summarize the group of tourists and the tours created for them in the name of eco-tourism.

As with the term "eco-tourism", there is similar confusion regarding the term "alternative tourism" that is often used as a generic term encompassing a range of variations such as eco-tourism and green tourism, all of which purport to offer a more benign alternative to conventional mass tourism. Indeed, eco-tourism has been described as "one of the most widely used and abused phrases of the last decade", which it is argued can mean anything to anyone.

A Few Definitions of "Eco-tourism":

"An enlightening nature travel experience that contributes to the conservation of the ecosystem while respecting the integrity of host communities".

"Responsible travel to natural areas, which conserves the environment and improves the welfare of local people".

"Purposeful travel that creates an understanding of cultural and natural history, while safeguarding the integrity of the ecosystem and producing economic benefits that encourage conservation".

Eco-tourism can contribute enormously to the management of protected areas. Benefits include foreign exchange revenues, employment opportunities, improving awareness of conservation objectives and stimulation of economic activity. While protected areas are major destinations for eco-tourists, private enterprise is playing an increasing role in the eco-tourism sector. In addition, eco-tourism is a major vehicle for realizing tangible benefits of conservation for local communities with wildlife populations occurring on their land. However, the benefits accruing to local communities from tourism have so far been overstated. The type and magnitude of the environmental impacts associated with eco-tourism vary with the type of tourist activity pursued. Some impacts are obvious and easily identifiable, while others are indirect and difficult to quantify.

Strategies to manage the impacts arising from eco-tourism may also be direct or indirect. Direct strategies include limiting the total numbers of visitors to an area; dispersing visitors; zoning; using fixed viewing points; and setting guidelines for minimum viewing distances. Indirect strategies are those that aim to modify the behaviour of tourists. One of the most important ways of achieving this is to educate visitors about the potential disturbance they can cause and to provide advice on how to reduce it.

Eco-tourism has the potential to be more damaging than mass tourism since they often occur in fragile or unique environments. Small-scale operations in environmentally sensitive locations may eventually turn into much larger and more destructive operations. Eco-tourism may simply represent the early stages of the conventional tourist destination life cycle. The life cycle concept essentially revolves around the premise that, unless intervention occurs, tourist destination areas and resources inevitably will become over-used and, consequently, will decline. The six stages of the cycle are as follows:

- Exploration (few tourists, poor access and facilities, environment unchanged);
- Involvement (local initiatives, some promotion, increasing numbers);

- Development (many tourists, locals lose control, deterioration of environment);
- Consolidation (tourist numbers exceed local residents, all major chains represented);
- Stagnation (numbers peak, destination falls out of fashion, environmental and social problems);
- Decline or Rejuvenation (or intermediaries).

This cycle has a number of obvious implications for sustainability, based on the consideration of factors such as carrying capacity, local participation, ownership, social and environmental impacts.

Mass tourists may have less impact than eco-tourists, because they tend to limit themselves to well known, easily accessible areas and insulate themselves from the local people. In some instances, the zoning of mass tourism (or enclave tourism) is adopted as a deliberate policy by a host country. For example, tourists in the Maldives are confined to self-contained, purpose built resorts on isolated, often formerly uninhabited islands, in order to avoid a culture clash between bikini-clad tourists and the conservative, Islamic islanders. Bhutan limits the annual foreign tourist entrance to their country to 3,000 pax only.

Eco-tourism proved to be a very lucrative sector of the industry, and commercial considerations of marketing the latest "undiscovered" paradise quickly overshadowed any concerns for environmental or cultural degradation. Indeed, the marketing of eco-tourism may well have accelerated social degradation, because more and more previously unknown destinations were discovered and subsequently opened up to mass tourism.

Turkey & Sustainable Tourism Development

Without giving due regard to the underlying principles of eco-tourism, tour operators and even governmental agencies seem to be securing the short-term economic benefits to sell regions or products.

As a developing country, Turkey's choice of pursuing a tourism development strategy is to create opportunities for economic improvement, since it suffers from deficit in the balance of payments. Tourism is also a tool for decreasing unemployment, because it is a labour-intensive industry. Turkey is trying to secure the short-term inflow of the foreign currency by increasing its bed capacity and trying to attract more tourists. Although the industry is centralized as being governed by the ministry, there are not any records available of any act for sustainable tourism development. Some accommodation units and travel agencies to a certain extent, as a tool for revenue generation, only use sustainable tourism. Accommodation units try to decrease the operational costs like usage of sun energy. Some demand less usage of towels. Clearly, the aim of these acts is not to maintain sustainable tourism, but to minimize their costs. Indeed, the travel agencies' main concern is to maximize the total number of tourists to increase their profit. Therefore, the carrying capacity is totally ignored.

Like many other developing country governments, Turkish governments have helped the fast development of tourism without taking into account the factors of local culture and environment. All governmental acts have been related to monetary gains, since Turkey have been used to economic crises during the last decade. Even IMF has expected certain tourism income figures in order to give credits.

Research Methodology

The purpose of the research was to explore the perceptions of and the possible commitments of Turkish travel agencies engaged in eco-tourism to sustainable tourism development. An exploratory study were undertaken since not much was known about the situation at hand, and there were not any information available on how similar problems or research issues have been solved in the past. In other terms, there were not any previously defined theoretical framework and any hypothesis to test, so this research was to develop related subjects and their groupings by content analysis.

In order to address the quality of information obtained about nature tour operators, substantial attention will be given to survey design and administration. The aim of the research was to examine how travel agencies perceive the impacts of their development and to evaluate their level of response to environmental concerns. In order to satisfy these aims, the objective was to obtain rich data. This pointed towards using a qualitative method involving relatively few people. According to Oppenheim (1992) 'the longer, the more difficult and the more open-ended the questions schedule is, the more we should prefer to use interviews.' In the light of this, a decision was made to undertake face-to-face, in-depth interviews.

In order to reach desired information, directors or senior personnel of ten TURSAB member agencies who are engaged in eco-tourism as the unit of analysis were interviewed. Having obtained the booklet of TURSAB listing the agencies as the population frame, the initial intention was to undertake systematic random sampling; however, this method of sampling proved unsatisfactory due to the high number of companies unwilling to participate and the fact that only around one-third of the population were in Istanbul, making the rest impossible to reach regarding the time limits. The choice of researcher was, therefore, very much decided on by the respondents' willingness to participate, i.e. the first ten agencies in Istanbul to agree. Given the seniority of all the interviewees, this was effectively 'elite interviewing': the individuals are influential and in a position to report on their organizations policies and future plan. Furthermore, 'elites respond well to... intelligent, provocative, open-ended questions'.

Among the total population of 362, 135 were located in Istanbul and the rest 227 were located especially where eco-tourism activities took place. A limitation should be noted that the number of agencies rapidly change and figures of 2000 may not be the exact values of today, yet helped us for a fair idea of the population, since links on TURSAB website of the updated lists of agencies did not work during research process.

The research was a cross-sectional study with respect to time horizon, because data were gathered by the interview once, for a period of days.

In-depth, face-to-face interviews with managers of travel agencies engaged in eco-tourism have been used as the data collection method. Other data sources were used during the literature survey such as publications, manuals, archives, journals and related books.

For qualitative data analysis, systematic coding by content analysis was used to analyze the transcripts of the interviews. In this method, the researcher analyzed interview answers and prepared a list of subjects. The researcher and one independent sorter categorized these subjects independently. After a discussion between the researcher and the independent sorter, who was a manager of one of the visited travel agencies, a common categorization was agreed upon. For reliability testing, two independent graduate students who have studied research methodology also categorized the subjects.

According to the reliability test, the results of the content analysis came out to be significant.

Findings & Discussions

Types of Tours

According to the segmentation like mass tourism and eco-tourism, travel agencies engaged in eco-tourism also sell tours for the mass market. When the respondents were asked to compare the two types of tours with respect to sustainability, there was a clear dichotomy between the two segments. At the first glance, special tours and eco-tours might be considered more sustainable; their volumes are lower, they are more likely to use local accommodation, local guides and services, and attract more environmentally aware clients. However, a differentiated tour for the mass market may attract eco-tourists as well. On the other hand, some specialist markets are evolving into mass markets, because of the increase in volume and the rapidly changing markets. This shows the danger of using broad statements, as eco-tours are more sustainable.

Types of Activities

According to the frequency order derived from the answers of the respondents, the following activities are marketed by the travel agencies: Walking/rambling, alternative water sports, trekking, golf, adventure, cycling, hunting, safari, photographing, mountaineering, rafting, horseback riding, fishing, alternative winter sports, bird watching. Many of the agencies sell more than one type of tours.

Why to Sell Alternative Forms of Tourism?

Travel agencies sell alternative forms of tourism in order to earn more money. Other reasons are to reach the young generation, to increase the variety of products and to enter a new market. Travel agency executives feel that their companies should be considered like markets or small shops in evaluation of any effects of operations, but they forget the fact that they do not sell products of another company like a market, but they produce the eco-tours themselves and sell them. Since those tours selling the nature are their products, they are responsible for the positive or negative effects of their products. These effects may be to the environment, to the local culture or to other aspects related to sustainable tourism. Travel agencies do not seem to accept the fact that some of the activities they make are acting against sustainable tourism by opening new areas to tourism without considering carrying capacity, using the nature as a marketing concept and allowing uncontrolled contact with local culture and tourists.

Sustainable Tourism

Sustainable development is a new subject of concern that many of us are not familiar with. Sustainable tourism development is also new, but it is being discussed in meetings of many international organizations. The first and obviously the main finding was that most of the interviewed senior personnel or managers of travel agencies in Turkey that are engaged in eco-tourism do not even know what sustainability is all about. Interesting answers on the definition of sustainability, which were totally unrelated to it, reminded the researcher the fact that many of the employees and managers in the tourism industry are uneducated or did not have their education on tourism. This was proved by the respondents' education levels, which were mostly high-school graduates. The most interesting answer for the researcher was: 'Sustainable tourism,... should be related to renovations of the hotels, planes... it should not be related with travel agencies, we sustain tourism'. No matter the answer is funny or dramatic, but it seemed to be the reality for general knowledge of travel agency executives in Turkey related to sustainability. So, the respondents did not take into consideration the important aspects of sustainability like local culture or environment, since they did not know the term.

Who is More Responsible for Realization of Sustainable Tourism?

Economically, travel agencies feel that any attempt to take steps on sustainable tourism will put them at a commercial disadvantage because of increasing costs. They agree on helping the realization of sustainable tourism only if the tourists accept to pay more. Therefore, they feel that governments are more responsible for imposing restrictions, limiting growth and controlling volumes and so helping sustainable tourism. The result of this study showed that, travel agencies are willing to comply with regulations if governments impose them to the whole sector. Another point that Turkish travel agencies engaged in eco-tourism mentioned is their operations are too small with respect to the whole market to make any influence.

Conclusion & Implications

This study has examined the social, environmental and cultural impacts of alternative tourism activities with regard to the travel agencies in Turkey engaged in eco-tourism. First conclusion is that it has become harder to segment the market into mass tourism and eco-tourism, since the two segments are becoming more integrated into each other and there are products, which cannot be put under a certain category. Second conclusion is that, although these travel agencies sell eco-tours and earn money, they believe that government has the major responsibility to ensure sustainable development. The third general conclusion is the fact that most of the travel agency executives has learned the definition of sustainability after the general explanation of the researcher.

It is easy to make an assumption like because travel agencies are small enterprises; their responsible behaviour may have a very small effect on sustainable tourism. Yet, specialist tours take tourists deeper into nature and sensitive local culture, and import the necessary skills instead using local work force.

Environmental policies and sustainable acts have become nothing more than a marketing ploy and a vehicle or eluding regulation. Environmental departments and affiliations with glossy campaigns have arguably become a PR exercise designed to meet the growing awareness in some markets to appear environmentally sound and to attract higher spending tourists. For sustainable tourism to be a marketable concept, tourists themselves have got to really buy on it.

To conclude, the researcher wants to point out that sustainability is mostly considered as an utopia and will probably never be achieved.

Limitations & Weaknesses of The Study

Since the respondents were not aware of the topic, it was hard to evaluate travel agencies' attitudes towards sustainable tourism. Most of the respondents did not want their company names to be published because of their lack of knowledge on the topic.

Certainly, as far as travel agencies are concerned, it is almost impossible to make generalizations, with each company having a different product, market segment, strategy and philosophy. Another weakness is that the respondents were busy with the new coming hot season. They demanded the time of the interview to be as short as possible. This limited the number of words used and so the frequency numbers.

Adult and Senior's Tourism

This status report summarizes the history of the Florida Library Literacy state grant program and outcomes achieved as a result of the grants. The Florida Library Literacy Grant program has reached over 6,000 adult learners through literacy programs at local public libraries from April 2000 through September 2001. Libraries have documented improvements in 63% of the adult learners attending their programs. Individual outcomes can be seen in the Activities and Accomplishment section of this document.

The Florida Library Literacy Grant program was established by the State Legislature in spring 1999. Its purpose is to support the development and implementation of innovative adult literacy programs through Florida public libraries.

Fifty-two grant applications have been received and 41 have been funded. Among those counties receiving funding are 17 of the 33 rural counties, certified as such by the Office of Trade, Tourism and Economic Development (OTTED). Florida Library Literacy Grants provide funding to 11 of the 13 counties and one of the four communities identified as in either the first or second Rural Area of Critical Economic Concern.

Of the 30 counties and two municipalities receiving funds, more than 50% have greater than the state's average of poor persons (15.2%). Nearly two-thirds of the grant recipients have more persons at Level 1 literacy, the lowest level of literacy, than the state average (24%). These individuals are unable to find information in text, such as newspapers; complete forms, such as social security card applications; or interpret graphs and charts, such as a table of employee benefits.

Twelve of the grants addressed English as a Second Language (ESL) instruction, either in whole or in part. Five grants received multiple years of funding. The need for ESL occurs across the board, and is not always known at the beginning of a grant cycle.

For example, Lake County discovered that of the people enrolling in the library's adult literacy classes, 94% are seeking to learn English as a Second Language. To meet this new-found demand, the library redefined their mission during the second year and successfully secured funding for the second and a third year. The accomplishments of ESL participants include learning to write letters to landlords and holding telephone conversations in English.

ESL instruction is also critical in many urban areas in Florida. Hialeah's Level 1 literacy rate is 59% and observational data gathered by staff indicates that many of the parents whose first language is Spanish are unable to help their children with their reading assignments. In counties such as Leon, the libraries have targeted specific neighbourhoods that are in desperate need of literacy services. Working through one of its branches, the Leon County public library has targeted a two-mile area, which includes five low-income housing complexes. While there is not in-depth data on each complex, only 10% of adults in one complex has a high school diploma or GED.

Adult learners are gaining literacy skills that enable them to get jobs or better jobs. For example, one disabled man learned to fill out forms, identify jobs in want ads, and read manuals to receive an Air Conditioning Repair certification. Adult learners are also gaining life skills at their own pace. For example, one of the libraries benefiting from the Florida Library Literacy Grant program wrote, "...our students benefit greatly from the fact that these grant funds are NOT tied directly to Workforce Development. Adult learners, seniors, and disabled adults not entering the workforce are "welcomed" by programs funded with these grant dollars."

Of the forty-one grants funded, forty have successfully leveraged funding with partners and the programs will be sustained. The 41st grant involved the purchase of materials that continue to be available to the adult learners. Twenty-two library systems have received funding.

Program Implementation

The Florida Library Literacy Grant program was established by the State Legislature in spring 1999. Its purpose is to support the development and implementation of innovative adult literacy programs through Florida public libraries. The legislature appropriated $500,000 during the first year of funding and reduced the appropriation to $250,000 for the second and third years of funding.

Secretary of State Katherine Harris appointed members to the Florida Library Literacy Grant Advisory Council who designed the focus of the grant program. The Department of State, Division of Library and Information Services developed procedures to implement the program. The first projects began in April 2000. Thus, the program has actually been in place for 21 months with the third year starting December 2001.

The program has evolved as the Florida library community better identified their needs in the area of adult literacy. In the first year, the grant program focused on the broad literacy needs of the family. The second cycle of grants resulted in programs with the adults as the central beneficiary. For the third year, the application guidelines were revised to support the development and implementation of innovative adult literacy programs through Florida's public libraries.

For the first year, the program had two outcomes, 1) adult learners' literacy skills improved and 2) parents or caregivers read to their children. In the second year, successful applicants were asked to put most of their effort on the outcome of improving adult learners' literacy skills. In the third year, the applicants addressed the outcome of improving adult learners' literacy skills in order to create lifelong learners and library users supporting their role as parents, workers and citizens. This evolution has resulted in a program increasingly targeting the hard to serve adult learner.

An important development in the implementation of this grant program occurred with the third year of funding. The Division revised the grant guidelines and application to incorporate the outcomes-based evaluation methodology originally developed with its Library Services and Technology Act (LSTA) grants. In addition to identifying outcome(s) the grant applicant anticipated achieving, they were also required to identify the indicators of the successful achievement of the outcome(s) and the method of data collection. For example, a grant applicant could identify as an indicator of success, the number and/or percentage of adult learners receiving one-on-one instruction who complete a skill book or attain a personal goal.

Many of the library literacy programs funded through the Florida Library Literacy Grant program use alternative assessment which involves site-developed tools to measure success in achieving life skills goals rather than standardized tests which measure reading level improvement. Literacy professionals view both means of assessment as valid. Standardized tests alone "...are limited in their ability to demonstrate the full range of growth shown by program participants."

3

The Management of Australian Educational Tourism

Introduction

Improving communication between scholars and the tourism sector requires us to explore the emerging possibilities of scholarly interaction with Australian educational tourism companies, as well as to understand the challenges for academics to engage with teaching and learning in this domain.

Challenges

136 of the academics surveyed expressed an interest in participating in educational tourism in the future. This included 79 who had previously participated, indicating that the experience was positive for most that had done so in the past. As with prior experiences, being a guest lecturer on a tour was the preferred experience. Significantly, being a tour leader was the least preferred experience for the future, despite being the second most common experience previously experienced.

Just as significantly, 47 academics indicated they would not be interested in participating in educational tourism; including 13 who had previous experience. Broadly speaking, the reasons concerned a series of perceptions about educational tourism that fell into the following categories

Description

As tourism matures as an academic subject and the number of tourism higher education providers continues to expand worldwide, there is an increasing interest in its educational aspects.

At the same time the development of research into education issues related to tourism means that there is now a developing literature on the subject. This international handbook offers a timely evaluation of the sate of the art of tourism higher education.

Its global survey of tourism education offers a comprehensive basis for comparative review. In addition to setting out the development and current provision of tourism education it also addresses cutting edge issues such PhD education, non-formal education, cultural issues in learning, research and teaching, e-learning and e-assessment. It offers practical advice for the design, delivery, evaluation and resourcing of courses and concludes with a reflective agenda of issues for the future.

Education Tourism: A Strategy to Strategy to Sustainable Tourism Development in Sub-Saharan Africa

Countries in sub-Saharan Africa are faced with bleak economic and grave human conditions. Protracted civil wars, political instability, and falling prices for agricultural and mineral exports have combined to wreak havoc on the economies in the sub-region. These countries are saddled with huge debt burdens resulting from foreign loans. Consequently, scarce resources needed for economic development are diverted to service these loans. According to Vice-president George Saitoti of Kenya, sub-Saharan Africa's debt in 1999 exceeded 250% of its export earnings, a figure that is over the 200% that the World Bank and other multi-lateral financial institutions consider sustainable for economic development.

The combination of a crippling debt burden, political instability, civil wars and falling export prices is that living standards are lower today in sub-Saharan Africa than they were at the time of independence in most countries.

Attempts are being and continued to be made by leaders in the sub-region to alleviate these conditions. Promotion of mass tourism is one of several strategies that has been tried. However, sub-Saharan Africa is still not a significant player in the world tourism industry. The sub-region accounted for less than one percent of the world's total tourism receipts in 1997. This paper suggests education tourism as an alternative strategy to the mass tourism development efforts. It calls for a coordinated, sustained and organised approach to education tourism to realise its social and economic potential.

What is Education Tourism? The term education tourism or edu-tourism refers to any "program in which participants travel to a location as a group with the primary purpose of engaging in a learning experience directly related to the location". It is comprised of several sub-types including ecotourism, heritage tourism, rural/farm tourism, and student exchanges between educational institutions. The notion of travelling for educational purposes is not new and its popularity in the tourism market is only expected to increase. Sub-Saharan African countries can increase their tourism earnings by tapping into this growing market phenomenon. The sub-region is endowed with abundant tourism resources that could serve as the basis for education tourism. These resources may be categorised into the following dimensions: cultural/historical, ecotourism/nature based tourism/rural tourism, and study abroad programs. Examples of themes that may be used for education tourism include: studying dolphins in South Africa to discover their ecological limits; monitoring bird migration to restore declining populations and manage habitat change; tracking the habitats of rare endemic carnivores; measuring the impact of public health education and clinical testing of intestinal parasites of remote villages; surveying traditional herbalists to preserve indigenous knowledge; finding the connection between global warming and termites by investigating South Africa's insect engineers. Cultural and historical themes include: arts and crafts, architecture, language, archaeological sites, music, dance, slave trade, etc.

Markets for Education Tourism in Sub-Sahara Africa The size of the word market for international education travel is estimated to have increased from 4.8 million trips in 1985 to almost 8 million trips in 1996. This figure represents more than a 66% increase. Over the same period, spending travel increased by 73%.

The Sub-region is currently not a major education tourism destination. The significant global edu-tourism destinations. However, trends from the U.S. market indicate the sub-region is increasingly becoming at destination of choice of many American students. The Open Doors Report 1998/1999 published by the Institute of International Education (IIE) indicated that the number of American students travelling to Africa increased by 20% between 1997 and 1998. Markets for education tourism in sub-Saharan Africa may be grouped into four categories:

(a) intercountry (domestic),

(b) intra-regional,

(c) European, and

(d) North American.

Countries in the sub-region cannot expect to develop a sustainable edu-tourism based solely on foreign tourists. These countries need to build and nurture the domestic capacity critical for the long-term success of edu-tourism. Education policies should be revamped to incorporate edu-tourism programs in school curricula from primary to tertiary levels. Students in these institutions should not only learn about these attractions/resources in their courses, but they also should be actively encouraged and required to make field trips to these sites. This is particularly important because research suggests that interest in the activities that most people engage in as adults were first developed during childhood and adolescence Consequently, by encouraging the involvement of school children in their formative and impressionable years, sub-Saharan African countries will be creating a cadre of future clients to sustain edu-tourism.

The second edu-tourism market results from intra-regional travels. According to the WTO, intra-regional travel, which is travel by Africans to other African countries, constitutes the most common form of tourism in the region. In 1998, almost 40% of tourist arrivals in Africa came from the continent. This figure represents a staggering increase of almost 118% compared with 1989 (WTO). Countries within the sub-region can tap into this vast potential market via education tourism.

To stimulate intra-regional edu-tourism travel, member countries can overhaul and strengthen existing travel and immigration protocols of their respective regional blocs to facilitate easy movement among nationals within the sub-region. Furthermore, conscious promotional efforts will have to be undertaken within the sub-region to heighten public awareness of available edu-tourism opportunities and their accessibility. In addition, national tourism organisations and universities will need to work in a coordinated manner to design and create edu-tourism programs that engender interests of nationals of the sub-region. For instance, in the area of foreign languages, universities in the sub-region rather than sending their students to metropolitan European capitals for practical experiences, may elect to send them to universities within the sub-region. Students from English-speaking African countries rather than travelling to Paris for their French language experience may travel to the Ivory Coast, Togo, Senegal, etc. Conversely, those from the French speaking African countries may travel to Ghana, Nigeria, Sierra Leone, Liberia, etc. for their English language requirements instead of to London. In addition. Countries with similar colonial experiences may encourage intra-regional travels by their nationals to learn more about their common colonial experiences and heritage.

The third edu-tourism market is represented by the European Union (EU). This region is a large tourist-generating market for Sub-Saharan Africa. Most of the countries in the sub-region still have strong ties to these former colonial powers. Education tourism could benefit from this market through several bilateral and technical agreements. Sub-Saharan African countries can negotiate with European institutions of higher learning to encourage European students to travel to the sub-region.

The fourth market is the North American market. It comprises of universities and institutions offering area studies relating to sub-Saharan Africa, Historically Black Colleges and Universities (HBCUs), and the largely untapped African-American market. Promotional efforts and direct contacts will have to be made with these entities to stimulate and tap into these latent markets currently under exploited by sub-Saharan African countries.

Organisational Framework for Implementing Education Tourism at the Country *Unit*

Countries in sub-Saharan Africa have to pursue the goal of education tourism separately as well as in a coordinated and structured way through regionalism. At the country level, each country through their National Tourism Organisations (NTOS), universities/colleges and tourism stakeholders will be responsible for identifying appropriate themes to form the framework for the education tourism strategy. In addition, inputs may be solicited abroad from universities/colleges travel agents/tour operators to shape the themes and course content.

Conceptual Framework for Implementing Education Tourism Strategy at the Country Unit. The NTOs will set the tourism development policies with advice from the universities and tourism stakeholders. The universities will have the responsibility of providing facilities and equipment, expertise and the necessary academic environment to facilitate learning. The stakeholders will make available the tourism attractions, lodging and transportation. Governments of these countries will provide the infrastructure and super-structure needed to facilitate the smooth operation of the strategy. The universities collaborating with tourism stakeholders, will produce a workable education program. This program will be divided into two sections: a) classroom experience and b) on-site experience. The program schedule should specify the length of the classroom segment and the on-site practical experience. The governments, through their NTOs, will provide resources to set up Community Communication Centres (CCC) in the various attraction sites.

These centres will have a resident expert on tourism attractions and subject matter in the curriculum to assist with the dissemination of on-site instruction. In addition, these centres will have up-to-date technological links to the universities. Lessons in education tourism could be delivered through distance learning, the Internet and email. Learning can take place in two phases. In the first phase, participants will spend some time in the university classrooms that are linked to the community centres. This arrangement makes it possible to provide participants the knowledge-base and the perceptual view of what is involved in the next phase. The second phase is the on-site experience where participants travel to the attraction location to actively participate and acquire skills that will reinforce the knowledge acquired in the classroom.

Organisational Framework Needed to Implement Regional Education Tourism

Strategy

The implementation of the education, tourism at the regional level will be based on the existing frameworks of regional blocs or institutions in the sub-region. Regionalism seeks to combine and coordinate efforts and functions of different sub-Saharan countries. The regional blocs include: (ECOW S (Economic Community of West African States), EAC (East African Cooperation) and SADC (Southern African Development Community). According to Dieke (1998), the benefits of regional strategies are as follows:

a) they provide countries a more co-ordinated approach to negotiations and strengthens their bargaining position with multinational corporations;
b) create a sizeable regional market-this is particularly important because over 40% of tourist flows in the sub-region resulted from intra-regional travel by residents to other sub-Saharan African countries); and
c) an increasing number of foreign tourists visiting sub-Saharan Africa are opting for tour circuits rather than resort holidays (the regional approach will prepare countries in the sub-region for this new demand).

The secretariats of the regional blocs, working with member countries, will create a composite education tourism product which is reflective of the region's diversity. The theme, curriculum, course content and schedule will be the outcome of joint efforts by both the regional secretariat and the individual countries. In addition, input may be solicited abroad from universities/colleges, travel agents/tour operators etc. To facilitate the delivery of the tourism education program, the regional blocs can take advantage of the new African Virtual University (AVU) established by the World Bank to serve countries in the sub-region. It is an interactive-instructional telecommunications network set up to build capacity and support economic development. AVU is currently in the pilot phase and is being implemented and tested in 14 English-speaking and 8 French-speaking universities across sub-Saharan Africa. The regional blocs may request AVU to include education tourism in their course offerings.

Description of the Process for Regional Tourism Education

The courses in education tourism from member countries will be transmitted at the regional level through the AVU. The regional blocs will serve as the link between A VU and: the sub-Saharan countries to facilitate this process. Each country will be responsible for providing the facilities, communication centres, local experts and other critical re-sources essential for linking that country with the AVU. Potential tourists may experience education tourism through Interactive Video Network Systems operated by the A VU and actual on-site visitations to the respective countries.

Interactive Video Networks allow for two-way voice activated video systems to transmit live, high-quality audio and colour video between several sites. An instructor or trainer at the home site is able to see and hear the students in a remote site. Conversely, students in remote sites are able to see and hear the instructor and other participants.

Pricing of Education Tourism Package

The tuition for the education tourism program at both the country and regional level may be calculated by, factoring in the cost incurred providing the education infrastructure and personnel. It should also be guided by competitive prices for similar attractions elsewhere in the world. At the country level, profit-sharing between entities involved will be determined by the size of each entity's investment and also by negotiations. A written contract should be signed by all parties before inception of the program.

Potential Problems and Possible Solutions

Potential problems associated with the education tourism strategy include:

1. limited financial resources to procure equipment, parts and other technology hardware;
2. lack of skilled personnel to facilitate the tourism instruction delivery via the Information Super highway; and
3. the sub-region's negative image in the tourist generating markets.

Countries and regional blocs can address the problem of limited financial resource by taking advantage of the World Bank's proposed loan and grants for Internet projects.

In addition, governments will have to liberalise their over-regulated markets to foster competition and attract potential external Internet providers. Skilled personnel may be trained through technical aid from the World Bank and other international agencies. In addition, countries could recruit qualified nationals residing abroad through the Reintegration of Qualified Nationals (ROQAN Program) based in Geneva. It was established to assist African countries to recruit their nationals who have acquired skills abroad through studies and work experience. ROQAN provides airfares, family support and luggage allowances to the individuals to help with their transition in their home countries. The negative image problem can only be effectively addressed through cooperative efforts of all the countries in the sub-region.

These efforts may be supplemented by the activities of the African Centre International (ACI) recently launched to give African business people an opportunity to trade in the U.S. According to its chairman, Emmanuel Chileshe, the centre would operate as a trade and tourism promotion initiative. Set the rules of behaviour for the visit. Emphasize the importance of the school or organization's reputation, local pride and the repercussions of the actions of any one person.

Prepare lists of DO's and DONTs covering such areas as good manners, their role as ambassadors, curfews, and use of drugs, cigarettes and alcohol. You might also want to elaborate on the following topics:

- Hotel behaviour: curfews, keys, phoning other rooms, running from room to room, etc.
- Restaurant behaviour: noise level, staying seated at the table, manners, etc.
- Amount of luggage, essential items to pack, amount of spending money, shopping time, etc.
- Always listening to the directions and other information given by the group organizers, chaperones, SEVEC-RVC guides or any other guide
- Respecting meeting times set by group organizers, chaperones and guides
- Wearing a watch and keeping track of time, and if some do not have one make sure they are with a friend who does
- Never going anywhere alone! Never leaving their buddy! Waiting for each other when going to the washroom or stopping to buy anything

- Being responsible for their own personal belongings and being careful with their back packs, cameras and jackets
- Not using an IPod, cell phone or other personal electronic device during scheduled activities
- Knowing the procedures to follow if lost. For example, participants should always have the emergency telephone numbers and a few quarters in their wallet in case they have to make an emergency phone call
- Sticking to the schedule and remaining with the group. Participants understandably look forward to opportunities for souvenir shopping, but shops at museums and attractions are often busy and there may not always be time to visit the gift shop

Code of Conduct

Make sure all group members understand the consequences of bad behaviour In extreme circumstances, they can even be sent home at their parent's expense.

Itinerary and City Map

All participants should have a copy of the itinerary in their handbook, plus any background information they have collected about any of the sites and attractions to be visited. A city map is also very useful.

What to Bring

The best kind of luggage is the lightest. Participants should not bring luggage or accessories that they cannot carry themselves. We suggest one piece of luggage so that participants are able to carry their own bag. It is recommended that you consult the airline you are travelling with to confirm their luggage policy. Here is a useful checklist of personal items that you will want to customize for your trip:

For all Seasons

- toiletries
- camera/film/batteries
- light backpack
- bathing suit/towel

- money belt/fanny pack
- lock
- watch
- spending money

Winter

- warm sweaters
- hat
- mittens/gloves
- scarves
- winter coat/hooded parka
- winter boots
- wool socks
- long underwear

Fall/Spring

- warm sweater
- wool socks
- walking shoes
- rubber boots
- waterproof rain jacket

Summer

- light clothing
- shorts and tee-shirts
- walking shoes
- wind breaker/waterproof rain jacket
- sunhat
- sunglasses
- sunscreen

Useful Vocabulary

It may be useful to have participants make a list of vocabulary and sentences that they may want to refer to during the trip.

Word Games, Puzzles, etc.

Word puzzles, crosswords and other games are great to occupy participants on the bus, train or plane.

Souvenir Page

Participants may want to have a few pages in their handbook to keep special souvenirs from their visit.

Autograph Page

Having an autograph page always seems to be very popular.

Participant Journal

Having participants write about their daily activities helps them remember what they have learned and makes for interesting reading in later years.

Emergency Procedures and Phone Numbers

Even with constant supervision, participants can occasionally get lost. It is a good idea to discuss this possibility with them beforehand, and to have them take note of the proper steps to follow if it happens.

Tourism

Tourism is travel for recreational, leisure or business purposes. The World Tourism Organization defines tourists as people who "travel to and stay in places outside their usual environment for more than twenty-four hours and not more than one consecutive year for leisure, business and other purposes not related to the exercise of an activity remunerated from within the place visited". Tourism has become a popular global leisure activity. In 2008, there were over 922 million international tourist arrivals, with a growth of 1.9% as compared to 2007. International tourism receipts grew to US$944 billion in 2008, corresponding to an increase in real terms of 1.8%. As a result of the Late-2000s recession, international travel demand suffered a strong slowdown beginning in June 2008, with growth in international tourism arrivals worldwide falling to 2% during the boreal summer months, and this negative trend intensified as international tourist arrivals fell by 8% during the first four months of 2009. Thereafter this declining trend was exacerbated in some regions due to the outbreak of the influenza AH1N1 virus.

Tourism is vital for many countries, such as the U.A.E, Egypt, Greece and Thailand, and many island nations, such as The Bahamas, Fiji, Maldives and the Seychelles, due to the large intake of money for businesses with their goods and services and the opportunity for employment in the service industries associated with tourism. These service industries include transportation services, such as airlines, cruise ships and taxis, hospitality services, such as accommodations, including hotels and resorts, and entertainment venues, such as amusement parks, casinos, shopping malls, various music venues and the theatre.

Definition

Hunziker and Krapf, in 1941, defined tourism as people who travel "the sum of the phenomena and relationships arising from the travel and stay of non-residents, insofar as they do not lead to permanent residence and are not connected with any earning activity." In 1976, the Tourism Society of England's definition was: "Tourism is the temporary, short-term movement of people to destination outside the places where they normally live and work and their activities during the stay at each destination. It includes movements for all purposes." In 1981, the International Association of Scientific Experts in Tourism defined tourism in terms of particular activities selected by choice and undertaken outside the home.

The United Nations classified three forms of tourism in 1994, in its "Recommendations on Tourism Statistics: Domestic tourism", which involves residents of the given country travelling only within this country; In bound tourism, involving non-residents travelling in the given country; and Outbound tourism, involving residents travelling in another country.

The UN also derived different categories of tourism by combining the three basic forms of tourism: Internal tourism, which comprises domestic tourism and in bound tourism; National tourism, which comprises domestic tourism and outbound tourism; and International tourism, which consists of in bound tourism and outbound tourism. *Intrabound tourism* is a term coined by the Korea Tourism Organization and widely accepted in Korea. Intrabound tourism differs from domestic tourism in that the former encompasses policy making and implementation of national tourism policies.

Recently, the tourism industry has shifted from the promotion of in bound tourism to the promotion of intrabound tourism, because many countries are experiencing tough competition for in bound tourists.

World Tourism Statistics and Rankings

Most Visited Countries by International Tourist Arrivals

The World Tourism Organization reports the following ten countries as the most visited in between 2006 and 2008 by number of international travellers. When compared to 2006, Ukraine entered the top ten list, surpassing Russia, Austria and Mexico, and in 2008 surpassed Germany. In 2008 the U.S. displaced Spain from the second place. Most of the top visited countries continue to be on the European continent.

International Tourism Receipts

In 2008, there were over 922 million international tourist arrivals, with a growth of 1.9% as compared to 2007. International tourism receipts grew to US$944 billion in 2008, corresponding to an increase in real terms of 1.8% on 2007. When the export value of international passenger transport receipts is accounted for, total receipts in 2008 reached a record of US$1.1 trillion, or over US$3 billion a day.

The World Tourism Organization reports the following countries as the top ten tourism earners for the year 2008. It is noticeable that most of them are on the European continent, but the United States continues to be the top earner.

International Tourism Expenditures

The World Tourism Organization reports the following countries as the top ten biggest spenders on international tourism for the year 2008. For the fifth year in a row, German tourists continue as the top spenders.

Most Visited Cities

History

Wealthy people have always travelled to distant parts of the world, to see great buildings, works of art, learn new languages, experience new cultures and to taste different cuisines. Long ago, at the time of the Roman Republic, places such as Baiae were popular coastal resorts for the rich. The word *tourism* was used by 1811 and *tourist* by 1840. In 1936, the League of Nations defined *foreign tourist* as "someone travelling abroad for at least twenty-four hours". Its successor, the United Nations, amended this definition in 1945, by including a maximum stay of six months.

Leisure Travel

Leisure travel was associated with the Industrial Revolution in the United Kingdom – the first European country to promote leisure time to the increasing industrial population. Initially, this applied to the owners of the machinery of production, the economic oligarchy, the factory owners and the traders. These comprised the new middle class. Cox & Kings was the first official travel company to be formed in 1758.

The British origin of this new industry is reflected in many place names. In Nice, France, one of the first and best-established holiday resorts on the French Riviera, the long esplanade along the seafront is known to this day as the *Promenade des Anglais*; in many other historic resorts in continental Europe, old, well-established palace hotels have names like the *Hotel Bristol*, the *Hotel Carlton* or the *Hotel Majestic* – reflecting the dominance of English customers. Many leisure-oriented tourists travel to the tropics, both in the summer and winter. Places often visited are: Cuba, the Dominican Republic, Thailand, North Queensland in Australia and Florida in the United States.

Winter Tourism

Major ski resorts are located in the various European countries, Canada, the United States, Australia, New Zealand, Japan, Korea, Chile and Argentina.

Mass Tourism

Mass tourism could only have developed with the improvements in technology, allowing the transport of large numbers of people in a short space of time to places of leisure interest, so that greater numbers of people could begin to enjoy the benefits of leisure time.

In the United States, the first seaside resorts in the European style were at Atlantic City, New Jersey and Long Island,

New York. In Continental Europe, early resorts included: Ostend, popularized by the people of Brussels; Boulogne-sur-Mer (Pas-de-Calais) and Deauville (Calvados) for the Parisians; and Heiligendamm, founded in 1797, as the first seaside resort on the Baltic Sea.

Adjectival Tourism

Adjectival tourism refers to the numerous niche or speciality travel forms of tourism that have emerged over the years, each with its own adjective. Many of these have come into common use by the tourism industry and academics. Others are emerging concepts that may or may not gain popular usage. Examples of the more common niche tourism markets include:

1. Agritourism
2. Culinary tourism
3. Cultural tourism
4. Ecotourism
5. Heritage tourism
6. LGBT tourism
7. Medical tourism
8. Nautical tourism
9. Religious tourism
10. Space tourism
11. War tourism
12. Wildlife tourism

Recent Developments

There has been an upmarket trend in the tourism over the last few decades, especially in Europe, where international travel for short breaks is common. Tourists have higher levels of disposable income and greater leisure time and they are also better-educated and have more sophisticated tastes. There is now a demand for a better quality products, which has resulted in a fragmenting of the mass market for beach vacations; people want more specialised versions, such as Club 18-30, quieter resorts, family-oriented holidays or niche market-targeted destination hotels. The developments in technology and transport infrastructure, such as jumbo jets, low-cost airlines and more accessible airports have made many types of tourism more affordable. WHO estimates that up to 500,000 people are on planes at any time. There have also been changes in lifestyle, such as retiree-age people who sustain year round tourism. This is facilitated by internet sales of tourism products. Some sites have now started to offer dynamic packaging, in which an inclusive price is quoted for a tailor-made package requested by the customer upon impulse. There have been a few setbacks in tourism, such as the September 11 attacks and terrorist threats to tourist destinations, such as in Bali and several European cities. Also, on December 26, 2004, a tsunami, caused by the 2004 Indian Ocean earthquake, hit the Asian countries on the Indian Ocean, including the Maldives. Thousands of lives were lost and many tourists died. This, together with the vast clean-up operation in place, has stopped or severely hampered tourism to the area. The terms *tourism* and *travel* are sometimes used interchangeably. In this context, travel has a similar definition to tourism, but implies a more purposeful journey. The terms *tourism* and *tourist* are sometimes used pejoratively, to imply a shallow interest in the cultures or locations visited by tourists.

Sustainable Tourism

"Sustainable tourism is envisaged as leading to management of all resources in such a way that economic, social and aesthetic needs can be fulfilled while maintaining cultural integrity, essential ecological processes, biological diversity and life support systems."

Sustainable development implies "meeting the needs of the present without compromising the ability of future generations to meet their own needs"

Medical Tourism

When there is a significant price difference between countries for a given medical procedure, particularly in Southeast Asia, India, Eastern Europe and where there are different regulatory regimes, in relation to particular medical procedures, travelling to take advantage of the price or regulatory differences is often referred to as "medical tourism".

Educational Tourism

Educational tourism developed, because of the growing popularity of teaching and learning of knowledge and the enhancing of technical competency outside of the classroom environment. In educational tourism, the main focus of the tour or leisure activity includes visiting another country to learn about the culture, such as in Student Exchange Programs and Study Tours, or to work and apply skills learned inside the classroom in a different environment, such as in the International Practicum Training Program.

Creative Tourism

Creative tourism has existed as a form of cultural tourism, since the early beginnings of tourism itself. Its European roots date back to the time of the Grand Tour, which saw the sons of aristocratic families travelling for the purpose of mostly interactive, educational experiences. More recently, creative tourism has been given its own name by Crispin Raymond and Greg Richards, who as members of the Association for Tourism and Leisure Education (ATLAS), have directed a number of projects for the European Commission, including cultural and crafts tourism, known as sustainable tourism. They have defined "creative tourism" as tourism related to the active participation of travellers in the culture of the host community, through interactive workshops and informal learning experiences.

Meanwhile, the concept of creative tourism has been picked up by high-profile organizations such as UNESCO, who through the Creative Cities Network, have endorsed creative tourism as an engaged, authentic experience that promotes an active understanding of the specific cultural features of a place.

More recently, creative tourism has gained popularity as a form of cultural tourism, drawing on active participation by travellers in the culture of the host communities they visit. Several countries offer examples of this type of tourism development, including the United Kingdom, the Bahamas, Jamaica, Spain, Italy and New Zealand.

Dark Tourism

One emerging area of special interest tourism has been identified by Lennon and Foley (2000) as "dark" tourism. This type of tourism involves visits to "dark" sites, such as battlegrounds, scenes of horrific crimes or acts of genocide, for example: concentration camps. Dark tourism poses severe ethical and moral dilemmas: should these sites be available for visitation and, if so, what should the nature of the publicity involved be. Dark tourism remains a small niche market, driven by varied motivations, such as mourning, remembrance, macabre curiosity or even entertainment. Its early origins are rooted in fairgrounds and medieval fairs.

Growth

The World Tourism Organization (UNWTO) forecasts that international tourism will continue growing at the average annual rate of 4 %.With the advent of e-commerce, tourism products have become one of the most traded items on the internet. Tourism products and services have been made available through intermediaries, although tourism providers can sell their services directly. This has put pressure on intermediaries from both on-line and traditional shops.

It has been suggested there is a strong correlation between tourism expenditure per capita and the degree to which countries play in the global context. Not only as a result of the important economic contribution of the tourism industry, but also as an indicator of the degree of confidence with which global citizens leverage the resources of the globe for the benefit of their local economies. This is why any projections of growth in tourism may serve as an indication of the relative influence that each country will exercise in the future. Space tourism is expected to "take off" in the first quarter of the 21st century, although compared with traditional destinations the number of tourists in orbit will remain low until technologies such as a space elevator make space travel cheap.

Technological improvement is likely to make possible air-ship hotels, based either on solar-powered airplanes or large dirigibles. Underwater hotels, such as Hydropolis, expected to open in Dubai in 2009, will be built. On the ocean, tourists will be welcomed by ever larger cruise ships and perhaps floating cities.

Latest Trends

As a result of the Late-2000s recession, international arrivals suffered a strong slowdown beginning in June 2008. Growth from 2007 to 2008 was only 3.7% during the first eight months of 2008. The Asian and Pacific markets were affected and Europe stagnated during the boreal summer months, while the Americas performed better, reducing their expansion rate but keeping a 6% growth from January to August 2008. Only the Middle East continued its rapid growth during the same period, reaching a 17% growth as compared to the same period in 2007. This slowdown on international tourism demand was also reflected in the air transport industry, with a negative growth in September 2008 and a 3.3% growth in passenger traffic through September. The hotel industry also reports a slowdown, as room occupancy continues to decline. As the global economic situation deteriorated dramatically during September and October as a result of the global financial crisis, growth of international tourism is expected to slow even further for the remaining of 2008, and this slowdown in demand growth is forecasted to continue into 2009 as recession has already hit most of the top spender countries, with long-haul travel expected to be the most affected by the economic crisis. This negative trend intensified as international tourist arrivals fell by 8% during the first four months of 2009, and the decline was exacerbated in some regions due to the outbreak of the influenza AH1N1 virus.

4

Hospitality Planning and Management

The marketing mix-the 4 Ps-target audience-segmentation-objectives-evaluation. These and other terms are all used in the process of "marketing." In tourism and tourism related industries, success means understanding this process. This bulletin is designed for those in the tourism industry who may not be completely familiar with marketing or who may simply wish to refresh their basic marketing skills. Covered will be important concepts used in marketing, the relationship of marketing to tourism, and a process for developing a marketing plan for tourism/recreation businesses and/or communities. It will be impossible to cover in detail all the aspects of marketing within the scope of this bulletin. There are, however, other bulletins in this series that will provide more in-depth information on the different components of a marketing plan.

What is Marketing

People hold a variety of misconceptions about marketing. Most common is its confusion with selling and advertising. Selling and advertising are actually types of promotion which is only a component of marketing. Marketing involves much more, including product/service development, place (location and distribution), and pricing. It requires information about people, especially those interested in what you have to offer (your "market"), such as what they like, where they buy and how much they spend. Its role is to match the right product or service with the right market or audience. Marketing, as you will see, is an art and a science. According to the American Marketing Association, marketing is "the process of planning and executing the conception, pricing, promotion, and distribution of ideas, goods, and services to create exchanges that satisfy individual and organizational objectives." Simply stated it is creating and promoting a product (ideas, goods or services) that satisfies a customer's need or desire and is available at a desirable price and place. Modern marketing is a way of doing business, heavily based on the "marketing concept" which holds that businesses and organizations should:

(1) design their products/services to meet customer needs and wants;

(2) focus on those people most likely to buy their product rather than the entire mass market; and

(3) develop marketing efforts that fit into their overall business objectives.

By adopting this concept you not only provide your customers with better products, you will avoid wasting valuable time and money developing and promoting a product or service nobody wants.

Recreation and Tourism Marketing

Earlier it was mentioned that a product can be "ideas, goods, or services." Since tourism is primarily a service based industry, the principal products provided by recreation/tourism (R/T) businesses are recreational experiences and hospitality. These are intangible products and more difficult to market than tangible products such as automobiles. The intangible nature of services makes quality control difficult but crucial. It also makes it more difficult for potential customers to evaluate and compare service offerings. In addition, instead of moving the product to the customer, the customer must travel to the product (area/community). Travel is a significant portion of the time and money spent in association with recreational and tourism experiences and is a major factor in people's decisions on whether or not to visit your business or community. As an industry, tourism has many components comprising the overall "travel experience." Along with transportation, it includes such things as accommodations, food and beverage services, shops, entertainment, aesthetics and special events. It is rare for one business to provide the variety of activities or facilities tourists need or desire. This adds to the difficulty of maintaining and controlling the quality of the experience. To overcome this hurdle, tourism related businesses, agencies, and organizations need to work together to package and promote tourism opportunities in their areas and align their efforts to assure consistency in product quality.

The Marketing Plan

One of the most important steps a business or community can take to improve the effectiveness and efficiency of their marketing efforts is to develop a written marketing plan. This plan will guide their marketing decisions and assist them in allocating marketing resources such as money and personnel time. The plan should include:

(1) the overall business objectives—what you want to accomplish;

(2) an assessment of the market environment—what factors may affect your marketing efforts;

(3) a business/community profile—what resources are available,

(4) market identification (segmentation)—the specific groups or clientele most interested in your product;

(5) the marketing objectives for each segment;

(6) the marketing strategies (or mixes) for different markets you target—the best combination of the 4 Ps (product, price, place, promotion) for each segment;

(7) an implementation plan—how to "make it work;"

(8) the marketing budget-how much you have to spend; and

(9) a method for evaluation and change.

A framework which can be used to develop a marketing plan. Each component will be briefly discussed in the remainder of the bulletin. For more information regarding different components of the plan be sure to consult other bulletins in this series.

Overall Business Objectives

Businesses, agencies, and communities should develop overall objectives and regularly monitor their progress. The objectives should provide guidance for all decisions including finances, personnel and marketing. They should be quantitative and measurable statements of what the business or community wants to accomplish over a specified period of time. Business objectives are often stated in terms of sales, profits, market shares and/or occupancy rates. Communities frequently establish objectives relating to such things as increasing the number of tourists, developing or changing their image, facility and activity development, cooperation among tourism related businesses and increasing length of stay and local expenditures. It is important that the objectives be reasonable given the market conditions and the firm's or organization's resources. Establish a few reasonable objectives instead of a long, unrealistic "wish list." This is especially true for new businesses or communities which do not have much experience in tourism development and/or marketing.

Market Environment Analysis

The next step in developing a marketing plan is to assess the impact of environmental factors (such as economic, social and political) on present and future markets. Changes in these factors can create marketing opportunities as well as problems.

Demographic and Lifestyle Trends

Changing demographics and lifestyles are having a major impact on R/T participation. An assessment of these trends is important to understand how they will likely affect your business or community. Some of the important trends that bear watching:

(1) population growth and movement;

(2) rural community growth compared to metropolitan areas;

(3) number of adult women employed outside the home;

(4) the number of households is growing, especially non family and single parent households, but family size is decreasing;

(5) the impact of two wage earner households on real family income;

(6) the number of retired persons with the financial ability to travel;

(7) better health to an older age; and

(8) continued aging of the population (we are becoming a middle aged society).

Economic Conditions

Overall economic conditions can have significant impacts on recreation and tourism markets. A marketing strategy that is effective during periods of low unemployment rates may have to be significantly adjusted if unemployment increases.

Businesses and communities should monitor and assess the likely impact of factors such as unemployment rates, real family income, rate of inflation, credit availability, terms and interest rates. Consideration should also be given to the prices of complementary products, such as lodging, gasoline and recreation equipment.

Laws and Government Actions

As a complex industry, tourism is significantly affected both positively and negatively by laws and by actions of governmental agencies. For instance, rulings on such things as liability issues or decisions regarding building and health codes may change or possibly prevent the construction of a proposed facility. If a public facility changes the prices of its services, this could affect the service offerings of associated private businesses. These actions may have both positive and negative effects on the marketing efforts of the business and community. To avoid wasting valuable resources it is important that R/T businesses, agencies, and communities continually monitor and evaluate governmental actions.

Technology

Technological developments are increasing rapidly. New recreation products, such as all-terrain vehicles and wind surfers, provide new ways for people to satisfy their recreational preferences. New production technologies and materials offer recreation and tourism businesses ways to reduce costs and improve the quality of their products/services. Advances in telecommunications have and will continue to create new promotional opportunities. Technological innovations, in relation to jobs and the home, have resulted in increased leisure time for many people.

Competition

Businesses and communities must identify and analyse existing and potential competitors. The objective of the analysis is to determine the strengths and weaknesses of the competition's marketing strategies. The analysis should include the competition's:

(1) product/service features and quality;

(2) location relative to different geographic markets;

(3) promotional themes and messages;

(4) prices; and

(5) type of customer they are attracting.

Business and Community Profiles

Too many communities attempt to market themselves as tourist destinations without accurate information about their resources (facilities, services, staff), image (projected vs. Actual), and how well their customers are satisfied. Without this information, it is difficult to make other decisions in the planning process. Included should be such things as recreational and entertainment facilities, cultural and historic sites, overnight accommodations, restaurants, shopping opportunities, special events and activities, staff size, and transportation. Each item of the "inventory" should also be assessed in terms of quality and availability.

Market Segmentation (Identification)

Recreation and tourism businesses and communities often make the mistake of attempting to be all things to all people.

It is difficult, and risky, to develop marketing strategies for the mass market. Strategies designed for the "average" customer often result in unappealing products, prices, and promotional messages. For example, it would be difficult to develop a campground that would be equally attractive to recreational vehicle campers and backpackers or promote a property to serve both snow mobilers and nature oriented cross country skiers.

Marketing is strongly based on market segmentation and target marketing. Market segmentation is the process of:

(1) taking existing and/or potential customers/visitors (market) and categorizing them into groups with similar preferences referred to as "market segments;"

(2) selecting the most promising segments as "target markets;" and

(3) designing "marketing mixes," or strategies (combination of the 4 Ps), which satisfy the special needs, desires and behaviour of the target markets.

There is no unique or best way to segment markets, but ways in which customers can be grouped are:

(1) location of residence—instate, out-of-state, local;

(2) demographics—age, income, family status, education;

(3) equipment ownership/use—RV's, sailboats, canoes, tents, snowmobiles;

(4) important product attributes—price, quality, quantity; and

(5) lifestyle attributes—activities, interests, opinions.

To be useful, the segment identification process should result in segments that suggest marketing efforts that will be effective in attracting them and at least one segment large enough to justify specialized marketing efforts.

After segments have been identified, the business or community must select the "target markets," those segments which offer them the greatest opportunity. When determining target markets, consideration should be given to:

(1) existing and future sales potential of each segment;

(2) the amount and strength of competition for each segment;

(3) the ability to offer a marketing mix which will be successful in attracting each segment;

(4) the cost of servicing each segment; and

(5) each segment's contribution to accomplishing overall business/community objectives. It is often wiser to target smaller segments that are presently not being served, or served inadequately, than to go after larger segments for which there is a great deal of competition.

Marketing Objectives for Each Segment

Marketing objectives which contribute to the accomplishment of the overall business objectives should be established for each target market. Objectives serve a number of functions including:

(1) guidance for developing marketing mixes for different target markets;

(2) information for allocating the marketing budget between target markets;

(3) a basis for objectively evaluating the effectiveness of the marketing mixes (setting standards); and

(4) a framework for integrating the different marketing mixes into the overall marketing plan.

The target market objectives should:

(1) be expressed in quantitative terms;

(2) be measurable;

(3) specify the target market; and

(4) indicate the time period in which the objective is to be accomplished.

For example, increase the number of overnight stays by people from the Chicago market over the next two years by five percent.

Remember, rank objectives by priority and carefully evaluate them to ensure that they are reasonable given the strength of the competition and resources available for marketing.

Marketing Strategy (Mix)

The marketing strategy, or mix, should be viewed as a package of offerings designed to attract and serve the customer or visitor. Recreation and tourism businesses and communities should develop both external and internal marketing mixes for different target markets.

External Mix

The external marketing mix includes product/service, price, place/location, and promotion.

Product

Earlier we said the principal products that recreation and tourism businesses provide are recreational experiences and hospitality. The factors that create a quality recreational experience often differ among people. A quality experience for one skier might include an uncrowded, steep slope. To another it might be a good restaurant and a chance to socialize. Decisions on what facilities, programs and services to provide should be based on the needs and desires of the target market(s). They should not be based on the preferences of the owner/manager or necessarily on what the competition is providing.

Recognize that a recreational/tourism experience includes five elements: trip planning and anticipation; travel to the site/area; the experience at the site; travel back home; and recollection. Businesses should look for ways to enhance the quality of the overall experience during all phases of the trip. This could be accomplished by providing trip planning packages which include maps, attractions en route and on site, and information regarding lodging, food and quality souvenirs and mementos. Recreation and tourism businesses should also view their service/product in generic terms. Thinking of products/services in this manner helps focus more attention on the experiences desired by customers and also the facilities, programs and services that will produce those experiences. For example, campgrounds are the business of providing recreational "lodging" not just campsites to park an RV or set up a tent. Marinas should provide recreational "boating" experiences, not just slippage.

Location and Accessibility—Place

Too many tourism businesses and communities fail to recognize their role in improving travel to and from their areas. They focus instead on servicing the customer once they arrive at the site/ community. A bad experience getting to or leaving an R/T site can adversely affect a person's travel experience. Ways to help prevent this include:

(1) providing directions and maps;

(2) providing estimates of travel time and distances from different market areas;

(3) recommending direct and scenic travel routes;

(4) identifying attractions and support facilities along different travel routes; and

(5) informing potential customers of alternative travel methods to the area such as airlines and railroads.

Potential businesses should also carefully assess alternative locations for:

(1) distance and accessibility to target markets;

(2) location of competitors with respect to target markets;

(3) modes of travel serving the area; and

(4) other attractions and activities that might induce travel to the area.

Pricing Price is one of the most important and visible elements of the marketing mix. When setting prices it is important to take into consideration all of the following:

(1) business and target market objectives;

(2) the full cost of producing, delivering and promoting the product;

(3) the willingness of the target market to pay for the product or service you provide;

(4) prices charged by competitors offering a similar product/service to the same target market(s);

(5) the availability and prices of substitute products/services;

(6) the economic climate (local and national); and

(7) the possibility of stimulating high profit products/services (such as boats) by offering related services (such as maintenance) at or below cost.

When establishing prices, R/T businesses should give attention to pricing strategies which may encourage off season and non-peak period sales, longer stays, group business, and the sale of package plans (combination of room, meals, and recreational facilities). For additional information on pricing.

Promotion

Promotion provides target audiences with accurate and timely information to help them decide whether to visit your community or business. The information should be of importance and practical use to the potential or existing visitor and also accurate. Misrepresentation often leads to dissatisfied customers and poor recommendations.

Don't make claims you cannot live up to. Developing a promotional campaign is not a science with hard and fast rules. Making decisions regarding which type or combination of promotion types to use (personal selling, advertising, sales promotions, or publicity) is not always easy. If, however, you follow a logical process and do the necessary research, chances for success will be improved. It will be necessary to make decisions regarding:

(1) Target audience—the group you are aiming at;

(2) Image—that which your community or business wants to create or reinforce;

(3) Objectives—those of the promotional campaign;

(4) Budget—the amount of money available for your promotion;

(5) Timing—when and how often should your promotions appear;

(6) Media—which methods (television, radio, newspaper, magazine) will most effectively and efficiently communicate your message to the target audience; and

(7) Evaluation—how can the effectiveness of the promotional campaign be determined.

Internal Mix

As stated, marketing services such as recreation and tourism differ from marketing tangible products. Recreation and tourism businesses must direct as much attention at marketing to customers on site as they do to attracting them. In this respect, internal marketing is important because dissatisfied customers can effectively cancel out an otherwise effective marketing strategy.

The success of internal marketing is dependent on creating an atmosphere in which employees desire to give good service and sell the business/community to visitors. To create such an atmosphere requires the following four important elements:

(1) Hospitality and Guest Relations—An organization wide emphasis on hospitality and guest relations, including a customer oriented attitude on the part of the owners and managers as well as the employees. If the owner/manager is not customer sensitive, it is unlikely the lower paid employees will be.

(2) Quality Control—A program which focuses on improving both the technical quality (the standards associated with what the customer receives) and the functional quality (the standards associated with how the customer receives

the service). All employees who come into contact with customers should receive hospitality training.

(3) Personal Selling—Training the staff in the selling aspects of the property (business) or community. This also includes rewarding them for their efforts. By being informed about the marketing objectives, and their role in accomplishing those objectives, they can help increase sales.

(4) Employee Morale—Programs and incentives aimed at maintaining employee morale. The incentives can be both monetary and nonmonetary.

A customer oriented atmosphere usually results in customers that are more satisfied, do less complaining and are more pleasant to serve. This helps build employee morale, their desire to provide good service and their efficiency.

Marketing Budget

Successful marketing requires that sufficient money and personnel time be made available to implement activities comprising the marketing strategy. A marketing budget is a financial plan which shows the total amount to be spent on marketing during different times of the year and how it is to be allocated among alternative activities. Separate marketing budgets should be developed for each marketing mix strategy. The separate budgets should then be aggregated to develop an overall marketing budget. If the total amount is too great it will be necessary to modify the overall objectives and the target market objectives, narrow down or drop target markets, or adjust marketing mixes. The final budget should be realistic given your objectives. When deciding on a marketing budget, consideration should be given to the job that needs to be done as defined by the objectives. Basing marketing budgets on some percent of sales or what the competition spends usually leads to over spending or under spending. Decisions should also be based on the costs, projected revenues, and desired profitability of different activities, not just costs alone. Successful marketing activities will generate additional revenues which can be projected based on the marketing objectives (such as increase off season stay by 5%).

Although budgets should be viewed as flexible plans, every effort should be made to adhere to them. Revisions in the budget should only be made after careful consideration of the likely impact of the change on the marketing mix and accomplishment of your objectives.

Implementation

Many well designed marketing plans fail because they are poorly executed. Businesses, agencies, and communities can increase the likelihood of successful implementation if they:

(1) Identify specific tasks which must be accomplished;

(2) Assign people or departments specific responsibility for different tasks;

(3) Provide employees with information on the marketing plan (rationale, objectives, strategies);

(4) Develop time lines and deadlines;

(5) Adhere as much as possible to the budget; and

(6) Regularly monitor and evaluate progress.

Evaluation

It is important that marketing efforts be continually evaluated. This will improve the effectiveness of marketing strategies by quickly identifying differences between actual results and expected performance and determining likely reasons for the success or failure to realize objectives.

A framework for evaluation would include:

(1) Determining which elements of the different marketing mixes are most important to evaluate.— —It is rarely possible or cost effective to evaluate all elements;

(2) Establishing performance standards to compare against actual results.—Marketing objectives, if properly formulated, should serve as performance standards;

(3) Development of formal and informal methods for collecting data on actual results.—There are many ways different elements of the marketing mix can be evaluated. For example, promotions can be evaluated with money off coupons. Special information request forms, telephone numbers to call or post office box numbers to write to can identify the area the request is coming from. Also, formal

(written) and informal surveys can be used to determine the promotional material the customer used in planning the trip;

(4) Comparison of results with objectives;

(5) Determination of needed change(s).

Conclusion

Customer satisfaction in tourism is greatly influenced by the way in which the service (hospitality) is delivered and the physical appearance and personality of the business. It is critical that these elements be communicated in the best possible manner to convince people to come and experience what your business or community has to offer. Equally important is the ability to generate repeat business because of your efforts. Thus, marketing becomes the method to reach potential visitors. It is a vital part of tourism management and can be done effectively and well, with sophistication and tact, or it can be done poorly in a loud, crass and intrusive manner. Hopefully, this bulletin has given you the basics for the former rather than the latter. Remember that to do an effective job at marketing:

(1) Adopt a strong customer orientation which includes regular research and assessment of their needs, wants and attitudes;

(2) Allocate sufficient resources and time to marketing;

(3) Assign formal responsibility for marketing to one person or department; and

(4) Develop and regularly update a marketing plan.

Information Supply in Tourism Management

Operators in tourism management, compared to other management sectors, are confronted with a vast field of complex aims, requiring different plans of action. The special working requirements of the services sector are a result of its business peculiarities. Problems instrategic, and frequently operational planning, are characterized by their complexity, often being intermingled, non-transparent, individualistically dynamic and requiring the achievement of multiple goals. The vast amount of information or complex weighting of the different sectors can present an insurmountable problem for human resources. As are sult there are high expectations of decision-makers' trouble-shooting abilities.

In order to solve complex problems, decision-makers need to have a factual knowledge of the industry (declarative knowledge) and the methodology used (procedural knowledge). The wealth of knowledge is drawn from two pools; that obtained from the "storage" of already existing experiences, and by generating knowledge in the respective field. Com-bining these two pools creates an arena for problem solving.

Declarative Knowledge – Decision Basis in Tourism Planning

Currently, information gains more and more importance, leading legitimately to the development of a fourth economic sector – the information sector. Information also plays a vital role in tourism for entrepreneurs and managers who spend the whole day involved in information processing. In the tourism industry there is no lack of market research data, on the contrary, there is a rather uncontrolled growth of various data sources, each having different survey purposes and survey designs. Tourism surveys of national and international market research institutes are published in ever shorter intervals and the level of itemization of market data increases rapidly. Information collected by these means has indicated data which can be organized into the following groups:

1. Information on markets and environment,
2. Information on customer behaviour,
3. Information on competition in the industry, and
4. Internal information for executive boards.

The first three information groups are predominantly non-discretionary from a manager's point of view as the information can very rarely be directly influenced by an individual company. Information from these groups are similar in nature and scope for most sectors represented in the tourism industry (hotel trade, restaurant trade, tour operators, travel agents, common carriers, pressure groups, etc.). In the fourth group however, there is a larger scope for variety. Due to high costs for primary market research many tourism managers abandon market research in general. Even the larger businesses and tourism organizations lack market research departments and employees rarely work exclusively on market research items. This results again in an inconsistent development of marketing aims and strategies, as businesses as often as not grope in the dark for their direction.

In Europe the most frequent or highly recognized of the commissioned tourism studies are either publicly financed, directly by national or local authorities, or indirectly by government agencies. This method of procuring market research, is important and often a condition for its development, as the expensive primary studies cannot be financed by the numerous small or medium-scale businesses. The resulting obligation to pass on information, created by the above mentioned research financing, has lead to a wider search-inregional tourism organizations, and other bodies representing tourism-to find means of successfully sharing and communicating information.

Traditional data resources in tourism market research are reports, records and statistics which may be presented either in printed format or are electronically driven (CD-ROM). Computer-based information systems (databases) are currently a rarity, but usually can be found either in connection with the official statistical data of a country or a region or international institutions. The information available by this method is rarely used since it ignores the special information requirements of the end-user (managers), or is simply inaccessible due to high fees, complicated application procedures or is simply not user friendly.

The lack of practical relevance, of these information systems, can be explained by their bias toward representing the economic interest of the sponsors and data collectors and/or by the universal requirements the systems have to meet in the collection, storage and search of statistical data from other industries. Market research results are mainly available in print and they can be obtained either in bookshops, online or directly from the author. From the consumer's perspective this way of passing on secondary information has a number of disadvantages:

- Due to the complex design of market research reports the surveyed data is not up to date any more.
- Data from different sources cannot be easily compared especially if it has been surveyed for different purposes.

- Information contained in reports is often of limited relevance for the particular problem.
- Presentation of data is either not detailed enough, not significant enough, or supplementary information is missing which prevents a faultless interpretation of results.
- Often only very specific data from a more comprehensive study is required and thus the cost-benefit-ratio becomes unattractive.

There is usually an overabundance of available information leaving managers to cope with determining which is the best source. Often the entrepreneur has to rely on external consultants and market research specialists resulting in additional costs.

Procedural Knowledge – Decision Basis in Tourism Planning

"The big problem with management science models is that managers practically never used them." More than 20 years ago John Little described the discrepancy between the scientific development of planning instruments, models, level of itemization and the fact that, when available, the knowledge gathered is rarely put into practice. This is caused by the numerous, often poorly documented assumptions of model architects, which was denoted as model plutonism by Hans Albert. As a response to this problem Little suggested that the manager is included in the model. He postulated in his article on the Decision Calculus, aniline models with the following features: robustness, ease of control, simplicity, completeness of relevant detail and suitability for communication.

The communication problem is of vital importance in the every day life of managers' daily events. It is still common practice to employ various levels of change rather than continue-ally observe the changes in market share and volume. Many entrepreneurs do not even know terms such as market segmentation or market positioning and they do not regard them as essential. They keep on looking for measures to expand seasonal business but lack knowledge of methods that will measure their success. Corporate planning only takes place if external financing is required and supporting documents have to be submitted to the lender. Heuristic forecasting methods are hardly ever used, accordingly quantitative methods are never used. Models of strategic market plan-ningportfolio analyses and analyses of the lifestyle of a product-employed in other industries are hardly ever used in tourism management. The grounds for the poor employment of methodological processes in tourism management can be divided into two groups; technological development and insufficient training. Issues related to the technological development of existing information processing and transmission systems are:

- Data required for the application of tourism models is either not up-to-date or unsuitable.
- Standard software is not able to support the relatively complex tasks in tourism management.
- Specially developed software is too expensive for single tourism businesses. Issues related to the insufficient training of tourism managers are:
- Managers have little knowledge of existing methods or available data.
- Managers are confronted with various data sources and different results and they do not know how to cope with this situation.
- Managers do not know which data sources and models are suitable.

The Transmission of Market Research Data in the Internet

Due to the vital role of tourism in many countries and regions in Europe a number of programs concerning tourism promotion have been installed. Government and private tourism organizations have been established in order to strengthen a tourism destination. Usually the aim is to increase the added value of a region. The major tasks of these bodies are:

- To provide consumers with information about the destination,
- To coordinate and implement sales promotion measures,
- Tourism advertising,
- Support in sales and distribution, and
- To coordinate and implement market research projects.

For most of their tasks (except the coordination and implementation of market research projects) these tourism promoting bodies provide efficient methods. The actual effect of the last item mentioned has been lost in the past due to inefficient instruments relating to the transmission and utilization of declarative and procedural knowledge. Now with the development of cheaper hard-and software many tourism organizations are reconsidering their promotion policy.

In almost all industries systems are being developed in order to support investment and marketing planning. Also the tourism industry has developed decision support systems and the most important applications are: (1) systems supporting marketing decisions in national tourism organizations, (2) travel counselling systems for shipping clerks, (3) systems supporting regional planning regarding the optimal selection of locations in which to invest (4) systems providing tourism portfolio analyses, (5) simulation tools for forecasting travel behaviour in certain regions. In Austria in 1982 the Austrian Society of Applied Research in Tourism (ASART) started a project aiming at the development of a marketing information system for the national tourism organization in Austria (Austrian National Tourist Office).

The first version of the tourism marketing information system (TourMIS) consisted of a database installed in a host system of the Scientific Computer Centre Vienna and an optimization programme for the advertising budget of the Austrian National Tourist Office.

Though the programmes were adapted in 1991 in favour of PC-software, and hence became accessible for a greater number of people (mainly employees of tourism organizations in the federal provinces), the area-wide information supply for top managers in the tourism industry did not begin until 1999 when the internet version was introduced.

Tourism Marketing Information System

The major aim of Tour MIS is an optimal information supply and decision support for the tourism industry. The first step is to provide aniline tourism survey data, as well as evaluation programmes to transform data into precious management information. Tour-MIS predominantly comprises:

1. A database containing tourism market research data (declarative knowledge),
2. Various program modules (method-base, procedural

knowledge) converting acknowledged methods/models into simple surfaces, and

3. Various administrative programmes which assist the maintenance of the database and track and control the information search behaviour of users.

The internet supports the transport and presentation of animated and unanimated pictures, sound and video recordings and text and numerical data and is expandable. A high-performance SQL-database and a functionally designed user interface for Tour MIS based on hypertext and Perl permits the development of interactive applications. The programme modules contained in the method-base are developed according to the specific requirements of tourism managers. The internet offers a number of advantages against the old PC-solution. Since changes in the database have immediate worldwide effect the speed of information transmission can be reduced to the availability of the information source. For example, Tour MIS makes the monthly projections of Statistics Austria available within only a few seconds to all regional managers of the Austrian National Tourist Office regardless of whether they are located in New York, Sydney, Tokyo or Madrid. Anybody provided with access to the internet and entitled to use Tour MIS may access data and information, make calculations or simulations send or receive data – without tiresome postal procedures, danger of loss, delays and costs. All these advantages have led to a significant expansion in the number of users.

Conditions for the Use of the System

In the beginning Tour MIS was provided with strict access control and used to be only accessible to certain users. In this respect the application did differ from traditional internet offers. However, the present concept is also not an Intranet. Unlike the Intranet which supports internal information management systems Tour MIS is not owned by a certain organization but is open to all authorized tourism organizations, societies, tourism consultants, companies, tourism training centres, pressure groups, etc. in Austria and abroad. By covering the maintenance costs, a consortium of 12 of the most important initiators of market research projects in Austria (Austrian National Tourist Office, nine provincial tourism organizations, the two special interest associations for Hotel Trade and Restaurant

Trade of the Federal Chamber of Commerce, Federal Ministry for Economic Affairs and Labour Tourism and Recreational Commerce Section) guarantee the continuous updating of the comprehensive database. Since 2000 this initiative has provided the Austrian tourism industry with free access to overall data and functions (with some exceptions) of Tour MIS. The necessary hardware resources are situated at the Institute for Tourism and Leisure Studies at the University of Economics and Business Administration in Vienna where a major part of the necessary maintenance work is carried out.

The Tour MIS Database

In the beginning Tour MIS contained data that was strongly influenced by the internal interests of its commissioner, the Austrian National Tourist Office. In this respect international tourism statistical data, empirical tourism studies and economic indicators for the most important markets of origin for the Austrian tourism industry have been collected in Tour MIS. The PC-version, developed in the early nineties, contained more than 10,000 time series. The periodicity of information was generally based on annual data, however the most significant time series have also been recorded for periods of less than a year.

Over the years the database has continually expanded. Due to the increasing importance of overseas markets further information has been required. Unequal needs of provincial tourism organizations led to additional statistics regarding the federal provinces and Vienna, being city and federal province at the same time, acquired an exceptional position.

Furthermore data on the Austrian and international city tourism has been added. This information was collected at the branch offices of the Austrian National Tourist Office, transmitted by fax and data was entered manually into the marketing information system in order to be available to users. Later based on international cooperation (European Cities' Tourism, European Travel Commission) the first online maintenance agreements with local tourism organizations were initiated.

The most important available data sources of Tour MIS are indicated in. Besides the basic information search functions the method-base has also been continually upgraded. In this respect the system more and more meets the requirements of an efficient decision support tool. In the next paragraphs the most important data sources and the facilities for analysis and reporting are discussed.

National Tourism Statistics Austria

One of the first data sources which was installed in Tour MIS was the official tourism statistics in Austria. Data generated from the registration with accommodation suppliers is one of the fundamental supports of the official inbound tourism statistics in Austria. Accommodation statistics are divided into two different kinds of survey: the accommodation for inbound travel and the accommodation capacity. The data on arrivals and over nights are surveyed for 50 generating countries related to 13 different accommodation types and 1,600 municipalities (= report communities) on a monthly basis.

Thus the official travel survey offers 25 million data points per annum which can be transformed into precious information for tourism managers. From the data material important information on tourism development, trends in markets of origin and accommodation types, evaluation of the competing situation can be derived. For example, for each of the 1,600 municipalities the database allows the user to regularly monitor the development of the average duration of stay, the seasonality, market shares, guest-mix structure, and, in connection with the capacity statistics, the occupancy rate.

Tour MIS presently offers official tourism statistics only at the provincial basis which nevertheless requires maintenance work of 11,700 data sets per month. The necessary data transfer from the host system of Statistic Austria (ISIS) to Tour MIS takes place automatically each time after the arrival of new data segments and in accordance with various maintenance routines.

The information supply of Tour MIS users takes place by means of predominate tables and reports created for the user in real time operations. The content and design of tables or reports plays an important role in the user's perception of the system's usefulness and usability. Only if the information supply meets the users' needs will the system achieve its aim of providing a high-performance usage of market data and improve the information supply in tourism management.

Source Feature Evaluation Period Update Data

Statistic Austria bed nights, arrivals, capacity (suppliers and beds) 50 countries of origin (markets), 13 types of accommodation – for Austria and her 9 provinces since 1960 monthly secondary data in time series format

Austrian Guest Survey 250 variables incl. intention to revisit, guest satisfaction, type of travel, means of transport, duration of stay, travel motive, expenses, selection of accommodation, activities, net income of the household, profession, education, etc. 16 countries of origin (markets) – for Austria and her 9 provinces since 1991 each third year primary data ETC (European Travel Commission) bed nights, arrivals, capacities (beds) 21 countries of origin (markets) – for 33 destinations (countries) in Europe since 1990 annually secondary data in time series format ECT (European Cities' Tourism) bed nights, arrivals, capacities (beds) 21 countries of origin (markets) – for 80 European cities since 1983 annually secondary data in time series format

Number of visitations in Austrian attractions (Austrian National Tourist Office) number of visits for 240 Austrian attractions federal provinces of Austria since 1998 annually secondary data in time series format Austrian Hotel and Restaurant Panel 60 variables incl. net product, fixed and working assets equity and debt capital,, cash flow, profitability-ures, etc. location, size, category and type of business. Since 1982 annually primary data.

- No particular database knowledge is required by the user,
- The data transformations and calculations implemented in the method-base of Tour MIS allow for adequate problem reporting, and
- The user interface refers to a familiar technical terminology.

Especially for the requirements of the managers in the provincial tourism organizations. The comparison with the developments in other (competitive) destinations permits an evaluation of the market share development in Carinthia.

The analysis in indicates for example that Carinthia could defend its position regarding the three most important markets (Germany, Netherlands, Italy), shown in the increase of market shares, despite the fact that Carinthia experienced a severe loss in bed-nights. On the other hand an apparent success regarding the increased demand of American guests (+ 7,7%) has to be put into perspective since the other federal provinces outperformed Carinthia in this segment. Due to the comparative analysis and a simple and informative presentation of the statistics (using sorting features and different colours to distinguish between market share gains (green) and losses (red)) the data material is upgraded. The analysis presented in may be used for historical or current data, for each Austrian province, based either on arrivals or bednights for each of the 13 different accommodation types.

Competitive Analysis for Austrian Regions

The opportunities for implementing tools which use official tourism statistics for bench-marking analyses, the implementation of early warning systems and forecasting tourism trends is obvious. Due to the refinancing interests of data collection authorities and the lack of financial resources in the tourism industry, however, the data analysis for smaller tourism regions or report communities has been prevented in the past.

This factor must be regretted since it can be assumed that the evaluation of key success factors in tourism marketing will significantly improve when they are measured in smaller regional units. Also tourism managers, especially those operating on a regional level, usually have only very little influence in the organization of nationwide surveys. Therefore, many of the statistical series are based on administrative regions that are not always congruent with actual regional use and by tourists and subsequent flows.

Number of Visitations in Austrian Attractions

The collection of statistical data on leisure-time activities and especially the measurement of visitor arrivals in attractions is a rather complex project. It is rarely executed internationally on a systematic or continuous basis.

The major problems lie in the delimitation of the study object and the methods of measurement. Since the early 90's the Austrian National Tourist Office has collected and distributed information on the visitation numbers in Austrian attractions. In close collaboration with the nine provincial tourism organizations a list of 240 Austrian attractions is checked for completeness and updated on an annual basis.

Number of Visitations in Austrian Attractions

Since 2001 this maintenance procedure is carried out online in Tour MIS. Here the market research specialists at the respective provincial tourism organizations enter their information into the system. Due to the newness of the database the reporting facilities are still very limited. The present tables either provide simple time series for a single attraction or list all attractions for one or more federal province(s) arranged according to frequency of visits.

Austrian Guest Survey

Since 1988 alternating each third year a comprehensive visitor survey in Austria has been carried out. The Austrian Guest Survey is one of the most important sources of information in tourism market research. It provides vital information on guest profiles, customer satisfaction, information and booking behaviour, type of travel, destination, means of transport, accommodation, activities, visitor expenditures and other current topics. The Austrian Guest Survey is financed and coordinated by a consortium of authorities responsible for tourism promotion in Austria (Austrian National Tourist Office and nine provincial tourism organizations), the Chamber of Commerce and the Federal Ministry for Economic Affairs and Labour (Tourism and Recreational Commerce Section). Since the Austrian Guest Survey is a primary study it presents some features which complicate the information diffusion in Tour MIS compared to the above mentioned secondary data sources. The main reasons for these additional difficulties are:

(1) The much wider scope of the study,

(2) The required data analyses are more demanding, and

(3) Interpretation possibilities are limited by the sample size and characteristics.

The Austrian Guest Survey has more than 200 features which are partially modified for each survey. Considering the scope of the study and that only descriptive evaluation is possible the Austrian Guest Survey offers more than 1 million findings per survey. Traditional forms of report (market research report, press releases etc.) cover just a small part of the real investigation and evaluation potential. Thus important questions managers would raise remain unanswered although theoretically the answers exist. Data of primary analyses are available unprocessed (disaggregated data format). Regarding the Austrian Guest Survey there are 10,000 interviews per survey, all of the features being available in quantitative form. However, information processing requires the application of analytical methods ranging from calculating simple mean values to complicated data mining procedures.

The necessary methodological knowledge has to be obtained from statistics experts who create costs which, in most cases, cannot be covered by the tourism industry. Therefore, due to a lack of know-how or lacking financial support, many questions managers raise remain unanswered although data actually would be available. Contrary to a census, as found in official statistics, sample surveys do not integrate all elements of the whole picture into the study. The major aim in statistics is to draw reliable conclusions regarding to the totality from a limited number of elements. The previously mentioned evaluation procedures take more effort and interpretation depends on the features of the sample (sample size and sampling technique).

Automatic Selection of Analysing Methods

In addition the user may select only a certain part of the overall data set for evaluation (i.e. data of a certain province or market). In order to prevent interpretation errors due to unreliability of results, those values based on a small sample are only indicated after informing the user about the problem.

The analysis takes place in real time. Tour MIS provides the facilities to evaluate more than one survey, at the same time offering two alternatives: longitudinal and cross section analyses. The first application informs the tourism manager about changes in the guest behaviour over a specified period of time. Query support is provided by offering only variables surveyed unmodified over the overall selected period of time (i.e. the standard questionnaire programme). The latter application increases the sample size (for 4 surveys more than 45,000 interviews) which makes answers to detailed questions possible (assuming a particular time invariance, of course). This function permits for example reliable results about the share of side expenses of Italian guests in the federal province of Salzburg during a particular season.

Comparison of Hotel and Restaurant Groups

The database supports regional planners and tourism managers in their decisions as well as managers in the hospitality industry. The results of the past 10 years of a project which has been executed by the Austrian Society of Applied Research in Tourism and commissioned by the Austrian Hotel and Restaurant Association situated within the Austrian Federal Chamber of Commerce are presented in Tour MIS. In this project operating data and annual financial statements for hotels and restaurants in Austria are compared on an annual basis. Information collected directly from the businesses with a high level of itemization is supplemented with comprehensive, compressed data stored at cooperative industry related organizations such as the Wirts chafts for derungs institute der Austrian Federal Economic Chamberund Tourism us bank and Burges Forder ungsbank of the Austrian Federal Ministry of Economic Affair and Labour. In connection with the design and evaluation of continually repeated surveys a number of new approaches for the diagnosis and comparison of industry groups are developed. Tour MIS presently provides the following applications:

- Industry information for more than 1,300 hotels and restaurants per year since 1991.
- Various functions supporting key ratio analyses in the hotel and restaurant industry.
- The chance for hotel and restaurant managers to participate online in the most significant hotel and restaurant panel survey in Austria.

Information about more than 50 different key ratios is provided in the form of arithmetic mean and median values for 30 distinguished industry groups. Within the industry groups additional evaluations for businesses of excellent profitability (best practice enterprises) are available. For the hotel and restaurant panel database Tour MIS users are provided with the following query and analysing facilities:

- Evaluation of a key ratio for all industry groups referring to a certain year.
- Comparison of all key ratios for a particular industry group.
- Development of a key ratio uncovering the main industry developments.

- Benchmarking analysis for a particular hotel or restaurant (only provided when managers are actively participating in the study).

The quality of information based on the results of the survey is strongly influenced by the number of participating businesses. Due to the chance for interaction in the internet the first results may be obtained straight after entering business data. In this context the problem of how to prevent participants from entering incorrect data occurs. Tour MIS offers a number of plausibility controls during data entry and records data in a second, temporary database. At regular intervals experts determine which records are qualified to be stored in the general database.

Analysis of the User Behaviour of Tour MIS

How do we know that we have successfully implemented a system? Researchers have not really agreed on an indicator for successful implementation. One appealing approach is a cost-benefit study. In this evaluation, one totals the costs of developing a system and compares them with the benefits resulting form the system. In theory, this sounds like a good indicator of success, but in practice it is difficult to provide meaningful estimates.

Obtaining the cost side of the ratio is not too much of a problem if adequate records are kept during the development of the system. However, an evaluation of the benefits of a computer-based information system is difficult. How can the value of improved information processing be measured? With transactions processing and some operational control systems, it is usually possible to show tangible savings.

For example, many transactions systems have resulted in increased productivity in processing paperwork without a proportional increase in cost.

Operational control systems, such as those used to control inventories in large hotels and restaurants, may reduce inventory balances, saving storage and investment costs while maintaining existing service levels. For systems that aid a decision maker, it is much more difficult to estimate the benefits. For a marketing information system, like Tour MIS, use of the system is voluntary. A manager or other user receives a report but does not have to use the information on it or

1. Council of the European Union, Council Directive 95/97/EEC of 23 November 1995 on the collection of statistical information in the field of tourism, Official Journal. L291 of 6 December 1995.
2. Commission of the European Communities Report to the Council, the European Parliament, the Economic and Social Committee and the Committee of Regions on the Application of the Directive of the Council 95/97/EEC on the compilation of statistical data in the field of tourism, 17 January 2001, even read the report.

In particular systems that provide aniline retrieval of information from a database can be classified as voluntary since the use of such a system is frequently at the discretion of the user. For this type of system where use is voluntary, it is generally accepted that high levels of use is a sign of successful implementation.

In this case the economic or personal success of its users is indirectly measured by the frequency of usage. Several authors have shown that the frequency of usage is determined by the perceived usefulness (textual component) and the ease of use (technical component).

The acceptance of Tour MIS can be determined by means of constantly updated and aniline available access statistics. Contrary to other internet applications the accesses to websites is not counted but the number of virtually answered queries is. Results of the Tour MIS statistics are therefore not influenced by website characteristics (number of graphics or distortions due to the application of window techniques), but do represent the 'genuine user acceptance'. In addition, the comprehensive protocol system permits the analysis of queries broken down into various user groups, information sources and the type of query.

The community of Tour MIS users has continually developed. In 1998 there were only 50 registered users at the Austrian National Tourist Office and at the end of 2001 more than 1,000 registered Tour MIS users have been counted. The distribution of user groups indicates that Tour MIS is not only favoured by tourism managers (44.6%), but also by employees, students and pupils of education and research institutes (31.6% of all queries) and other non-tourism professionals or private persons (23.8%). The distribution of various user groups is present. The average number of queries per user in 2001 and therefore indicates the frequency of use for a specific Tour MIS user group. The employees of provincial tourism organizations use Tour-MIS most (92 queries per user) due to the comprehensive data material available on the federal provinces. The students, as the largest user group, show a relatively low number due to only temporal interest (for a seminar paper or a diploma thesis they need access to data material only once). The number of accommodation providers and F&B managers using the system is, considering the number of existing businesses, very low. A reason for this is probably that the most interesting information source for this user group (the Austrian hotel and restaurant panel database) is a relatively new data set that is simply not known by the managers. Overall, 34.538 queries have been processed in 2001, signifying an increase of 35.5% in comparison to the previous year (25,492 queries).

About half of all queries are made regarding the official tourism statistics in Austria. The industry appears to be very interested in the development of the major markets of origin and accommodation types in the federal provinces (on average approx. 50 queries per day). Regarding the official statistics for Austria most queries are made in connection with information concerning monthly statistics (20% of all queries). The international data sources ECT and ETC gained 18.7% respectively and they rank behind the official Austrian statistics. The significant increase of queries regarding these two international data sources as well as the tendency towards English queries, however, indicate a growing international interest in Tour MIS.

The assessment of demand of information certainly needs a more detailed investigation than simply monitoring the current use of market research resources. However, in Tour-MIS 'demand of information' not only refers to the principal (statistical) sources, but also to the sort of data transformations (analysis) and formats of automatically generated reports available to the users. The functional characteristics and the design of the system have always been developed in close collaboration with the affected managers. For instance, concerning the development of the decision support tools part of the international data sources in the system, the developers have met more than 20 times in form of working group meetings and seminars with representatives (CEOs and research directors) of European Cities Tourism and the European Travel Commission. The involvement of the managers in the design and operation of the information system resulted in favourable user attitudes and perceptions of the information system and led to higher levels of use. In the beginning only a few members were able and willing to actively contribute to this project by entering their data on a regular basis. Today, more than 100 managers working in different tourism destination marketing organizations, based in more than 30 different European countries, and speaking more than 15 different languages, are obviously convinced by the significance of the project and the value of the system as they regularly and voluntarily enter their data into the system.

Conclusions

Generally speaking tourism managers benefit from access to the internet in two ways: the internet provides the opportunity to communicate and serves as a platform for new distribution channels. The present article does not deal with new distribution channels and new booking systems in the tourism industry. This undoubtedly important topic has been discussed in an number of publications and symposia.

The present article introduced Tour MIS, an aniline accessible decision support tool for tourism and hospitality management which has been successfully used by more than 1,000 users for three years. According to Ritchie and Ritchie for the development of an industry supported destination marketing information system, information must be both generally accessible and widely advertised so that managers are aware of the benefits it offers. In lieu of a more preferable cost-benefit analysis, the success of Tour MIS was analysed by studying actual system use observed from various log files generated by the system. The merits of this form of evaluation lie in the objectivity of the findings, the cost-effective procedure, and the comparability of the estimates when the analysis are performed on a regular basis.

The major reason for the poor application of management science models and methodologies in tourism management is the insufficient education of practitioners and the inadequacy of problem solving features of standard software solutions. The development of simple, affordable (shareware) programs, downloadable for every tourism manager, is the first step into a new era of dialogue between research and practice. Within a short time, for internal diagnosis, forecasts and simulations on the net there will be high-performance computer languages available which are now being developed by major international software producers.

Technological progress will also offer benefits for the electronic transmission of tourism market research data. Interdisciplinary research projects will be challenged with tourism research, research in statistics and commercial information technology. For example there are still a number of problems to be solved in order to be able to jointly use ecoscopic and demoscopic tourism data within a marketing information system. These combination options require a constant standardization of information sources as well as new approaches towards the methodological processing of data gained from various studies. Another vital research initiative will be the development of information systems about themselves? Optimizing the knowledge presentation of 'service quality in information services' has been neglected in the past. By applying and accepting decision support systems the significance of this field of research will increase. Another important factor will be the role system imminent? Protocol presentations play, which are continually improved. Thus data on the user behaviour offers not only information on necessary improvements in the data processing of tourism market research results, but also on the future focus of tourism market research.

The sudden explosion of data and the growing need for information challenges basic research as far as data reduction and decision support methods are concerned. Therefore existing concepts for qualitative forecasts and market reaction models and their calibration options in a marketing information system have to be reconsidered. In this respect projects which aim at a systematic and regular compilation of experiences experts made with regard to various technical subjects (i.e. short-term development of singular markets of origin) are considered to be promising. It is their aim to provide an improved evaluation of future market developments and eventually to integrate the findings into the strategic planning of national and regional tourism organizations and businesses. Another necessary development regards already existing data collections and the processing of the European cities' statistics. In this respect this author has observed many shortcomings relating to the international comparability of the data. The improved communication possibilities provided by the new medium stimulates critical discussions and behavioural learning among all participants. Within European Cities Tourism, among other things, new initiatives to evaluate one city's major competitors have been released due to the managers' increased awareness of the importance of this problem.

The trend towards globalization in research, where the internet plays a vital role, refers also to tourism research. To those critics who refer to the internet as uncontrolled growing, complicated and in its applications too playful, supporters used to point out that one day smart and profitable applications would be found. That is where we stand now. The new areas of responsibility regional and national tourism managers are confronted with today, not only suggest shortcomings in education but also promise new opportunities for the next manager generations to acquire status.

5

Contemporary Food Marketing-Challenges & Ethical Issues

Today's consumers are more flirtatious gazing for an increasing level of fun and variety. Anything that surrounds them for too long jades them. With the dawn of every fresh day, these modern day customers demand for quality and healthy food that is offered as per their convenience and changing cultural needs. The survival of any food outlet or the industry is also highly dependent on them – their palate can either make or break the existence of these companies. This has wrought a great challenge on the marketers of the food industry who intentionally resort to unethical practices that had sourced many lively international debates on ethical and marketing practices of the food industry besides the intervention of regulatory authorities to implement necessary legislation wherever required to reduce the ill-effects on the society.

There has been an increase in the number of tourists (both in-bound and outbound) due to the boost in tourism resulting in the exchange of cultural and traditional ideas among different countries; the development of communication, infrastructure, and information technology due to the liberalization, globalization and various other good reasons has turned the world into a global village; the spending capacity of the middle-class people has also risen due to availability of highly disposable income and increasing economy of the country for the past few years. All these reasons were enough for the food industry to bring into the country a multitude of different gastronomy from across the globe – like the pastas & spaghettis from Italy, the ever-popular chowmein from China, the tacos and enchiladas from Mexico, the Continental pizzas and burgers, the French flambe etc., to name a popular few which were normally ever heard of and were limited within the precincts of star hotels and among those people who could afford them. But of late, there have been a slew of contemporary foods pouring into the market at affordable prices that are targeted at the growing numbers of fashionable consumers. Some of the latest additions to the already existing modern foods include –

- the ready instant mixes that consumes less cooking time (like the idli mix, dosa mix, sambar powder and so on that are added with preservatives to increase their shelf life),
- the ready-to-eat foods like ITCs paneer butter masala, nav ratan kurma, dal makhani and so on (under the Aashirvaad's ReadyMeal brand), that just requires pre-heating through a baine-marie,
- the fusion of cuisines customizing to Indian palate-Italian pizza in the form of Indian Tandoor pizza.

With increasing demands largely from the perpetually growing niche segment – the children and the young adults, there is also rigorous sale of junk foods that mainly includes energy-dense fast foods like the puff pastries and burgers containing large quantity of margarine, mayonnaise, butter or cheese; carbonated soft drinks with high calorie content like Pepsi or Coke; sugary breakfast cereals like the Kelloggs Choco Pops; salty snacks like Haldirams or Leher namkeens; and other baked goods like patties, cookies, doughnuts etc.,

Though these food products are claimed to be manufactured using the best technology under most hygienic standards by trained professionals, they generally tend to be nutrient-poor and High in Fats, Sugars and Salt (HFSS foods) contributing to an environment of more obese people with diet-related non-communicable diseases like the cardiovascular diseases, diabetes, osteoporosis, certain forms of cancer, and high blood pressure.

The Pill with a Sugar Coat

The marketers exploit many innovative practices and use wide unethical deeds and techniques to promote their products to capture the gullible segment. Though most of the practices used by the food marketers seem upright and lawful, it would be found to be immoral only when appropriately examined where it becomes difficult for one to judge and draw a clear line between normal marketing practice and unethical behavior of the marketer. All of us have encountered the marketing gimmicks of many companies in some form or the other – like the buy two get one free; the offer is only for employees of certain organizations; some pop-ups sprouting on the screen when browsing the Internet informing that we have won a prize; or a banner of some sponsor placed at the venue during an event attended, etc. Once the consumer gets attracted by this publicity stunt, he is further lured to become a customer and then a permanent customer. As Vikram Bakshi, MD, McDonald's puts it in one of his recent interviews-

"McDonald's is a family restaurant. We believe that we are here to make our customers feel at home and enjoy their time out with their family when they are at McDonald's. Extra care has been taken to make our restaurants child friendly, by providing play areas wherever possible so that the parents can relax and have a good time when they are visiting McDonald's. Our tables are rounded so that a child does not hurt himself while in the restaurant, our counters are low and the menu pictorially depicted so that a child can order a meal for himself very easily and his parents don't have to bother. At McDonald's, customer always comes first. Every employee strives to provide 100 percent customer satisfaction – for every customer – for every visit. This includes friendly and attentive service, accuracy in order taking, and anticipation of customer's needs. We have hostesses who keep circulating in the lobby helping children and adults alike with straws, napkins, souffle cups, sauce sachets etc., and any other assistance that they may require"

Anyone would hardly resist such royal treatment. These food outlets take into concern not only the comfort and convenience of their guests, but also to convert their first time visitors into repeat business. Meticulous plan is done as per the behavioural patterns and feedback from the target consumers – like from "McDonald's mein hai kuch baat" caption when it first started operations ten years back in India to "Toh aaj McDonald's ho jaye" after getting established properly in the market. Notice the change of talk from the experience of a first time visit to about an everyday experience i.e. the customers are encouraged to visit more often with their family and enjoy their time out. And the segment that wishes to have the food delivered at its place, then there is Domino's

Pizza at the neighborhood, a global 'Pizza Delivery Expert' known world over for providing freshly baked pizzas topped with quality ingredients and cheese. This was the first pizza chain in the world committed to the promise of delivering pizzas in 30 minutes or less and most of their outlets in India are delivery-based with only about 25% being both delivery and "sit-down" outlets.

None would get misled or infer anything wrong with the above points against the food industry or its strategies used. As already stated, it is very difficult to draw a clear line between normal marketing practice and unethical behavior. But how far it is ethical on the part of the food companies to offer junk and unhealthy food to its valued customers and again chase them to visit almost daily? Mind you, there is nothing to criticize the food industry here as such with regard to its quality of products or services offered or even doubt on its credibility. It is only on the type of food that they offer that is having its negative impact on the society.

It is agreed that there is nothing called bad food as such, but it is mainly the kind of food that does not add any value or significance to the health of the people. It rather acts as nutrition-less junk food showing its ill effects on the health that affects the mortality rate of the civilization. Again concurring that the modern day consumer is too busy and insists on such kind of food, but how far is it good on the part of the marketer to lure and tempt these innocent gullible with attractive offers and promotions who are unaware or limitedly aware of the consequences. The insistence from the consumer to provide such food does not come on its own unless shaped by the industry in order to survive and earn huge profits. This is created through the heavy dose of advertisements and promotions, the peer pressure, and with the rapid expansion and opening of new branches even in smaller towns of the country.

Ethical Challenges

Naturally, a company will exist and grow in the market by expecting repeat business only when it satisfies its customers' needs i.e. it understands what its customer wants. But, there are some instances where the customers' wants are not good for him or her. Like a child buying a cigarette for his father but smoking himself or an obese patient having more of sweets, oily food. Similarly, it may also happen that some demands of the customers may be good for them but are not good for the society or the environment like the recent killings of the extinct, endangered species to celebrate a high profile dinner, a premarital abortion, etc.

Examining these points from different perspectives i.e.

a) interests and behaviors of the marketers,
b) the extent of consumers' concern to reduce the negative side effects of the products they buy and
c) the steps to be taken to reduce the consumption of products that have ill-effects on the general public at large and the appropriate intervention.

Interests and Behaviors of the Marketers

Any food manufacturer will always strive to increase the sale of his product or service to the maximum extent and leave the negative consequences to be the result of the free choice of consumers – a natural phenomenon. Some food products like burgers, sweets, and carbonated soft drinks are not so harmful as compared to alcoholic drinks, cigarettes or drugs etc., but as mentioned are poor in nutrients with rich fat, sugar and salts content causing obesity and other diseases. Most people especially the young children and the teenage group get addicted to them quickly mainly due to reasons like emulating of Western culture, the environment of nuclear family with sometimes both the parents working, peer coercion in the school/college/office etc. These addicted categories are the company's treasures who later become heavy users as the days pass by accounting for their high profits. Let us understand this with an example:

Presume a teenager is addictive of eating a cheese pizza daily. This promises the company a patron for life and each such new addict expectedly generates a 25-year to 30-year profit stream for the pizza company if the consumer continues to favour the same brand. Suppose the teenager starts eating at the age of 15, eats for 25 years and stops further consumption due to obesity and doctor's advice. If she spends an average of Rs. 10,000/-a year on the pizza, she will spend Rs. 2,50,000/-till she reaches 40. If the company's profit rate is 20%, she is worth Rs. 50,000/-to the company. Which company will not try to attract such a heavy user who is contributing Rs. 50,000/-to its profits? And this profit is the minimum as the lady stopped eating at 40. What if the addiction continued and she consumed the same for another few years neglecting its ill effects? This is the thing that generally happens, as most of the people are unable to control themselves due to the temptations created by these food marketers with their innovative methods.

Are you aware that Coca-Cola is aiming to get people to start drinking Coca-Cola for breakfast instead of orange juice?

Then, McDonald's is encouraging customers to choose a larger hamburger, a larger order of French fries, and a larger cola drink.

And with best of the marketers working for them, it is just a cakewalk to transform the consumer eating habits.

Consumers' Concern to Reduce the Negative Side Effects

Would anybody be ready to reduce their sales or restrain consumption of their products? Never. Hence, there should be at least some kind of pressure from the government or the public. Recently, in the interest of the consumer, the Cola companies were directed by Supreme Court to list the composition of contents on all bottles including the pesticide residues but the company is utilizing the opportunity of time given to approach the High Court on the phraseology. Surrogate advertising though banned is still observed and continued on television, generally seen at places like sports stadiums, art exhibitions in the form of sponsorships of the event. Some of them under close scrutiny of the regulations are McDowell's Mera Number One, Gilbey's Green Label ads, Bagpiper soda water, Kingfisher mineral water, 8PM apple juice, ITC-GTD's (greeting cards division) Expression Greeting Cards, Red & White Bravery Awards and Wills sportswear as they are the titanic advertisers under this category.

Most of the companies, as part of their Corporate Social Responsibility give a statutory warning on their products. For example, like the statutory warning on the cigarette packs, some of the food companies also warn in similar way – on products that contains Monosodium Glutamate (MSG) i.e. Ajinomoto. MSG if consumed in large quantities causes migraines, hormonal disorders and Chinese restaurant syndrome. But still people keep continue to buy such product and the companies who just try to behave in a socially responsible manner know this and are aware that the sales loss resulting from their CSR 'cooperation' is very slight.

On the other hand, there is sometimes resistance from the consumers themselves when the companies genuinely struggle to find avenues to reduce the ill effects of too much consumption of their products. When Mc. Donald's offered a reduced-fat hamburger or salad, consumers rejected it. Keeping the calorie conscious people in mind, Coca-Cola and Pepsi introduced the Diet Coke and Pepsi One brand with low calorie content. Coca-Cola also recently announced the launch of Coca-Cola Zero, a new, zero-calorie cola drink sweetened with a blend of aspartame and acesulfame potassium.

All these modifications and new product development from the company are the results of feedback and behavior from the consumers themselves as well as the pressures from the Government.

Right to Intervene and Reduce the Consumption

Infinite numbers of debates ensued with regard to the right to intrude by the government or any public interest groups in the free choices of individuals whether to reduce or ban the consumption of foods that show their ill effects on the health of the people in due course. On one end, it is detested with remarks like the job of marketer is not to make society a better place or to save the world. He is mainly there to sell more and earn good profits for the shareholders in a legal way. On the other side, there are few people concerned with the personal and societal costs of unregulated consumption. Very sensitive issues are created on certain food products and statistics are developed on the heavy health costs of various diseases caused because of failure to reduce the consumption of such kind of products. These costs affect everyone as they lead to higher medical costs and taxes. Thus, even those who don't consume such products are harmed because of unenlightened behavior of others.

The Finale Act

What legislations have to be brought out by the regulatory authority that would create a check on the marketers while promoting and selling of their products? What ethical practices does the marketer need to carry out in order to create a good image among his customers and also to develop a healthy society? Let us look at this issue from both the perspective.

Promotional Regulations

The regulatory authority of various countries have brought into force various regulations and restrictions with regard to the promotional activities of the food marketers in order to reduce its usage and avoid the related ill effects on the society. As the marketers particularly target the children and the young adults who are found to be the most influential decision makers during any purchases, their promotional activities have created a very high impact on the society that have shown more of negative results. Let us observe few of the strategies of the marketers and the legislations put upon them by the legal authorities.

1. *Television :* The strongest of all the media in the modern world, television is highly used by food marketers to advertise their products with particular target on children. Breakfast cereals, soft drinks, snacks, and fast foods are the common food products advertised frequently through this medium. The effect has been so great over the past few years that there have been strong proposals to restrict television advertising, particularly to children in many countries including India, Australia, Brazil, Germany, United Kingdom, Ireland, Italy, New Zealand, Poland and France. Television ads carried various clauses emphasizing companies not to exploit the credulity of people; be harmful to their physical, mental or moral health; make them feel inferior to others who possess the products; or induce them to unduly pressurize their parents/guardians into purchasing the product.

2. *In-premises marketing:* The food marketer visits the place of customer like schools, colleges, offices or homes and promotes the products. This strategy is used to target all categories of people as all of them would gather together at their respective places. This strategy is found to be second best to television advertising as it has also attached lot of controversy and debate in recent years. The techniques used are direct advertising (e.g. Signage in canteens), indirect advertising (eg. Sponsorship of events) and product sales. Most of the items like soft drinks, confectionary, snacks, ice-creams, instant noodles, etc., which do not even contain the minimum nutritional value

(MNV) required are usually sold. Some of the restrictions used especially in schools are prohibiting commercial solicitation, non-distribution of advertisements and other marketing material without the consent of the parents in advance, not allowing the marketing activities unless the head teacher believes it has an educational objective. In Japan, the meal provided under the school lunch program is the only food to be eaten within school premises.

3. *Sponsorship:* In sponsorship, the food companies provide funds and other resources to an event or activity in return for access to the exploitable commercial potential associated with that event. Sponsorship has the benefits of reaching globally at less cost than conventional advertising when the event sponsored is broadcast worldwide. Food companies sponsor wide range of activities like sporting events, television programs and musical events. The main advantage to the marketer under this strategy is that being a sponsor, he may have influence on the program content and cause program dilution where much publicity for his company and products would be demanded and created among the audience. Some of the regulations under sponsorship include banning sponsorship of children's program, not encouraging purchase or rental of the products or services of the sponsor, etc.

4. *Product Placement:* Under product placement, a visual or graphic uses the message, logo, or object of the food company in exchange for payment. It is found in many forms of visual entertainment like films, television programs, music videos, computer games, etc. This powerful marketing tool of 'surreptitious advertising' and indirect or non-regular advertising is widely used to market food and beverage products. It is a cost-effective technique when compared with the purchase of normal airtime, it is less disruptive than commercial breaks as the viewer is held captive, giving the product his undivided attention because it is part of the program. It is explicitly banned in countries like Austria, Belgium, UK, Norway and is used with restricted time in Philippines.

5. *Internet marketing:* Consumers at present are widely targeted with this new but rapidly expanding strategy with a range of internet-based marketing techniques. The cross-border marketing is especially changing the entire world into a global village. The ideal target group under this strategy is mainly young people, as they tend to browse the net for longer durations. The strategies used are interactive games and activities, competitions, attractive sites with flashy graphics, chat and e-mail facilities. Keeping the children and teenagers in mind, the website is made more interactive, providing free downloadable games & general information. Subsequently, personal data of the visitors are collected for future promotions and sale of database. There are statutory guidelines and restrictions with self-regulatory codes specific to Internet marketing, e-commerce, data collection, consumer protection, broadcast advertising, link to other websites which are still in the budding stages.
6. *Sales promotion:* Under the sales promotion technique, the marketer creates an incentive scheme to make the consumer buy a product or service at the point-of-sale. Door-to-door selling, ballyhoo, prizes, hawking, price discounts all come under sales promotion. With regard to sales promotion, there are very general regulations like sales promotion must be fair and sometimes are very specific like not allowing any sweepstakes, etc.

Likewise, the food companies may reflect on the following few brief opinions that would act as guidelines for meeting their challenges without foregoing the ethical values. Some of the international food marketers may be already treading on them while some may make use of these for exercising in their organizations.

1. *Following the basic ethical norms and values:* The first and foremost being marketers must do no harm and work for which they are appropriately trained for by adhering to applicable laws and regulations. This will automatically make them actively add value to their organizations and customers. The products should be appropriate for their intended and promoted uses for which intentionally

deceptive or misleading communication should be avoided. The ethical values should be embraced, communicated and practiced so as to improve the consumer confidence; they should show honesty by being truthful or forthright in their dealings with customers, employees, investors, Government and other stakeholders. They should be responsible and accept the consequences of any marketing decisions and strategies, should be fair by trying to balance justly the needs of the buyer with the interests of the seller, respect the basic human dignity of all stakeholders, be open by creating transparency in their marketing operations and finally fulfill the economic, legal, philanthropic and societal responsibilities that serve the stakeholders in a strategic manner.

2. *Using appropriate and ethical marketing strategies:* The ethical and appropriate marketing strategies include the packaging or serving the food in reasonable portion sizes without encouraging overeating that generally food marketers do to increase their product sale. The products also should be reformulated to reduce the size of the portions, the amount of calories, the sodium content along with refined sugars and saturated fats. Emphasis should be to improve the nutritional value of the food by concentrating more on fruits, vegetables, whole grains and low-fat milk contents in the food products. There should be strenuous efforts to promote healthy eating habits by portraying healthful foods in a positive way. The advertisements should not focus on nutritionally poor food products especially on those channels that are particularly watched by children.

3. *Concentration on some specific issues:* Marketers should concentrate on some specific issues as given below particularly in case of marketing the food products for children –

    a. Not to mislead the child regarding the emotional, social or health benefits of a product.

    b. Not to market any food by negatively portraying the parents, teachers or any other popular personalities.

    c. Not to suggest that a person who buys a certain product for the child is better than the person who does not.

d. Not to link the child's self-image to consumption of his company's food, use any peer pressure or arouse any kind of unrealistic expectations in relation to consuming his company's food (like a child will be more fit physically, will be more happy or popular if he eats a particular food).

e. Not to use pictures of healthful foods like fruits or vegetables to market the low-nutrition foods.

4. *Making safer products:* The foods to be manufactured and marketed to the consumers should be lighter with minimum quantities of fat and calories. This can be done alternatively by means of selling more of salads and healthy sandwiches. The beverage companies can think of producing nonalcoholic beer in huge quantities as the young population largely consumes it, soft drinks companies can focus on increasing their packaged drinking water that are healthier than carbonated soft drinks. The soft drinks that are sold in underdeveloped countries can be added with nutrients and vitamins so as to deliver better health benefits to the deprived people there.

5. *Support the efforts to foster healthy eating habits:* As most of the people have limited proficiency in nutritional aspects of any food, the companies who have extensive expertise in persuasive techniques should make it a point to support the Government in communicating the effects of various foods on the health of a person. Hence, communicating with the target audience by means of effective media like television through cartoon characters, celebrities, contests etc., about the low-nutrition foods that does not benefit in any way and rather harm their health, along with discouraging them from buying cigarettes, drugs or alcoholic beverages etc., will indirectly help the society to improve itself.

6. *Restrict the sale or use of certain products:* Whenever a product is of any harm to the consumer, such items should be either restricted or totally banned from the market. There have been successful and unsuccessful attempts of frequent prohibitions of alcoholic beverages in different states of the country at different times. Such products should also

neither be advertised nor promoted to prevent any illegal usages. This could be effective only with the adequate support of the companies who should take responsibility and show more concern for the society than on its own profit motive. Of course, equal support is required from the society as well to make it a successful accomplishment.

The regulatory authority has put itself on the static end by turning a Nelson's eye simply ignoring the misdeeds of the marketers and giving them more opportunity and space to create a situation which has an unbearable effect on the society. The marketers, being the responsible citizens should be concerned more about the civilization and the environment instead of focused concentration on their company's bottom-line. To conclude, it is not only in the hands of the food companies or the Government or the interested groups at large to create a healthy society but a more patronage and sustaining is required from the consumers themselves to make the world a better place to lead a quality life.

Food & Beverage

The food and beverage industry faces many challenges as companies struggle to keep up with changing consumer tastes and demographics. Today's consumers demand bolder flavours, timesaving conveniences and tempting service options. They understand food safety and environmental issues and are concerned with supply chain protection and whether an operation has gone green. Moreover, current and future consumers embrace technology, an area in which the food and beverage industry has historically lagged.

Consumer lifestyle changes also add new complexity. The days of the three-martini lunch are long gone. New data shows that 50 percent of employees take 30 minutes or less for lunch, and 58 percent eat at their desk. These hurried lunch breaks equate to lost revenue for contract and self-operated dining facilities, making it more difficult for food and beverage businesses to remain profitable.

As investors and private equity firms increase their holdings in the food and beverage industry, it is important for them to understand a company's true potential and the trends affecting each segment.

If this is Your Situation

- You want to identify ways to increase revenues and improve profitability in your geographically dispersed restaurant portfolio.
- You want to understand your brand's ability to grow in a variety of markets.
- Your company needs to reduce the cost of your contract-managed foodservice operations while keeping your employees and guests satisfied.
- You want to invest in or purchase a food and beverage company or ready your own company for sale.
- You are a hotel or residential facility and want to determine the best blend and use of food and beverage facility offerings.
- You need to assess your internal controls to improve accountability.
- You want to mitigate the risk of a supply chain breach or a food-borne illness outbreak.

How Pricewaterhouse Coopers can help You

Pricewaterhouse Coopers' (PwC's) hospitality and leisure practice includes food and beverage specialists with extensive knowledge and global experience in all aspects and segments of the industry. Our team works closely with clients to identify and analyse issues, implement innovative solutions, and build strong, trusting relationships. Because we understand that each business has unique needs, we design custom solutions for each client. Clients have relied on PwC to help them grow brand concepts, increase profitability of brands, ready their companies for sale, provide potential buyers with the insight they needed to make sound investment decisions, and identify significant savings. Our team has also worked with companies responding to food-borne illness outbreaks to help them implement proactive strategies to reduce the potential of an outbreak and assess supply chain risk. PwC's extensive food and beverage advisory services include:

Asset analysis and monitoring: We work as an independent third party to inform companies of potential risks and opportunities that may affect operational performance and profitability.

Operational and financial assessments: We conduct four-wall evaluations to analyse infrastructure, labour models, procurement/ supply chain practices, internal controls, current appeal of menu selection, quality of operations, dining experience and historical financial results. Through these evaluations, we provide clients with independent observations and actionable recommendations to mitigate risk, increase revenues and improve profitability.

Self-operating and contract dining foodservice assessment and development: Our experienced team can assess clients' current contract foodservice environment and identify areas of potential improvement and savings.

We also work with companies to define and articulate programmatic needs and financial goals to design a relevant foodservice strategy that meets the needs of both the company and its employees. We assist in creating targeted requests for proposal, identify potential contractors and evaluate responses.

Transaction services/strategic assessment: We identify the core financial and operational strengths and weaknesses of a business: assess segment-specific industry trends and evaluate the competitive environment to identify barriers to entry/growth and market appeal. Our multilayered approach, which often includes four-wall analysis of multiple locations, allows us to provide clients with a clear picture of a brand's internal strengths and external opportunities for growth, increased revenues and potential savings.

Market research: The PwC team gathers primary and secondary data and uses advanced analytical techniques to provide clients with recommendations to enhance their business. Our research includes location and industry-specific demographic, sociographic and competitor data.

Infrastructure enhancement: We analyse current strategies and recommend a focused, disciplined model to build a sound infrastructure and organization that increases brand equity and profitability.

Restaurant concept creation/readying concept for franchising: Our specialists recommend compelling, differentiated concepts that will allow growth for independent, multi-unit and franchise clients. We take existing brands and develop the operational support materials needed to ready the concept for franchising.

Profile of Key Responsibilities

Our department is responsible for food safety control, import control on live food animals, management of food incidents and environmental hygiene services and facilities. We have two major areas of responsibilities: environmental hygiene services and food and public health services.

Environmental Hygiene Services

We strive to provide and maintain a clean and hygienic living environment for the people of Hong Kong through organizing and delivering high standard environmental hygiene services in the following major areas-

- Public cleansing services;
- Licensing and control of food businesses;
- Provision and management of environmental hygiene facilities; and
- Control of street trading activities.

Public Cleansing Services

We are committed to keeping public places clean, tidy and free of litter. Direct public cleansing services range from street sweeping and washing, collection of household waste and on-street litter, gully emptying, desludging, to providing toilets for public convenience.

These services are provided by our 5 300 cleansing staff or by our private contractors whose services are under our close supervision. We provide more than 16 000 litter containers and 400 dog excreta collection bins throughout Hong Kong. These containers are emptied at least once a day. On household waste, we collect about 5 940 tonnes of household waste daily by a fleet of 387 modern refuse collection vehicles.

Licensing and Control of Food Businesses

We license food businesses to safeguard public health and safety and conduct regular inspections to ensure hygiene standards of licensed food premises are met. We also take law enforcement actions such as prosecutions, summary arrests, imposition of court orders, daily fines and suspension or cancellation of licences against unlicensed and unhygienic premises.

Provision and Management of Environmental Hygiene Facilities

We manage 36 cooked food centers, 24 freestanding cooked food markets and 81 public markets where some 13 000 stalls offer a wide variety of commodities ranging from fresh produce, meat and poultry to household items. We are also responsible for the management of 11 public cemeteries, six crematoria and eight gardens of remembrance.

Control of Street Trading Activities

On-street hawking is an accepted social and economic activity and has become part of Hong Kongs way of life. We are the authority responsible for hawker management. Through licensing and enforcement of legislation, environmental nuisance caused by street trading activities is minimised.

Food and Public Health Services

We monitor the safety of imported and locally produced food to ensure that food available for human consumption is wholesome, unadulterated and properly labelled. We also aim to safeguard public health through testing and control of live food animals; to prevent vector-borne diseases and provide advice to the public on proper food and environmental hygiene practices. The major areas of work include-

- Food surveillance and certification;
- Risk assessment and communication; and
- Pest control.

Food Surveillance and Certification

We take samples at import, wholesale and retail points for chemical, microbiological, radioactivity and toxicological tests to ascertain their fitness for human consumption. Prepackaged food is also checked for compliance with food labelling laws.

Risk Assessment and Communication

We conduct risk assessment on food safety, set food standards and recommend food safety control measures. On risk communication, we introduce and promote the Hazard Analysis Critical Control Point (HACCP) approach to ensure food safety and provide food safety information to the public and the food industry on a regular basis.

Pest Control

We give advice on pest control and prevention to government departments and the general public. Our work includes surveillance and monitoring of pest problems to prevent local transmission and investigation of vector borne diseases. Operational services on pest control are carried out by district pest control sections.

Environmental Policy

Our statement on environmental policy is as follows-

Food and Environmental Hygiene Department is committed to ensuring that all our services are delivered in an environmentally responsible manner, particularly in the collection, recycling and reduction of waste, conservation of energy and water, and prevention of air, noise, water and soil pollution. We will also promote green housekeeping in premises that we manage.

Environmental Objectives and Performance

In line with Governments efforts to protect the environment, we have incorporated environmental considerations in the formulation of our policy and the delivery of our services to ensure that all our operations are conducted in an environmentally responsible manner. The following is an account of our main objectives and performance for our operations and services in 2001.

Objective : To Reduce Waste in our Operations

Our Performance

Waste Recycling in Waste Collection Programme: In support of the Governments Waste Reduction Framework Plan 1998-2007, we have increased the provision of waste separation bins for the collection of waste paper, aluminum cans and plastic bottles from 203 sets in 2000 to 565 sets in 2001. The sets of three waste separation bins are placed at convenient public locations including MTR exits, KCR exits, bus termini, ferry piers and refuse collection points. Our contractors collect and deliver the recyclable waste to recyclers for recycling purpose.

Chemical Waste Recovery and Waste Water Drainage at Vehicle Depots: Waste lubrication oil, spent batteries and air conditioning refrigerants from vehicles are properly recovered and collected by approved contractors. During the year, we have increased the quantity of waste lubrication oil recovered from vehicles to 11 000 litres per annum, compared to 8 000 litres per annum in 2000. Proper drainage systems are also provided for vehicle washing bays to avoid pollution to storm water drainage. All the departmental depots are in compliance with the requirements under the Waste Disposal (Chemical Waste) (General) Regulation and Water Pollution Control Ordinance and are issued with relevant licences by the Environmental Protection Department (EPD).

Food Safety and Control

The amount and the way in which unwholesome food is destroyed is interrelated with the overall environmental objective of producing less waste and mitigating nuisances arising from waste disposal. To this end, we exercise tight control on the import of certain categories of high-risk food including game, meat, poultry, milk and frozen confections. We also conduct food surveillance programme through sampling at different stages of the food supply chain-from import and manufacture to the wholesale and retail stages.

Objective : To Minimise Pollution in the Delivery of our Services

Licensing Control and Enforcement on the Operation of Food Premises.

To ensure that waste generated from the operation of food premises is properly handled, we conduct regular inspections to licensed food premises to check that-

- grease traps installed in food premises are functioning properly to prevent discharge of oil or grease into public drains or sewers;
- plumbing systems in food premises are properly maintained to prevent discharge of offensive or noxious effluents into public places;
- fumes and hot air are discharged in such manner as not to be a nuisance. Metal hood, air-ducts, extraction fans, grease filters/water scrubbers of exhaust systems are maintained in good order;
- waste is properly stored in dustbins for collection; and

- no smoking area together with sufficient and proper no smoking signs are provided in restaurants having more than 200 seats for customers.

Enforcement action will be taken on those food premises not compiling with the licensing conditions. In 2001, we conducted 403 408 inspections to food premises and took 7 229 prosecution actions against food premises.

Cremation Services

To control the quality and volume of emissions generated from cremation services, we

- ensure regular servicing and maintenance of the cremators by Electrical and Mechanical Services Department (EMSD);
- install a Telemetry and Monitoring System with online computerised network supplying information to EPD for monitoring the pollution level. Monitoring system with temperature recorders are installed in major crematoria;
- use the less sulphur content (0.05%) diesel for cremation; and
- enlist the support of the public and funeral service operators to use environmental-friendly coffins through the issue of pamphlets and regular meetings with the funeral trade.

On cremation facilities, the construction of a new crematorium in Kwai Chung with four cremators to replace the existing one has started in early 2001. The works are expected to be completed in late 2002.

Environmental Hygiene Facilities

Efforts are made to improve the drainage systems in our venues including markets, hawker bazaars and refuse collection points (RCPs). All cooked food markets have proper drainage systems with grease traps to prevent the discharge of excessive pollutants into surface channels.

To prevent odour and pollution from RCPs, newly built RCPs will be installed with a water scrubber system, while existing RCPs will be retrofitted with water scrubber system or activated carbon filtration system in phases if circumstances permit.

Objective: To Minimise the Environmental Impact of Pest Control Operations

In the prevention and control of public health pests, we have adopted an Integrated Pest Management approach to rationalise the work to minimise the impact of pest prevention and control on nontarget animals and the environment. It includes finding out the causes of pest infestation and then determining the choice of control method(s). Pest control operations are evaluated regularly and will be terminated if no longer necessary. Advice on environmental improvement for solving pest problems is given to the parties concerned.

Environmental-friendly methodologies, technologies and products are used. Non-chemical means will be considered before adopting the use of pesticides. We are also very cautious in the choice of pesticides so that pest disinfestations are carried out effectively and with the least impact on the environment. Pests and nuisance causing animals are disinfested judiciously to avoid unnecessary disturbance to the ecological system.

Non-chemical Prevention and Control

Mosquito breeding can be forestalled by killing the insect at its adult or/and larval/pupal stages. Application of pesticides has an immediate effect but kills other insects as well. We strive to improve the environment so that it becomes unfavourable for mosquitoes to breed. We shall apply larvicidal oil or pesticide strictly on a need basis and to specific spots only. In 2001, the amount of larvicidal oil applied in streams was 28 421 litres, representing a 34% decrease as compared to the amount used in 2000.

In preventing malaria transmission, an environmental control approach has been adopted and found to be successful. The prevention programme is mainly confined to densely populated areas with a high risk of malaria transmission. In the year, we have put in place a control programme against malaria transmissible mosquitoes, covering a total of 647 streams.

In areas where malaria vector mosquitoes are detected but with a low population, mosquito larvae eating fishes are released to abate mosquito breeding. To further reduce the impact on the environment, *Bacillus thuringiensis israelensis* are used for killing mosquito larvae. *Bacillus thuringiensis israelensis* produce crystal proteins which can be converted into toxins in the gut of the mosquito larva. The toxins act on larvae of limited species including mosquitoes, blackflies and non-biting midges.

Pesticides

The use of pesticides is sometimes unavoidable in pest prevention and disinfestations but they are usually also harmful to nontarget animals and plants. To minimise the detrimental effect to nontarget living organisms, we choose synthetic pyrethroid insecticides which generate less hazards to human beings.

In rodent disinfestations, anticoagulants are used although it takes a longer time to kill the animal. With the right dosage, chosen bait, selected baiting locales and a well-designed baiting programme, the use of anticoagulants is considered much safer than acute rodenticides. Trapping of rodents is preferred to using chemicals. In drawing up rodent disinfestation programmes, we always take into account the environmental concern. During the year, we laid poison baits at 58 724 points and 3 247 traps, disposing of 48 944 rodents.

Judicious Disinfestations

Although some arthropods such as wasps, wild bees, ants, millipedes, motes, etc. are harmful or cause nuisance to human beings, they are not killed unless they pose a threat. When these insects have to be disinfested, non-chemical means will be considered before resorting to pesticides. The control measures include a choice of physical, environmental, biological, legal or chemical methods.

Promotion of Environmental Awareness

To promote a green office environment and to achieve continual improvement in the efficient use of resources, we constantly remind our staff of good green housekeeping measures and organise education programmes and campaigns.

To Promote Green Housekeeping Within the Department

We continue our efforts to use and purchase more green products. In 2001, we have established a list of green products such as recycled photocopying and duplicating papers, recyclable toner cartridges for printers and photocopiers, mercury-free batteries and environmental-friendly soap and liquid detergent as our standard stock items to meet the daily operational requirement.

In the near future, we plan to replace the conventional black lead pencil with green products like Clutch Pencil and Lead Refill. They will become our standard stock range.

To Reduce Consumption of Paper

We constantly remind our staff on paper-saving measures such as-

- keeping photocopying to the minimum;
- sharing copies of circulars, memoranda or publications on a team or division basis instead of making personal copies;
- reviewing distribution lists regularly to keep duplication to the minimum;
- not sending a covering memorandum and fax leading page when forwarding a document without additional message;
- using A5-size paper for short letters and memoranda; and
- using paper on both sides.

In 2001, we have successfully reduced the consumption of paper by 9.6 % when compared with the consumption in 2000.

To Promote the Use of Electronic Communication

We provide PCs and email facilities to all officers with operational needs to promote electronic communications. In 2001, the number of email users has increased to over 1 750. We encourage our staff to communicate through electronic mail as far as practicable. We post notices, circulars, telephone directories and other information that require wide circulation on the department¡¦s electronic bulletin board for sharing.

To Reduce Consumption of Other Stationery

We remind our staff to exercise economy in other stationery such as-

- not using envelopes for unclassified documents;
- reusing envelopes or using transit envelopes;

- monitoring the number of brochures/forms requiring printing or reprinting to keep the requirement to the minimum; and
- encouraging the use of ball pen refills.

In 2001, the number of envelopes used was reduced by 10% when compared with the consumption in 2000.

To Economise on Electricity Consumption

We constantly remind our staff of energy saving practices such as-

- reducing lighting for illumination to the minimum;
- switching off lights when not needed;
- switching off lights/air conditioners, communal facilities (e.g. photocopiers) outside office hours;
- switching on computers only when required;
- using Venetian blinds to reduce direct sun heat;
- closing doors to separate an air-conditioned area from a non-conditioned one;
- controlling the use of personal electrical appliances in the office;
- urging staff to use staircase for inter-floor traffic;
- reducing water consumption as the treatment and distribution of water consume energy; and
- ensuring that the indoor temperature of air conditioned offices and public waiting areas is not lower than 23¢J in the summer months.

To Collect Waste Paper for Recycling

In 2001, we collected 18 372 kg of waste paper in our offices/ venues for recycling, compared to 20 409 kg in 2000. The decrease was probably due to our efforts in reducing paper consumption.

To Maintain No-smoking Workplace Policy

We maintain a smoke-free workplace policy in all offices as well as government vehicles. In 2001, we reissued the circular on smoke-free workplace policy and distributed no-smoking signs to remind all staff to maintain a healthy and smoke-free workplace.

To Incorporate Environmental Considerations in Using Departmental Vehicles

We procure vehicles with engines that meet the latest legislative environmental standard. During the year, we planned for the procurement of vehicles running on cleaner energy. Forty-six light buses using liquefied petroleum gas will be put into service in 2002. Our vehicles are maintained on schedule to minimise the emission of excessive fumes and particles. We participate actively in trials that facilitate assessment of pollutant reduction devices on vehicles, especially those for heavy-duty vehicles like refuse collection vehicles. We will continue to work together with EMSD and Government Land Transport Agency to explore the feasibility of using pollutant reduction devices to protect the environment.

Objective : To Promote Environmental Awareness Through Educational Programmes and Campaigns

Internal : We support green initiatives launched by other government departments and organizations. In 2001, we encouraged our staff to join the "No Plastic Bag, Please" and the "No Smoking Day in Workplace" Campaigns.

External : The Health Education Exhibition and Resource Centre organises talks for kindergarten and primary school students throughout the year. Apart from messages on personal hygiene, food hygiene and environmental hygiene, the economical use of paper and the reduction of waste are also covered. A total of 100 school talks were organised in 2001. During the year, in collaboration with other government departments, we organised the "Anti-rodent Campaign" and the "Anti-mosquito Campaign" with the theme of "Lets Remove Stagnant Water, Eliminate Mosquitoes for Healthy Living". The campaigns have enhanced public awareness of the importance of rodent and mosquito control.

The Way Forward

Our senior management places great importance on environmental issues and initiatives and monitors related performance and achievement closely. To strive for continuous improvement, we will-

- monitor the effectiveness of the green measures we have put in place, and modify and improve them as necessary.

- review our environmental objectives regularly and incorporate new techniques that bring about good environmental impact when delivering our services; and
- promote staff awareness and knowledge on environmental issues and support green initiatives and campaigns organised by other organizations.

Future Activities

Looking ahead, we plan to take forward the following environmental initiatives, which will bring about good environmental impact.

Clean Hong Kong Programme : We have launched since December 2000 a three-year Clean Hong Kong Programme with a view to bringing about visible and sustainable improvements on the ground through active cleansing operations, public education and publicity efforts, and to instilling a sense of belonging and pride in the community for the clean environment. In 2002, we will intensify our efforts in Clean Hong Kong and take the following actions-

- implement new action-oriented initiatives addressing district concerns such as cleanup actions all over the territory, face-lifting work to village-type refuse collection points and aqua privies, and public toilet refurbishment programme;
- implement the fixed penalty system against minor cleanliness offences; and
- continue the seasonal thematic activities for cleanup operations (harbour and beaches in summer, country parks and countryside in autumn and year-end operations in winter/spring).

Upgrading of Cremation Facilities **:** To enhance efficiency and minimise environmental nuisances, we are actively planning for the replacement of cremators at the Fu Shan Crematorium and the Diamond Hill Crematorium, which allow us to increase the capacity and speed for cremation for the provision of a better service.

Improvement of Refuse Collection Points **:** To further improve waste collection services, we plan to build more off-street RCPs equipped with features to minimise environmental nuisance to nearby residents. New RCPs, which are designed to be visually attractive as well as odourless, are equipped with water scrubber systems, vehicle exhaust extraction systems and high pressure water jet cleaners. In addition to these, upgrading works to another 49 RCPs in the New Territories to enhance pollution control are under active planning.

Using Transport Efficiently : The department is installing electronic vehicle monitoring devices to its special purpose vehicles to monitor the performance of the vehicle fleet. This can help maximise the utilisation of the vehicles and in turn reduce the fuel consumption and pollutants as a result.

Use of Retread Tyres : In support of the Governments initiative on waste reduction and environmental protection, we are exploring the feasibility of using retread tyres for our vehicle fleet. In the initial stage, refuse collection vehicles are selected for trial. If the trial is successful, it will be extended to other types of vehicles.

6

Hospitality Markets

Creating Jobs and Wealth

Travel & Tourism is the world's largest industry and creator of jobs across national and regional economies. WTTC/WEFA research show that in 2000, Travel & Tourism will generate, directly and indirectly, 11.7% of GDP and nearly 200 million jobs in the world-wide economy. These figures are forecasted to total 11.7% and 255 million respectively in 2010.

Jobs generated by Travel & Tourism are spread across the economy-in retail, construction, manufacturing and telecommunications, as well as directly in Travel & Tourism companies.

These jobs employ a large proportion of women, minorities and young people; are predominantly in small and medium sized companies; and offer good training and transferability. Tourism can also be one of the most effective drivers for the development of regional economies. These patterns apply to both developed and emerging economies.

Contributing to Sustainable Development

The 1992 United Nations Conference on Environment and Development (UNCED), the Rio Earth Summit, identified Travel & Tourism as one of the key sectors of the economy which could make a positive contribution to achieving sustainable development. The Earth Summit lead to the adoption of Agenda 21, a comprehensive program of action adopted by 182 governments to provide a global blueprint for achieving sustainable development.

Travel & Tourism is the first industry sector to have launched an industry-specific action plan based on Agenda 21. Travel & Tourism is able to contribute to development which is economically, ecologically and socially sustainable, because it:

- has less impact on natural resources and the environment than most other industries;
- is based on enjoyment and appreciation of local culture, built heritage, and natural environment, as such that the industry has a direct and powerful motivation to protect these assets;
- can play a positive part in increasing consumer commitment to sustainable development principles through its unparalleled consumer distribution channels; and
- provides an economic incentive to conserve natural environments and habitats which might otherwise be allocated to more environmentally damaging land uses, thereby, helping to maintain biodiversity.

Providing Infrastructure

To a greater degree than most activities, Travel & Tourism depends on a wide range of infrastructure services-airports, air navigation, roads, railheads and ports, as well as basic infrastructure services required by hotels, restaurants, shops, and recreation facilities (e.g. telecommunications and utilities).

It is the combination of tourism and good infrastructure that underpins the economic, environmental and social benefits. It is important to balance any decision to develop an area for tourism against the need to preserve fragile or threatened environments and cultures.

However, once a decision has been taken where an area is appropriate for new tourism development, or that an existing tourist site should be developed further, then good infrastructure will be essential to sustain the quality, economic viability and growth of Travel & Tourism. Good infrastructure will also be a key factor in the industry's ability to manage visitor flows in ways that do not affect the natural or built heritage, nor counteract against local interests.

Challenge for the Future

Travel & Tourism creates jobs and wealth and has tremendous potential to contribute to economically, environmentally and socially sustainable development in both developed countries and emerging nations. It has a comparative advantage in that its start up and running costs can be low compared to many other forms of industry development. It is also often one of the few realistic options for development in many areas. Therefore, there is a strong likelihood that the Travel & Tourism industry will continue to grow globally over the short to medium term.

Of course, if Travel & Tourism is managed badly, it can have a detrimental effect-it can damage fragile environments and destroy local cultures. The challenge is to manage the future growth of the industry so as to minimise its negative impacts on the environment and host communities whilst maximising the benefits it brings in terms of jobs, wealth and support for local culture and industry, and protection of the built and natural environment.

Industry Initiatives for Sustainable Tourism Problems

10. Travel & Tourism takes many different forms-from a trip only a few hours away from home to long distance travel overseas. A common belief is that most Travel & Tourism involves large numbers of visitors from developed countries travelling by air to destinations in emerging countries. In fact, in most countries, the domestic tourism market is larger than the inbound market. Of course, the social and cultural impact of inbound visitors is often greater than that of domestic tourists. Whether tourism is domestic or international, it involves visiting a destination away from the area in which one lives and using the services available in that destination. Therefore, tourists' requirements are for travel services to reach their destinations and once there, for services such as shelter, water, food, sanitation and entertainment.

What makes tourism special is that, many of these different products and services are often supplied by different operators: usually small or medium sized businesses in local ownership. This makes tourism a highly fragmented and diverse industry and so coordinated, industry-wide action is difficult to achieve. The influence of Travel & Tourism's demand also extends far beyond traditional tourism companies, into upstream suppliers like aircraft manufacturers or food producers and into the downstream service providers for travellers, like retail shops.

Despite the difficulties caused by fragmentation and lengthy supply chains, there has been a steady growth in environmental good practice across the industry in recent years. There are examples of-airlines and airports reducing pollution and noise impacts; cruise liners practising marine conservation; hotels implementing energy consumption and waste disposal programs; car rental companies investing in increasingly fuel efficient fleets and railways sound proofing to dampen noise. The result is that there are a number of excellent initiatives in place designed to improve the environmental management of Travel & Tourism businesses. Of course, more needs to be done.

Solutions

Providing Leadership

WTTC with 105 members is the global business leaders' forum for the Travel & Tourism industry.

The WTTC have set in place an extensive strategy to promote a culture of sustainable development and have put in place a three-tiered structure for its achievement. This involves:

Policy

In 1996 the WTTC, the World Tourism Organization and the Earth Council, joined together to launch an action plan entitled "Agenda 21 for the Travel & Tourism Industry: Towards.

Environmentally Sustainable Development"-a sectional sustainable development program based on the results of the Rio Earth Summit in 1992. Since the launch of the document, the three organisations have begun a series of regional seminars to increase awareness of the conclusions, and to adapt the program for local implementation. The program has held regional seminars in London and Jakarta in 1997 and Victoria Falls and Dominica in 1998.

WTTC has recently introduced a major addition to the program– the "Alliance for Sustainable Tourism", which invites public and private sector Travel & Tourism organisations to record their

Agenda 21 based activities on a central web site and commit to co-operation with all other partners. In order to develop the program from global principles to community based action, WTTC is also discussing with the International Council for Local Environment Initiatives (ICLEI) on how the principles of "Agenda 21 for Travel & Tourism" can be built into Local Agenda 21 programs. Furthermore, WTTC is considering pilot projects in 5 cities around the world to serve as models for other destinations.

Practice

In 1994, WTTC initiated the *"Green Globe"*, an Agenda 21 based industry improvement program, which provides guidance material and a certification process linked to both ISO standards and Agenda 21 principles. There are now 500 *"Green Globe"* members in 100 countries dedicated to improving environmental practice. The first certification has commenced with hotels groups in Jamaica and Manchester (UK). *"Green Globe"* has also developed a specific Destination Program, which provides a methodology for Travel & Tourism destinations to implement sustainable development. The ultimate aim is that *"Green Globe"* will become the primary global standard of environmental commitment by the global Travel & Tourism industry and will be recognised by the public as such. Currently, *"Green Globe"* has the support of over 20 international industry organisations representing thousands of businesses worldwide and the support of the World Tourism Organization, the United Nations Environment Program and the Earth Council.

Information

WTTC have also developed "ECoNETT", a website containing advice and data on good practice and sources of help and advice. "ECoNETT" is increasingly recognised as a focal point for environmental information, good practice, new techniques and technologies.

The International Hotel & Restaurant Association (IH&RA), based in Paris, represents over 700,000 establishments in more than 150 countries. Its membership comprises some 50 national and international hotel and restaurant chains, over 110 national hotel and restaurant associations, independent hotel operators and restaurateurs, industry suppliers and 130 hotel schools. The

IH&RA has offices in Asia-Pacific and Latin America. It is also the voice of the world's hotels and restaurants and plays a global role in representing, protecting, promoting and informing the industry to enable its members to achieve their business objectives.

Corporate Initiatives

The International Hotel Environment Initiative (IHEI), based in London, England, is a program of The Prince of Wales Business Leaders Forum. Founded in 1992 by a consortium of chief executives from 10 multinational hotel groups, IHEI is an educational charity designed to encourage continuous improvement in the environmental performance of the global hotel industry. It does this through:

- raising environmental awareness in the hotel industry by promoting good practice internationally;
- developing hotel-specific guidance, enabling hotels of all sizes to implement environmental programs; and
- multiplying the reach and impact of IHEI by working with partners, including hotel associations, governments, NGOs, tourism bodies and businesses.

IHEI is a catalyst and conduit for hotels to pool their resources and to share experience via a noncompetitive platform. In 5 years it has evolved into an organisation with global impact. IHEI has worked in 111 countries, stimulating and assisting with the establishment of local initiatives such as

New Zealand's "Environmental Hotels of Auckland, the Asia Pacific Hotel Environment Initiative" and the Caribbean Action for Sustainable Tourism. Member hotels now represent over 1 million guest rooms and more than 8,000 hotels on 5 continents.

The Co-operative Research Centre for Sustainable Tourism, based in Australia, was established in 1997 to enhance the strategic knowledge available to the Travel & Tourism industry through:

- long-term high-quality scientific and technological research which contributes to the development of an internationally competitive tourism industry;
- strengthening the links between research and its commercial and other applications;

- promoting cooperative research; and
- stimulating education and training, particularly in graduate programs, through active involvement of researchers from outside the higher education system in educational activities, and of graduate students in major research programs.

Company Initiatives

The Kandalama hotel in Sri Lanka has been a recipient of the "GREEN GLOBE" award, 3 years in a row, for its commitment to environmental excellence. The hotel has undertaken measures in the following areas to ensure that its operations are more sustainable:

- cultural and social-hotel employment, providing community infrastructure and development;
- natural environment-soil erosion measures and planting forests;
- pollution-sewage, solid waste and noise pollution reduction programs; and
- environmental communication-construction of an Eco Park where all waste is treated within the park, a dry debris sorting centre, a lecture room to promote environmental awareness and a sustainable development library.

Canadian Pacific Hotels, the largest hotel conglomerate in Canada, has developed an environmental program, which is recognised as the most comprehensive in the North American hotel industry. Based on the results of a survey, employee suggestions and the recommendations of a professional environmental consultant, Canadian Pacific Hotels developed a list of 16 goals to be attained by all hotels. In addition to individual projects implemented at each of the 26 hotels, the goals set for the chain as a whole were ambitious: (I) to reduce the amount of waste sent to landfill by 50% across the chain, by launching an extensive recycling program; (ii) to redesign purchasing policies to ensure that waste is reduced at source, and supplies used in the hotels are nature friendly.

Inter-regional level

The Caribbean Action For Sustainable Tourism (CAST) is an

alliance for sustainable growth developed by the Caribbean Hoteliers Association with the support of the WTTC, the IHEI and the Caribbean Tourism Organisation. CAST has developed workshops, training courses and guidance material for its members on a wide range of environmental issues, including:

- setting up environmental management systems;
- energy efficiency;
- renewable energy; and
- waste water management.

Agents and Partnerships for Change

The public sectors, particularly national and local government, have an important role to play by setting the agenda and providing the framework in which action should take place. The regulatory environment also plays an important role in creating the conditions suitable for sustainable tourism. Self-regulation involving the agreement and co-operation of industry is always likely to be the most effective solution. Therefore, the role of trade associations and industry organisations in distributing information among their members and encouraging participation is essential.

The major partnerships to be formed are between:

- industry and the public sector-to ensure consistency with the framework;
- industry and the voluntary sector-to tap into the enormous resources of expertise and good will that this sector is able to generate; and
- industry and the public-both travellers themselves and the people who live in the places they visit to develop more sustainable forms of tourism.

Influencing Consumer Behaviour to Promote Sustainable Tourism Problems

At the 1998 World Travel Market, WTTC hosted, as a part of its Environmental Awareness Day, a seminar entitled "Does the Consumer Care?" At this event, MORI presented the latest findings from their Business and the Environment survey-an annual UK survey devoted to public attitudes to the environment. The survey is now in its tenth year and illustrates the challenge facing the

Travel & Tourism industry in influencing consumer behaviour to promote sustainable tourism.

According to this survey, Travel & Tourism is now more associated with environmental damage than it has been in the past. Despite this decline in perception, the industry's economic success is not dependent on its green record-public sensitivity to environmental problems on holiday/business trips has not increased and is no more of a deterrent to repeat travel than it was previously.

There is a downward trend in the public's willingness to pay extra for environmental protection and environmentally friendly products, including "green" Travel & Tourism. Awareness of companies making environmental commitments is only marginally up. Therefore, the challenge is to persuade the consumer that it is in their interests to adopt and promote a sustainable approach in their activities and purchasing decisions. Education programs and the development and widespread acceptance of codes of conduct are useful tools in achieving this step. Once this message has been conveyed, it is then important to back this up with the necessary information to enable consumers to make informed choices. It is here that "ecolabels" and award programs have value.

Solutions

Education Programs

The Foundation for Environmental Education in Europe (FEEE) seeks to promote environmental education by carrying out campaigns and improving awareness of the importance of environmental education. It is composed of a network of international organisations. The FEEE (headquarters in Denmark) runs three major campaigns in Europe for providing safe and clean beaches and marinas.

The award itself is given annually to beaches and marinas that satisfy a number of essential criteria in three separate areas: water quality; beach management and safety; and environmental information and education.

"Green Globe"'s Dodo Campaign, is based on a cartoon character, who features in 65 Travel & Tourism videos. Dodo explains and promotes the actions that visitors can take to reduce the impacts of their travels. The videos are aimed at children and are designed to be fun, whilst conveying important messages about sustainable Travel & Tourism. The aim is to have these videos shown on inflight and in-room television channels to raise awareness and influence consumer behaviour.

Codes of Conduct

Codes of conduct are also used to try and influence consumer behaviour. For example, "Guidelines for Responsible Environmental Tourism" are prepared and distributed by the American Society of Travel Agents to all customers who book holidays through their members' branches. The Guidelines aim to "encourage the growth of peaceful tourism and environmentally responsible travel" and include 10 recommendations to encourage tourists to act responsibly and show respect for their hosts and the environment of their destination(s).

The Pacific Asia Tourism Association (PATA) is an industrial association, which promotes the Pacific Asia area's Travel & Tourism destinations, products and services. PATA also serves as a central resource of information and research, travel industry education and training, as well as quality product development with sensitivity for culture, heritage and environment. In 1992, PATA introduced its "Code for Environmentally Responsible Tourism" to strengthen the principles of preservation in the region. Businesses, organisations and individuals wishing to affirm their support for the PATA Code are encouraged to participate in the PATA Green Leaf program.

The Africa Travel Association has produced "Responsible Traveller Guidelines"; the Japanese Association of Travel Agents has produced the "Declaration of Earth Friendly Travellers" and there are many more examples of industry codes aimed at educating and influencing their customers.

Eco Labelling

There are numerous examples of industry sponsored labelling schemes, whose aim is to recognise good industry practice and influence consumer behaviour into purchasing the labelled products. For example, the "Green Key, Denmark" certificate operated by the Hotel, Restaurant and Leisure Industry Association (HORESTA) has 56 criteria that includes environmental information, water & energy consumption and waste management. Special features also include ecological food products, outdoor areas, non-smoking rooms, and adaptations for access by disabled persons.

Awards

There are a number of industries that runs and sponsors award programs to highlight and promote examples of good practice. For example, British Airways has run the "Tourism for Tomorrow" awards since 1992 to encourage action to protect the environment. The awards are directed at tour operators, hotels, national parks and heritage sites, and other activities associated with tourism. By selecting projects showing best practice in their field as role models, others are encouraged to follow suit and consider the environment in the everyday running of their tourism business. The awards are run annually, with a winner selected from each of five regions and an overall winner. In addition, two special awards are made for mass tourism destinations. The awards are run in association with the British Tourist Authority, the Association of British Travel Agents, the Pacific Asia Travel Association and the American Society of Travel Agents. Entries to the awards have been increases every year.

American Express also sponsors a variety of environmental awards for international tourism organisations.

Agents and Partnerships for Change

A broad based approach is called for which requires Travel & Tourism to work with:

- national governments to raise the profile of environmental and social issues within the education system;
- NGOs to raise awareness of tourism issues in their work and activities and provide feedback to the Travel & Tourism industry;
- development organisations to communicate with host communities to understand their needs and requirements;
- local authorities to engage local people through the inclusion of tourism issues in Local Agenda 21 plans;
- national and international trade associations, labour representative organisations and training providers to

increase awareness and training of staff in environmental and social issues;

- Travel & Tourism publications (such as travel guides);
- ravel & Tourism journalists to raise the profile of reporting environmental and social impacts of tourism among consumers and tourism businesses; and
- the Internet as a source of information for potential travellers.

Areas for Further Action

The WTTC/MORI data shows the scale of the task still remaining. The industry has developed a number of initiatives to influence consumer behaviour. However, if consumers do not understand or are not aware of the issues involved and do not demand more sustainable products then, in the long term, it will not be in the industry's interests to move in that direction. The priority for future action, therefore, should be to raise awareness among travellers of the issues associated with tourism and the impact their activities can have on local destinations and cultures.

Destinations

"Green Globe" has developed a specific "Destinations" program to recognise those tourist destinations where there is a concerted effort by all those involved in the local tourism industry to improve the quality of the environment. The Destinations process provides a framework to guide tourist locations towards achieving sustainable development based on the principles of Agenda 21. The Destinations programs are tailor made to reflect local circumstances, such as the level of environmental awareness, action taken to date and available resources.

Each program is based on achieving progressive environmental improvements. Targets are set within a realistic timetable and are developed by a steering group made up of key partners. The island of Jersey has become the first "*Green Globe*". For example, in 1996 Lusotour SA, a tourism development company, enacted a management plan for Vilamoura whereby employees are given responsibility for individual environmental tasks.

The company has invested money into rehabilitating the surrounding natural environment, which includes pine forests and a lake that has significance to local wetland areas. Guests are provided with a copy of the environmental policy and are encouraged to participate in the scheme through specialized brochures.

The campaign includes recycling; treating diseased pine areas; regular cleaning of the beaches and marinas; development of a sewage treatment plant and new buildings in the resort are designed to minimise visual and environmental impacts. For its work in Vilamoura, Lusotour SA is also a winner of the British Airways Tourism for Tomorrow Awards.

The "Afrikatourism" brand has been developed by the Open Africa Foundation to encourage products, which embraces sustainable ecological, economic and social development based on Africa's unique cultural, natural and wildlife heritage. "Open Africa" is also developing a continuous network of "Afrikatourism" routes from the Cape to Cairo, known as the "African Dream". The Dream helps to create awareness of the many rural and environmental projects, which exist throughout Africa. "Team Africa", a transcontinental alliance of governments, corporations, institutions, professionals and individuals, provides leadership and motivation in the development of the "African Dream".

Host Communities

"Whale Watch Kaikoura" is an initiative of local Maori people from a small town on the East Coast of New Zealand's South Island. Within a kilometre of the Kaikoura shore is an area ideal for whales, where visitors are guaranteed to see them all year round. The Whale Watch began 11 years ago and is now a booming tourist destination, run by indigenous people with a strong sense of heritage and a view of the future based on strong principles of sustainability.

Jordan Tourism Investments, has revitalised the traditional village of Taybeh, in Jordan, into a cultural tourist resort, with the help and agreement of villagers. With many of the younger generation moving to the cities, the village was losing its character. By restoring its 19th century buildings and reviving old crafts, the village is now thriving again. The village lies 9km south east of the historic city of Petra. Opened in July 1994, the village now accommodates around 60,000 guests each year.

Uluru and Kakadu National Parks are both owned by indigenous Australians, the local Aboriginal communities, and jointly run with the National Parks and Wildlife Service. They are both major tourism destinations and involve indigenous participation in planning, management, and ownership of tourism infrastructure, as well as interpretation for visitors. They bring significant economic, social and cultural benefits to the local indigenous communities.

The Conservation Corporation in Africa has established a series of high quality game parks in which local communities are major stakeholders and beneficiaries of tourism. This initiative is also helping to re-invigorate local crafts.

Agents and Partnerships for Change and Areas for Further Action

The challenge facing the tourism industry in moving towards a more sustainable future is set out in "Agenda 21 for the Travel & Tourism Industry". To achieve the goals set out in this document will require a partnership between government departments, national tourism authorities, international and national trade organisations and Travel & Tourism companies. Working together in close co-operation such partnerships should aim to deliver the following:

- Close co-operation between the public and private sectors to deliver a regulatory regime, which encourages voluntary action but supplement, where necessary, with regulation in areas such as land-use and waste management.
- Agreed common standards and tools to enable the measurement of progress towards achieving sustainable development.
- Certification criteria developed and more widely applied to industry initiatives.
- A commitment to the controlled expansion, where appropriate, of infrastructure.
- Environmental taxes, where applied, should be fair and non-discriminatory. They should be carefully thought out to minimise their impact on economic development, and revenues should be allocated to Travel & Tourism associated environment improvement programs.

- International, national and local funding bodies should include sustainable development as a part of their criteria, so that in time, all funding would be dependent on sound environmental practice.
- Contemporary research into sustainable tourism needs to be funded and developed. Issues requiring attention include design, carrying capacity, tour operator activities, environmental reporting, auditing and environmental impact assessments.
- Environmental education and training should be increased, particularly in schools, for future hotel and tourism staff.
- Greater investment and commitment to the use of new technology.

Coastal Impact of Tourism

Problems

Tourism provides an essential lifeline for many coastal communities. Faced with the prospect of increasing financial hardship, more and more coastal communities have turned to tourism as a means of generating income and survival. Tourism's impact on the coastal zone has, therefore, been largely positive. Of course, as in any area, if Tourism is not properly managed and developed, it can be harmful.

Impacts arise from the construction of infrastructure (hotels, marinas, transport, waste treatment facilities, groynes etc.) and from recreation (golf courses, water sports, theme parks etc.). Coastal communities are now faced with tourism on a considerable scale, and the host to guest ratio can be very high in such areas. At the same time, coastal communities must try to maintain the resort's attraction as tourist demands change, sometimes quite rapidly. With coastal regions being primary tourist destinations, sensitive marine and coastal environments can suffer dramatically. For example, as a result of large-scale sea-front tourist development,considerable beach and dune erosion can occur. Tourism also impacts on environmental quality in the following ways:

- ribbon development, infrastructure requirements, particularly transport links;

- the treatment and disposal of solid and/or liquid wastes, particularly during peak tourist seasons, may be inadequate or at worst non-existent; and
- water is often consumed excessively, not only for drinking but for showers, laundry, swimming pools, maintenance of golf courses etc. This can affect the quantity and quality of fresh water available to indigenous coastal populations.

Recreational activities can also have a significant impact on the coastal zone:

- golf course's impact can be considerable, with those situated directly on coastal habitats (especially sand dunes) in particular;
- erosion of reefs and coral from divers and swimmers;
- pollution from boats and jets skis; and
- noise from motor boats and jet skis, cars and buses, nightlife and other activities.

Solutions

The development of a sustainable tourism industry in the coastal zone offers numerous opportunities. Opportunities includes, those for nature conservation – which, given the increasing interest in high quality natural and cultural experiences, can help to reverse the decline in market share of many coastal destinations. Tourism also provides important opportunities for strengthening local industries. Where industries are in decline, tourism ventures can help supplement declining income. The following examples illustrate what can be done to make the most of the opportunities offered by tourism in the coastal zone:

Calvia is a Municipality on the Mediterranean coast that has undertaken an Agenda 21 project to assist the sustainable development of its tourism sector, in order to counter the negative impact of short-term tourism development since the 1960s. The local council has now implemented a transferable policy aimed at modernising, improving and diversifying the local tourist industry, involving all stakeholders, including the local population. A Project Plan was enacted, and achievements so far include:

- indigenous development, based on the sustainable use of available resources;

- high quality services and an appropriate bed night capacity;
- a ban on new development on 1,700 acres;
- active participation of the residents in community life; and
- environmental management of municipality buildings, waste recycling, reduction in spending on electricity, and use of environmentally friendly materials for office use.

Quicksilver Tours, Queensland, Australia, is owned by one of the largest tourism operators to the Great Barrier Reef. Quicksilver have five large catamarans, which take about 1,000 tourists a day to dive on the reef.

They have their own reef site with fixed diving platforms. They employ a team of biologists, both for environmental management and assessment as well as widespread environmental interpretation. Recent assessment of the reef, in the vicinity of the operation, shows that it is being maintained in pristine condition.

Kingfisher Bay Resort is found at Fraser Island, Queensland. It is a large five star "ecotourism" resort built in a beautiful, but fragile environment off the Queensland coast.

Its concept, design, construction and management were conceived using the latest ecologically sustainable principles. It is a state-of-the-art "ecotourism" resort, which has won Australia's top tourism awards, and its economic and environmental success has influenced new coastal tourism developments.

Maho Bay's camps and studios in the US Virgin Islands have based their product on a commitment to minimise impact on the environment, conserve natural resources, engage in active and passive environmental education of their guests, and contribute to the local economy. Specific initiatives introduced at Maho Bay include the following: use of new technology; purchasing policies; waste management; environmental education; energy and water conservation; and support for local communities and culture.

These initiatives show an appreciation of the need for alternative solutions to issues such as packaging and waste disposal through landfill. These are issues, which as the industry grows, will be increasingly important for the Travel & Tourism industry as a whole to address.

Agents and Partnerships for Change and Areas for Further Action

The agents, partnerships for change and areas for further action in relation to tourism in the coastal zone are similar to the development of broad based sustainable tourism in general as set out in Section D.

A number of issues do, of course, have particular importance for the coastal zone. Above all, the key to success is better participation at destination level among all the stakeholders concerned (such as at). In the case of the coastal zone, there are a number of additional organisations with an interest in coastal policy, marine conservation, shipping etc., which needs to be identified and included in partnerships for the coastal zone.

Successful planning for tourism is very important for the future of the industry in coastal regions, because a significant percentage of tourism occurs within the geographical parameters of the definition of a coastal zone. Concerted support from all countries involved (and the industries within them) is vital to protect the shared natural resources that coastal zones represent.

Historically, the influence most hoteliers have on the environmental impact of their business is limited to working within existing buildings, or after a new site has been completed. In April 1998, the IHEI convened a group of hoteliers, tour operators, architectural firms and sustainable development specialists with the goal of creating a partnership to be called the "Siting and Design Programme". The new initiative's mission will be to define responsible planning and design specifications that will cause minimal environmental damage at new sites. Particular attention will be paid to sites located within ecologically sensitive areas and upon waterfronts. The "Siting and Design Programme" will strive to reach hotel owners, investors and developers to bring these issues to the attention of the entire industry.

Conclusions

Travel & Tourism has a number of advantages over other industry sectors:

- it creates jobs and wealth whilst;
- at the same time, it can contribute to sustainable development;

- it tends to have low start-up costs;
- is a viable option in a wide range of areas and regions;
- is likely to continue to grow for the foreseeable future; and
- the industry is, in a large part, aware of the need to protect the resource on which it is based-local culture and built and natural environment-and it is committed to these resources' preservation and enhancement.

The industry is, therefore, making a concerted effort to build up programs for sustainable development. However, it cannot do this alone. If Travel & Tourism is to continue to flourish and to contribute to sustainable development, it needs help from national Governments. This assistance is needed in two forms:-both positive encouragement for sustainable tourism initiatives and an understanding that policy decisions in other areas can effect Travel & Tourism. In practical terms, what this means is the following:

The first point of action needed from Governments is to incorporate Agenda 21 principles into tourism policies at international and national level, and to promote their inclusion in regional and local tourism strategies. By providing such a lead and establishing a coherent global framework based on Agenda 21, national governments will make a vital contribution to developing a more sustainable tourism industry. Governments should also recognise that Travel & Tourism is a core service sector which should always be considered when looking at policies to expand trade, increase employment, modernize infrastructure and encourage investment-at both domestic and international level. It should also be included in national statistics with its economic impact calculated by means of a national tourism satellite account.

Governments should also consider helping Travel & Tourism by seeking to minimise regulatory impediments and by offering appropriate investment incentives. By supporting tourism and allowing it to compete in open and fair markets, tourism's benefits can be more easily secured.

Finally, governments can address some of the fundamental barriers to tourism growth by looking at how to expand and modernise infrastructure, to apply taxes fairly and to invest in human resource development.

If the program of action outlined above can be undertaken by national governments in co-operation with continued industry commitments and initiatives for sustainable tourism then we can look to a brighter future.

Tourism, Terrorism, and Tomorrow

As fewer overseas travellers pack their bags this holiday season, millions of tourism industry workers worldwide are losing their jobs. Before September 11th, travel and tourism was the world's largest industry, accounting for one in every 12 jobs. When the massive $3.6 trillion industry almost ground to a halt after the terrorist attacks, the ripple effects extended well beyond the United States, exposing the vulnerability of countries too dependent on international tourism, reports the Worldwatch Institute, a Washington, DC-based environmental research organization. "The aftermath of September 11 has shown us how important travel and tourism are to the global economy, but also how over-dependence on tourism can devastate lives and derail economies,". "Now, more than ever, it is time to put issues of sustainability at the top of the global tourism agenda." Revenues from tourism have been especially important in the developing world, which stands to suffer severe economic losses from the slowdown. "Tourism is the only economic sector where developing countries consistently run a trade surplus,". "It's especially significant in poorer countries that have few other options: for the world's 49 so-called least developed countries, tourism is the second largest source of foreign exchange after oil."

Businesses in the developing world are particularly worried about the sharp drop in bookings as the winter high season nears:

- India and Nepal, which are close to Afghanistan, are already feeling the effects of a drop in demand.
- In October, resort company Club Mediterrane was forced to close 15 of its holiday villages in the Caribbean, Central America, the Middle East, Europe, and Asia.
- Operators in Costa Rica report a 30 percent decline in bookings from last year.
- International tourism is now expected to grow by only 1.5 to 2 percent in 2001, compared with the robust 7.4 percent rise in 2000.

- The International Labour Organization estimates that as many as 9 million of the world's 200 million hotel and tourism workers could lose their jobs in the wake of the attacks. Nearly three quarters of these positions are outside the United States and Europe, many in countries with weak social safety nets.

Even in the best of times, the consequences of tourism's rapid growth have not always been positive. On average, as much as 50 percent of tourism earnings ultimately "leak" out of the developing world-in the form of profits earned by foreign-owned businesses, promotional spending abroad, or payments for imported goods and labour. And uncontrolled tourism development-on mountaintops, along coastlines, or in remote jungle areas-stresses many fragile ecosystems and cultures.

"Tourism does not have to have such negative impacts,". "Many governments and businesses, local communities, and tourists themselves are already paying more attention to the social, cultural, and environmental impacts of their activities."

Such changes can save money as well. Some hotels, tour operators, and other businesses are taking formal steps to restructure their management and operations along environmental lines-often at considerable cost savings. Between 1988 and 1995, for example, Inter-Continental Hotels reduced its overall energy costs by 27 percent, saving $3.7 million in 1995 alone. The Green Hotels Association reports that hotels that have adopted such conservation measures and green practices have been better able to weather the revenue loss, falling occupancies, and higher energy costs in the aftermath of the September attacks.

Improving Sustainability

Regulation and Accreditation

Because the regulation of ecotourism is poorly implemented or nonexistent, ecologically destructive greenwashed operations like underwater hotels, helicopter tours, and wildlife theme parks are categorized as ecotourism along with canoeing, camping, photography, and wildlife observation. The failure to acknowledge responsible, low impact ecotourism puts these companies at a competitive disadvantage. Many environmentalists have argued for a global standard of accreditation, differentiating ecotourism companies based on their level of environmental commitment. A national or international regulatory board would enforce accreditation procedures, with representation from various groups including governments, hotels, tour operators, travel agents, guides, airlines, local authorities, conservation organizations, and non-governmental organizations. The decisions of the board would be sanctioned by governments, so that non-compliant companies would be legally required to disassociate themselves from the use of the ecotourism brand.

Crinion suggests a Green Stars System, based on criteria including a management plan, benefit for the local community, small group interaction, education value and staff training. Ecotourists who consider their choices would be confident of a genuine ecotourism experience when they see the higher star rating.

In addition, environmental impact assessments could be used as a form of accreditation. Feasibility is evaluated from a scientific basis, and recommendations could be made to optimally plan infrastructure, set tourist capacity, and manage the ecology. This form of accreditation is more sensitive to site specific conditions.

Guidelines and Education

An environmental protection strategy must address the issue of ecotourists removed from the cause-and-effect of their actions on the environment. More initiatives should be carried out to improve their awareness, sensitize them to environmental issues, and care about the places they visit.

Tour guides are an obvious and direct medium to communicate awareness. With the confidence of ecotourists and intimate knowledge of the environment, they can actively discuss conservation issues. A tour guide training program in Costa Rica's Tortuguero National Park has helped mitigate negative environmental impacts by providing information and regulating tourists on the parks' beaches used by nesting endangered sea turtles.

Small Scale, Slow Growth and Local Control

The underdevelopment theory of tourism describes a new form of imperialism by multinational corporations that control ecotourism resources. These corporations finance and profit from the development of large scale ecotourism that causes excessive environmental degradation, loss of traditional culture and way of life, and exploitation of local labor. In Zimbabwe and Nepal's Annapurna region, where underdevelopment is taking place, more than 90 percent of ecotourism revenues are expatriated to the parent countries, and less than 5 percent go into local communities.

The lack of sustainability highlights the need for small scale, slow growth, and locally based ecotourism. Local peoples have a vested interest in the well being of their community, and are therefore more accountable to environmental protection than multinational corporations. The lack of control, westernization, adverse impacts to the environment, loss of culture and traditions outweigh the benefits of establishing large scale ecotourism.

The increased contributions of communities to locally managed ecotourism create viable economic opportunities, including high level management positions, and reduce environmental issues associated with poverty and unemployment. Because the ecotourism experience is marketed to a different lifestyle from large scale ecotourism, the development of facilities and infrastructure does not need to conform to corporate Western tourism standards, and can be much simpler and less expensive. There is a greater multiplier effect on the economy, because local products, materials, and labor are used. Profits accrue locally and import leakages are reduced. However, even this form of tourism may require foreign investment for promotion or start up. When such investments are required, it is crucial for communities for find a company or non-governmental organization that reflects the philosophy of ecotourism; sensitive to their concerns and willing to cooperate at the expense of profit.The basic assumption of the multiplier effect is that the economy starts off with unused resources, for example, that many workers are cyclically unemployed and much of industrial capacity is sitting idle or incompletely utilized. By increasing demand in the economy it is then possible to boost production. If the economy was already at full employment, with only structural, frictional, or other supply-side types of unemployment, any attempt to boost demand would only lead to inflation. For various laissez-faire schools of economics which embrace Say's Law and deny the possibility of Keynesian inefficiency and under-employment of resources, therefore, the multiplier concept is irrelevant or wrong-headed.

As an example, consider the government increasing its expenditure on roads by $one million, without a corresponding increase in taxation. This sum would go to the road builders, who would hire more workers and distribute the money as wages and profits. The households receiving these incomes will save part of the money and spend the rest on consumer goods. These expenditures in turn will generate more jobs, wages, and profits, and so on with the income and spending circulating around the economy.

The multiplier effect arises because of the induced increases in consumer spending which occur due to the increased incomes — and because of the feedback into increasing business revenues, jobs, and income again. This process does not lead to an economic explosion not only because of the supply-side barriers at potential output (full employment) but because at each "round", the increase in consumer spending is less than the increase in consumer incomes. That is, the marginal propensity to consume (mpc) is less than one, so that each round some extra income goes into saving, leaking out of the cumulative process. Each increase in spending is thus smaller than that of the previous round, preventing an explosion.Ecotourism has to be implemented with care.

Natural Resource Management

Natural resource management can be utilized as a specialized tool for the development of ecotourism. There are several places throughout the world where the amount of natural resources are abundant. But, with human encroachment and habitats these resources are depleting. Without knowing the proper utilization of certain resources they are destroyed and floral and faunal species are becoming extinct. Ecotourism programmes can be introduced for the conservation of these resources. Several plans and proper management programmes can be introduced so that these resources remain untouched. Several organizations, NGO's, scientists are working on this field.

Natural resources of hill areas like Kurseong in West Bengal are plenty in number with various flora and fauna, but tourism for business purpose poised the situation. Researcher from Jadavpur University presently working in this area for the develeopment of ecotourism which can be utilized as a tool for natural resource management.

In South-East Asia government and Non-Government Organisations are working together with academics and industry operators to spread the economic benefits of tourism into the kampungs and villages of the region. A recently formed alliance, the South-East Asian Tourism Organisation - SEATO is bringing together these diverse players to allay resource management concerns.

Tour Operators, Travel Agencies & Retailers

Some companies specialise in ecotourism, designing their trips to be environmentally, culturally and socially friendly. Companies such as Intrepid Travel, Adventure Life, Frontier, and Marine Conservation Society, Family Nature Summit, Peregrine Adventures, World Expeditions, greentraveller, Explore Worldwide and Exodus offer trips catering for the thoughtful traveller. Some tour operators are keenly aware of the impacts that they may have on specific areas and rotate clients around to different sites for snorkelling, bird watching, and other activities. Others are just beginning to see the advantage of "green" travel destinations.

Connecting the Sustainable Livelihoods Approach and Tourism

Tourism has been increasingly used for, and directly linked with, rural poverty reduction in developing countries. However, the application, and to an extent the principles, of the widely used organising framework for considering poverty reduction, the Sustainable Livelihoods Approach (SLA), may not fit fully the tourism situation, and vice versa. Based on a review of the literature we first suggest that sustainable livelihoods for tourism should be viewed in a broader tourism context, rather than merely taking tourism as a development tool. Second, the SLA seeks household livelihood sustainability at the individual or household level, while tourism sustainability is often applied to the industry and destinations at wider, more macro level scales. Thus, a reconciliation of the tensions and opportunities between the SLA and tourism needs to be found. Third, tourism research has demonstrated local residents" increasing concern about participation in political governance associated with tourism development, with less participation jeopardising local people's assets from a livelihood perspective. Therefore, an additional concept of institutional asset (mainly community participation) needs to be incorporated within the SLA. Given the above understandings, a sustainable tourism livelihood was defined and a Sustainable Tourism Livelihoods Approach (STLA) is proposed. The potential applications of the STLA are discussed and future research is recommended.

Although poverty is one of the most compelling challenges confronting humankind, there remains numerous issues when considering scale, form, and evaluation of response within the multiple poverty contexts. As the World Bank points out, 'policies targeted directly to the poor can hardly succeed unless governments know who the poor are and how they respond to policies and to their environment'. Based on this understanding, the World Bank adopted different approaches to rural and urban poverty, respectively, in implementing projects towards poverty reduction. This article focuses on the rural poverty context because up to 75% of the world's poor are in rural populations, and mostly in the 'third world' (World Bank, 2008).

Key economic activities aimed at rural poverty reduction continue to be primary industries including agriculture and fishing. While professionals tried to improve rural conditions through approaches to soil fertility improvement, land reform and advanced technology, these development approaches did little to alleviate rural poverty. In the 1980s, a new approach to poverty reduction, sustainable livelihoods (SL) and the Sustainable Livelihoods Approach (SLA) was proposed. It emphasised holistic and integrated thinking about poverty reduction and rural development, and soon gained popularity among researchers, practitioners and developers, while still typically being focused on agricultural practices.

Tourism is now the biggest and fastest growing industry in the world, having experienced enormous growth over recent decades (UNWTO, 2002). But only recently has tourism's potential of contributing to rural poverty reduction been widely recognised by policy-makers and others. Unlike agrarian change, the concept of tourism in rural areas originates from developed countries. Research regarding rural tourism has centred on aspects of tourism products, marketing, planning, and impacts. This trend has, however, recently been criticised for its reduced focus on rural livelihoods and poverty reduction, with some contending that this deficiency can be addressed by using the SLA. Thus, the question that arises is: will the SLA fit the case in which tourism is taken as a livelihood strategy for rural development? This paper addresses this question by reviewing the theoretical evolution of both the SLA and tourism. Possible gaps between their applications are explored and a sustainable livelihoods framework for tourism is proposed and discussed.

Rural Development

The SL approach arose from the broad context of rural development. In summary it can be seen that rural development has moved through three main bodies of thought since the mid 20th century, namely the population and technology model, political economy theories, and agricultural development.

In the 1950s the population and technology model was the main discourse. The model emphasises that rural population growth will increase agricultural productivity. Surplus agricultural output closely relates to the advancement of farming technologies, a major driver of agricultural productivity. In the 1960s, concerns with increasing income disparities in the rural economy led to the theory of political economy of agrarian change focusing on the equality of job opportunity and income, including appropriate social reform (Aziz, 1978).

This theory, however, failed to stress livelihood diversification away from agriculture on which the rural poor have always survived (Ellis, 2000). The third stage of rural development, agricultural development theory, prevailed in the 1970s. Its emphasis on small-farm agriculture was very successful in raising agricultural productivity, so that for nearly 20 years it remained the dominant rural development philosophy (Ellis, 2000). In the 1980s, the notion of rural development in developing countries was critiqued and questions were asked about the overall success of 'small-farm enterprises'.

While small-farm agriculture raised agrarian productivity it helped little to alleviate poverty, and worse, social inequality and unbalanced income distribution increased. More holistic, integrated, rural development thinking was called for. Thus, the sustainable livelihoods concept was proposed in the late 1980s, a concept that has subsequently undergone substantial theoretical and practical development.

Sustainable Livelihoods Approach

SL is a way of thinking about rural development. It calls for integrative thinking for poverty reduction rather than conventionally alleviating poverty through raising crop productivity and external aid (Cahn, 2002). Although the term Sustainable Livelihoods has been used widely in poverty and rural development research, there is no broadly accepted definition, and different governments, organisations and individuals have adopted their own understandings.

The notion of SL can be traced back to the first proposition of sustainable development in the Brundtland Commission Report of 1987 (Solesbury, 2003). In the same year the Advisory Panel on Food Security, Agriculture, Forestry and Environment produced a report to the World Commission on Environment and Development (WCED), in which the concept of SL was first, and officially, proposed (WCED, 1987). This report reversed the normal view that always starts with things rather than people, urban rather than rural, the rich rather than the poor (Conroy & Litvinoff, 1988).

Reviewing the WCED panel definition, Chambers and Conway put forth their understanding of SL:

A livelihood comprises the capabilities, assets (stores, resources, claims and access) and activities required for a means of living: a livelihood is sustainable which can cope with and recover from stress and shocks, maintain or enhance its capabilities and assets, and provide sustainable livelihood opportunities for the next generation; and which contributes net benefits to other livelihoods at the local and global levels and in the short and long term.

Chambers and Conway (1992), in their definition, accentuated the importance of capabilities, not only the ability of being and doing, but also the ability of recognising and recovering from the potential shocks and stresses which they consider are key features of sustainability. Ellis (2000) however, points out that the meaning of 'capabilities' in the above definition overlaps greatly with assets and activities, and use of the term 'capabilities' can bring confusion. Therefore, he argued that access to assets and activities mediated by institutions and social relations should be highlighted, rather than capabilities. When applied to Pacific cultures, Cahn (2002) notes that culture and tradition are prominent in a Pacific livelihood, and proposed a sustainable Pacific livelihoods model incorporating the integration of culture and tradition. Such deliberations indicate that a 'one size fits all' SL approach is neither possible nor appropriate—context is important.

World Travel and Tourism Council

The World Travel & Tourism Council (WTTC) was conceptualized in the early 1980s when a group of CEOs came to the realization that although Travel & Tourism was the largest service industry in the world and the biggest provider of jobs, nobody knew it. There was no consolidated data or voice for the industry to give the message to elected official and policy makers.

WTTC was established in 1990 and today the Council is positioned as the global business leaders' forum for Travel & Tourism, comprising the Chairmen and Chief Executives of 100 of the world's foremost organizations, representing all regions and sectors of the industry; a membership list is attached.

Mission

WTTC works to raise awareness of Travel & Tourism as one of the world's largest industries, employing approximately 220 million people and generating 9.4 per cent of world GDP, WTTC works together with governments to raise awareness of the economic and social importance of the industry across the world.

WTTC's mission focuses on three main areas:

Driving the Agenda: Raising awareness of the impact of Travel & Tourism and working with governments to make the industry an economic and job-creating priority. The Facilitator: Helping industry participants to understand, anticipate, interpret and act on global key regional development The Networking Forum: WTTC is the business leaders' forum to which Travel & Tourism players aspire

Blueprint for New Tourism

By 2003, events around the world such as the September 11th attacks, war in Iraq, the SARS crisis and increased terrorism meant that WTTC had to work to rebuild confidence among travellers. The Global Travel & Tourism Summit in 2003 was opened up to global press and media for the first time and the theme – Building

New Tourism – came out of the atmosphere at the time. The outcome of the Summit shaped the Council's future vision and led to the launch of the Blueprint for New Tourism. The Blueprint for New Tourism provides a new strategic framework to ensure that Travel & Tourism works for everyone in the future. It promotes Travel & Tourism as a partnership between the private and public sectors, matching the needs of economies, local and regional authorities and local communities with those of business. The three main messages that form the framework for the Blueprint for New Tourism are: 1. Governments recognizing Travel & Tourism as a top priority 2. Business balancing economics with people, culture and environment.

Activities

WTTC Research

When the World Travel & Tourism Council (WTTC) was established in 1990, the founding Members decided that the quantification of Travel & Tourism's impact on world and national economies would be the most important contribution they could make to achieve their goal of raising awareness among policy leaders and decision-makers of Travel & Tourism's economic contribution and its potential for creating wealth and employment around the world. The subsequent 19 years of investment in research made a significant contribution to the development of the new international standard for Tourism Satellite Accounting (TSA) research, adopted in 2001 by the United Nations Statistical Commission. WTTC has also developed a Crisis Impact Forecasting Model to assess the potential impact of a crisis on the industry within 48 hours. It was put into place following the crises of the London and Egypt bombings in 2005.

TSA Commissioned Reports

Over the years, WTTC and its research partner, UK-based Oxford Economics (OE), have endeavoured to create a system of Tourism Satellite Accounting research, which now covers 181 economies around the world. Using a combination of macro-economic research and forecasts, national accounting data/ information, Travel & Tourism variables and econometric modelling, WTTC/OE have produced a system of research covering many concepts of Travel & Tourism 'Demand', from personal consumption to business purchases, capital investment, government spending and exports. This information is then translated into economic concepts of production, such as gross domestic product (GDP) and employment, which can be compared with other industries and the economy as a whole to provide statistical information that can assist in policy- and business decision-making. Today, WTTC produces annual TSA forecasts for 181 countries and 13 regions and carries out commissioned TSA reports for a growing number of countries, regions, and cities each year..

Global Travel & Tourism Summit

The Global Travel & Tourism Summit is an annual WTTC gathering for both public and private sector leaders of travel and tourism. The Summit aims to facilitate meaningful dialogue among the world's Travel & Tourism industry and government leaders. Past locations of the Summit include Vilamoura, Doha, New Delhi, Washington D.C., Lisbon, and Dubai. The 9th Global Travel & Tourism Summit took place from 14-16 May 2009 in Florianópolis, Brazil.

Tourism for Tomorrow Awards

The Tourism for Tomorrow Awards were set up in 1989 by the Federation of Tour Operators to encourage action from all sectors of the industry to protect the environment. WTTC took over the Awards in 2004. Awarded annually, they recognise and promote the world's leading examples of best practice in responsible tourism development across four categories:

Destination Stewardship Award, Conservation Award, Community Benefit Award, Global Tourism Business Award

Winners and finalists are taking the stage in a Awards special session during WTTC's Global Travel & Tourism Summit.

7

Services for Hospitality Markets

Concepts of Service Quality Measurement in Hotel Industry

The domination of the service sector today is confirmed by the fact that 70% of the world GDP is realized in the service sector. The same sector sees the concentration of 70% of workforce. In order to ensure and keep the quality expected by today's customer/ tourist, we need to differentiate two aspects of quality in general with particular attention to tourism, namely: design quality and the quality of conformity with design. The design quality is a concept implying the presentation of products/services directed to the needs of the clients.

The hotel company can satisfy the demands of the client (tourist) only if they are included in its design, i.e. in order to do that, his demands need to be included or "built into" the product/ service of the hotel. The hotels do market research in order to determine who their customers are and which of their demands require special attention. The quality of conformity with the design completes the first aspect because it represents the level to which the product/service meets the demands of the market.

The quality represents the satisfaction of the client's needs and in order to achieve it and keep it in time, we not only need a continuous research into the demands of the clients but also of our own capabilities. Such an approach would ensure the pursuing of constant improvements according to the demands of the clients. The harsh competition on tourist market requires the development of a new approach to management known as TQM– Total Quality Management. When introducing the quality management system, hotel companies use various approaches adapted to their business conditions. The following part of the paper describes the most common service quality measurement criteria, in particular the model of internal service quality and the Servqual model.

Review of the Literature

Service quality is a way to manage business processes in order to ensure total satisfaction to the customer on all levels (internal and external). It is an approach that leads to an increase of competitiveness, effectiveness and flexibility of the entire company.

Benefits arising from a high quality are reflected in a more competitive positioning on the market, but also in a better business result. This statement can be proved by measuring the increase of profitability and market share. The results of a research carried out in the USA on a sample of 2600 companies in the period between 1987 and 2002, show a direct connection between the level of quality of goods and services and their financial performances. As a matter of fact, it was observed that all indicators of success of a company, like market share, return on investments, property turnover coefficient, show significantly more value in companies with a higher level of goods and services.

The efficiency of the whole system is possible only if we monitor and analyse the demands of the customers, as well as define and control the process and implement constant improvements.Quality is a complex term, made up of several elements and criteria.

All quality elements or criteria are equally important in order to obtain one hundred percent quality. If only one element of quality is missing, the complete quality of product or service is impossible to obtain.

Besides the mentioned general elements of quality, the product or service have to satisfy specific elements of quality, according to the demands of the profession in their pertaining activity. Today quality is the result of growing and increasingly diverse needs of the consumers, along with a highly increasing competition, market globalization and the development of modern technology.

Problems in service quality measurement arise from a lack of clear and measurable parameters for the determination of quality. It is not the case with product quality since products have specific and measurable indicators like durability, number of defective products and similar, which make it relatively easy to determine the level of quality.

The most important characteristics of services, separating them neatly from products, are the impossibility to separate production from consumption; the impossibility to store services; their non material quality; transience and heterogeneity.

The impossibility to separate production from consumption and the impossibility to store services implicitly includes a simultaneous production and consumption, which is characteristic for most services. Since the services are performances, ideas or concepts rather than objects, they cannot be seen in the same way as products and are, therefore, characterized by their being immaterial.

Furthermore, it is impossible to preserve services, which raises the issue of harmonizing offer and demand for services. The same service can be provided by different persons in an institution, and each of them might provide it in their own way so that heterogeneity also counts among characteristics of services that differentiate them from products.

The quality system is based on principles such as commitment of the management, focus on the customers, employees and facts, constant improvement and co-operation of all the participants to the process.

Research carried out in 101 companies in the service provision field (Zemke, Schaff, 1989) show the following results:

- Managers are "obsessed" with listening to the changeable wishes, needs and expectations of their customers, and the wish to respond to them.
- A solidly defined strategy of servicing "inspired by consumers" is created by managers in their companies, and transferred to the staff.
- Managers develop and maintain a *customer-friendly* system of providing services.
- Managers look for, and then inspire and develop staff that is in direct contact with consumers.

Two basic approaches to service quality have been identified in the early nineties of the twentieth century. The first approach is "technical" and product oriented, while the second approach is customer related. These two approaches have been recognized as results of managerial efforts to consider the aspect of quality when providing services from two angles: on one hand, the manager tends to abide by the set standards, while on the other, he wishes to satisfy the customer. The first approach is production oriented and tends to the consistency of service by impeding or minimizing the influence of the personnel directly involved in providing a service.

The service providing process is defined as a standard performance. The role of the staff providing services is reduced to the realization of the defined performance and the staff's discretion, i.e. its influence on the performance itself is minimized. In that way we can achieve maximum efficiency. Such a "product based" approach to the process of service provision is the result of the managerial view on this process as a series of elements that require a trained coordination and control, while the service itself is strictly standardized. The "product based" approach is contradictory to the aspirations of the consumers to be treated as individual people with marked personal tendencies and expectations. Besides, such an approach, "industrial" and cliche, is in contrast with the wish of the consumer to find warm and friendly manners when *consuming* the service. The second approach is consumer oriented. Expectations are the basis for satisfaction. After consuming the service, they compare their earlier expectations with experience. Results can range from satisfaction to dissatisfaction. The consumer anticipates the service standards in his expectations. Wilkie claims: "The seed of the consumer's dissatisfaction is sown in the pre-purchase stage, before reaching the decision to purchase." According to this, the consumer creates his own, individual *benchmark*, and the rating of his satisfaction is the result of his after purchase state.

Normann, the creator of the concept "moment of truth", points out that the first generation of researchers in the field of service sector management, had the task to determine the specificities of the services as opposed to other sectors, which paved the way for the second generation of researchers who focused on the relations in the service industry, the behaviour when providing service and service design, with the aim to optimize the "moment of truth". On the basis of the above exposed thesis, the understanding of service quality is based on the *paradigm of service*. In that sense, the service sector company manager looks for a "balance between the human factor and technology, between expenses and profit and, after all, between quality and productivity" (Gummesson, 1993).

The organization has to strive for success. When the set goals are achieved, we set other goals, striving for higher levels of product, processes and service efficiency. Accepting the concept of constant improvement means changing the management style. A total quality cannot be a program of changes with a set duration, it is a continuous, constant process. The questions set before the organization are the following: How do you keep up the constant striving for new improvement? What kind of measures and revisions of the business process do you have to use? How do you convince the employees that the business success and survival of the organizations can only occur if all employees accept constant actions to improve all their activities in the organizations? A successful organization constantly identifies and tackles the causes of problems or potential problems that employees have in doing their jobs. For that reason every employee has to be trained to identify such problems. The management and the employees must work together on implementing suitable corrective and preventive measures.

Each business process is subject to variability. Process variability is considered a normal phenomenon that is usually counted on. Parameter variability in the field of transformation of incoming values into outcoming values of the process affects the variability of the entire business process. For example, a lack of a specific product on the supplies market may require a substitution with another product of similar characteristics. Departure from the usual process (*variability*) can affect the quality of meals as results of a process, the timing of a process cycle, expenses of process quality, the level of satisfaction of the consumer/user with the process result.

Each episode of variability and a departure from the optimal process does not necessarily have a negative impact on the quality level of the process results. However, if the process is moving away from its optimal course so much as to get close to the acceptable limit or it has surpassed the limit, cost incur due to poor quality. The process becomes too expensive, jeopardizing the quality of the results and thus seriously risking dissatisfaction on the part of the client/consumer, in other words, it becomes irrational.

Service Quality Measurement in Hotel Industry

In order to achieve rationality the models of business excellence also, in a way, determine whether the criteria have been met, but the evaluation of business excellence is based not only on the fulfilment of the set criteria but also on the determination of the level up to which the criteria have been fulfilled (systems of points).

When analyzing the quality of service it is desirable to analyse the largest possible number of companies supplying the same type of service. As we already mentioned, if a company carries out a research and finds that the results are negative, it can interpret this information in the wrong way and conclude that it provides services in a totally wrong way. On the other hand, when analyzing a large number of companies, it is possible to compare data and obtain a realistic picture of the position of an individual company compared to others regarding quality.

The upper part of the model includes phenomena tied to the consumer, while the lower part shows phenomena tied to the supplier of services. The expected service is the function of earlier experiences of the consumer, their personal needs and oral communication. Communication with the market also influences the expected service. Experienced service, here called perceived service, is the result of a series of internal decisions and activities.

The management's perceptions of the consumer's expectations is the guiding principle when deciding on the specifications of the quality of service that the company should follow in providing service. If there are differences or discrepancies in the expectations or perceptions between people involved in providing and consuming services, a "service quality gap" can occur, as shown in image 1. Since there is a direct connection between the quality of service and the satisfaction of clients in hotel industry, it is important for the company to spot a gap in the quality of service.

The first possible gap is the knowledge gap. It is the result of the differences in managing knowledge and their real expectations. This gap can lead to other gaps in the process of service quality and is, among other things, caused by:

- incorrect information in market researches and demand analysis;
- incorrect interpretations of information regarding expectations;
- lack of information about any feedback between the company and the consumers directed to the management;
- too many organizational layers that hinder or modify parts of information in their upward movement from those involved in contact with the consumers.

The second possible gap is that of standard. It is the result of differences in managing knowledge of the client's expectations and the process of service provision (delivery). This gap is the result of:

- mistakes in planning or insufficient planning procedures;
- bad management planning;
- lack of clearly set goals in the organization; and
- insufficient support of the top management to service quality planning.

The management can be right in evaluating the client's expectations and develop business methods to satisfy these expectations, without the employees being correct in providing service. For example, a restaurant can order the waiters to serve the customers in two minutes after they sit at the table. Nevertheless, the waiters can ignore that specification and talk between them on the side. The fourth possible gap is the communication gap arising when there is a difference between the delivered service and the service that the company promised to the clients via external communications.

The reasons are:

- the planning of communication with the market is not integrated with the services;
- lack or insufficient coordination between traditional marketing and procedures;
- organizational performance not in keeping with the specifications, while the policy of communication with the market abides by the given specifications; and

- tendency to exaggerate in accordance with exaggerated promises.

Should any of the mentioned gaps arise, the "service gap" will also appear because the real service will not satisfy the client's expectations. Hotel companies try to detect the "service gap" with survey questionnaires. Gap analysis is the file conducteur for the management to find the causes of problems regarding quality and to find suitable ways to remove such gaps. For this reason the first four gaps are also called organizational or internal gaps. Although there are several models (scales) for the measurement of service quality and the satisfaction of customers, they are often too generalized or ad hoc, and as such hard to apply in the hotel industry. As opposed to TQM, which began before all in companies that dealt with products, due to the specificities of services (the basic are: impalpability, inseparability from provider

and receiver of service, impossibility of storage), a specific concept called Servqual (SERVices QUALity Model) was created. 8 The Servqual model offers a suitable conceptual frame for the research and service quality measurement in the service sector. The model has been developed, tested and adapted during various researches in cooperation with the Marketing Science Institute from Texas and numerous companies operating in the service sector. The model is based on the definition of quality as a comparison of the expected and the obtained as well as a consideration of gaps in the process of service provision. Servqual is based on the client's evaluation of service quality. The described concept is based on the gap between expectations and perception of the clients. Service quality·represents a multidimensional construction. The choice of the most important characteristics was an issue dealt with in various ways. One of these is a logical attempt to work out a list of desirable attributes from the basic needs of the clients. A variant of a scale containing desirable characteristics of services, known as Servqual scale, is currently quite popular in literature. It was developed in marketing circles with the aim to measure service quality (Bakoviæ, Lazibat). In the original Servqual instrument, Parasuraman et al. (1985) define service quality through ten dimensions which they sum up in five in 1988:

1) Reliability,
2) Assurance,

3) Tangibles,
4) Empathy,
5) Responsiveness.

Each of the listed dimensions has different features. Just like dimensions have different influence on the final service quality, so do these features have different influence on the grading of success of a single dimension. Despite its popularity and wide application, Servqual is exposed to numerous criticisms, from both the conceptual and the operational aspect.

Theoretical Criticism

- pattern objections: Servqual is based rather on an affirmation pattern than on the pattern of understanding; it does not manage to tie in with proved economical, statistical and psychological theories.
- Gap model: there is little evidence that the consumer evaluates service quality in the sense of perception – expectation gaps.
- Direction to the process: Servqual is directed to the process of service delivery and not to the result of service experience.
- Dimensionality: the five dimensions of Servqual are not universal; the number of dimensions that encompass service quality is connected to the context; there is a high degree of inter-correlation between RATER dimensions. RATER is a mnemonic acronym where R = reliability, A = assurance, T = tangibles, E = empathy and R = responsiveness. Operative criticism:
- Expectations: the term of expectations has multiple meanings; in evaluating services consumers use standards instead of expectations; Servqual cannot measure the absolute expectations of service quality.
- Content of the elements: four out of five elements cannot encompass the variability inside each dimension of service quality.
- Moment of truth: the consumer's rating of the service can vary from one to the next moment of truth.

- Polarity: the reverse polarity of the scale elements causes wrong reactions.
- Scale grading: Likert's scale with 7 ratings is inadequate.
- Dual administration: dual administration of instruments causes boredom and confusion.

The most important criticism of Servqual was the usage of gap analysis results (difference between expectations and perception of the received service) in measuring service quality. Comparing the expectation-perception gaps with perception only, called Servperf, Cronin and Taylor concluded that measurement of service quality based only on perception was enough.

Servqual Model in Croatian Hotel Industry

The Faculty for Tourist and Hospitality Management in Opatija constructed an empirical model for the measurement of service quality in hotel industry on the model of hospitality on the Opatijska Riviera. Its use shall be simple and effective in hotel practice.

The aims of the research were:

a) Evaluate expectations and perceptions of hotel guests on the studied sample,
b) Evaluate and calculate the Servqual gap,
c) Test the reliability of the Servqual model in hotel industry,
d) Determine the dimensions of service quality in hotel industry by applying the method of factor analysis.

From a practical point of view, the research intended to test the adapted Servqual model for the measurement of service quality of hotel guests (Markoviæ: 2005). It represents the difference between the average ratings of perceptions and the average expectations ratings. The wider the gap, the greater the difference between expectations and perception.

The results of the quantitative application of the Servqual model in Croatian hotel industry show that the expectations of hotel guests are higher than their perception. This proves the existence of a negative Servqual gap. It is visible that tourists from Great Britain have the highest total expectations, followed by guests from Australia and USA, while the Japanese tourists have the least expectations. Compared to clients in other services, "reliability" and an "impeccable" service is important to all hotel guests, regardless of their country of origin. Hotel guests prioritize this dimension, and so should hotel managers and personnel.

Dimensions of Countries

The need for the application of Servqual model in hotel industry is confirmed by the fact that, in the observed sample, hotel managers do not know the expectations of their guests because the dimensions of service quality they consider most important, do not match those that are most important for the clients, which is confirmed by the total Servqual gap.

Conclusion

Servqual can be widely applied, not only in science but also in practice in various services. The aim of the scientists is to work out and test useful instruments for managers in order to help them determine those organizational variables (policy, staff, structure, technology, processes) that will guarantee the best service quality with minimal costs. This methodology can assist hotel managers in assessing the position of the hotel regarding its competition and strategic and operative decision-making.

In hotel industry, service quality, as an extremely subjective category, is crucial to the satisfaction of the client. It is therefore imperative for managers in hotel industry to apply the Servqual model for the measurement of service quality in their own hotel company, in order to satisfy the guest's expectations and ensure a position on the growing global tourist market.

The results of the quantitative application of Servqual instrument show that this model can provide managers with useful information for the assessment of expectations and perception of hotel guests, with the aim of learning about gaps in individual service quality dimensions. To sum up, this article tend to clarify the Servqual model as not only provider to the managers with a clear picture of the quality of the provided service, but also helping in discovering the needs, wishes and expectations of the guests. The same is analyzed by determining thecharacteristics of service quality that are most important for guests. We can say that it helps managers in setting the standards for the provision of services in the hospitality industry.

Marketing Strategies in Hotel Industry

Strategic or institutional management is the conduct of drafting, implementing and evaluating cross-functional decisions that will enable an organization to achieve its long-term objectives. It is the process of specifying the organization's mission, vision and objectives, developing policies and plans, often in terms of projects and programs, which are designed to achieve these objectives, and then allocating resources to implement the policies and plans, projects and programs. A balanced scorecard is often used to evaluate the overall performance of the business and its progress towards objectives.

Strategic management is a level of managerial activity under setting goals and over Tactics. Strategic management provides overall direction to the enterprise and is closely related to the field of Organization Studies. In the field of business administration it is useful to talk about "strategic alignment" between the organization and its environment or "strategic consistency". According to Arieu (2007), "there is strategic consistency when the actions of an organization are consistent with the expectations of management, and these in turn are with the market and the context."

"Strategic management is an ongoing process that evaluates and controls the business and the industries in which the company is involved; assesses its competitors and sets goals and strategies to meet all existing and potential competitors; and then reassesses each strategy annually or quarterly [i.e. regularly] to determine how it has been implemented and whether it has succeeded or needs replacement by a new strategy to meet changed circumstances, new technology, new competitors, a new economic environment., or a new social, financial, or political environment."

Strategy Formulation

Strategic formulation is a combination of three main processes which are as follows:

- Performing a situation analysis, self-evaluation and competitor analysis: both internal and external; both micro-environmental and macro-environmental.
- Concurrent with this assessment, objectives are set. These objectives should be parallel to a time-line; some are in the short-term and others on the long-term. This involves

crafting vision statements (long term view of a possible future), mission statements (the role that the organization gives itself in society), overall corporate objectives (both financial and strategic), strategic business unit objectives (both financial and strategic), and tactical objectives.

- These objectives should, in the light of the situation analysis, suggest a strategic plan. The plan provides the details of how to achieve these objectives.

Marketing Action Plan

- Placement and execution of required resources are financial, manpower, operational support, time, technology support
- Operating with a change in methods or with alteration in structure
- Distributing the specific tasks with responsibility or moulding specific jobs to individuals or teams.
- The process should be managed by a responsible team. This is to keep direct watch on result, comparison for betterment and best practices, cultivating the effectiveness of processes, calibrating and reducing the variations and setting the process as required.
- Introducing certain programs involves acquiring the requisition of resources: a necessity for developing the process, training documentation, process testing, and imalgation with (and/or conversion from) difficult processes.

As and when the strategy implementation processes, there have been so many problems arising such as human relations, the employee-communication.

Such a time, marketing strategy is the biggest implementation problem usually involves, with emphasis on the appropriate timing of new products. An organization, with an effective management, should try to implement its plans without signaling this fact to its competitors. In order for a policy to work, there must be a level of consistency from every person in an organization, specially management. This is what needs to occur on both the tactical and strategic levels of management.

Strategy Evàluation

- Measuring the effectiveness of the organizational strategy, it's extremely important to conduct a SWOT analysis to figure out the strengths, weaknesses, opportunities and threats (both internal and external) of the entity in question. This may require to take certain precautionary measures or even to change the entire strategy.

In corporate strategy, Johnson and Scholes present a model in which strategic options are evaluated against three key success criteria:

- Suitability (would it work?)
- Feasibility (can it be made to work?)
- Acceptability (will they work it?).

Suitability

Suitability deals with the overall rationale of the strategy. The key point to consider is whether the strategy would address the key strategic issues underlined by the organisation's strategic position.

- Does it make economic sense?
- Would the organization obtain economies of scale, economies of scope or experience economy?
- Would it be suitable in terms of environment and capabilities?

Tools that can be used to evaluate suitability include:

- Ranking strategic options
- Decision trees.

Feasibility

Feasibility is concerned with whether the resources required to implement the strategy are available, can be developed or obtained. Resources include funding, people, time and information.

Tools that can be used to evaluate feasibility include:

- cash flow analysis and forecasting
- break-even analysis
- resource deployment analysis.

Acceptability

Acceptability is concerned with the expectations of the identified stakeholders (mainly shareholders, employees and customers) with the expected performance outcomes, which can be return, risk and stakeholder reactions.

- Return deals with the benefits expected by the stakeholders (financial and non-financial). For example, shareholders would expect the increase of their wealth, employees would expect improvement in their careers and customers would expect better value for money.
- Risk deals with the probability and consequences of failure of a strategy (financial and non-financial).
- Stakeholder reactions deals with anticipating the likely reaction of stakeholders. Shareholders could oppose the issuing of new shares, employees and unions could oppose outsourcing for fear of losing their jobs, customers could have concerns over a merger with regards to quality and support.

Tools that can be used to evaluate acceptability include:

- what-if analysis
- stakeholder mapping.

General Approaches

In general terms, there are two main approaches, which are opposite but complement each other in some ways, to strategic management:

- The Industrial Organizational Approach:
    - o based on economic theory — deals with issues like competitive rivalry, resource allocation, economies of scale
    - o assumptions — rationality, self discipline behaviour, profit maximization.
- The Sociological Approach:
    - o deals primarily with human interactions
    - o assumptions — bounded rationality, satisfying behaviour, profit sub-optimality. An example of a company that currently operates this way is Google.

Strategic management techniques can be viewed as bottom-up, top-down, or collaborative processes. In the bottom-up approach, employees submit proposals to their managers who, in turn, funnel the best ideas further up the organization. This is often accomplished by a capital budgeting process. Proposals are assessed using financial criteria such as return on investment or cost-benefit analysis. Cost underestimation and benefit overestimation are major sources of error. The proposals that are approved form the substance of a new strategy, all of which is done without a grand strategic design or a strategic architect. The top-down approach is the most common by far. In it, the CEO, possibly with the assistance of a strategic planning team, decides on the overall direction the company should take. Some organizations are starting to experiment with collaborative strategic planning techniques that recognize the emergent nature of strategic decisions.

The Strategy Hierarchy

In most (large) corporations there are several levels of management. Strategic management is the highest of these levels in the sense that it is the broadest-applying to all parts of the firm-while also incorporating the longest time horizon. It gives direction to corporate values, corporate culture, corporate goals, and corporate missions. Under this broad corporate strategy there are typically business-level competitive strategies and functional unit strategies. Corporate strategy refers to the overarching strategy of the diversified firm. Such a corporate strategy answers the questions of "which businesses should we be in?" and "how does being in these businesses create synergy and/or add to the competitive advantage of the corporation as a whole?"

Business strategy refers to the aggregated strategies of single business firm or a strategic business unit (SBU) in a diversified corporation. According to Michael Porter, a firm must formulate a business strategy that incorporates either cost leadership, differentiation or focus in order to achieve a sustainable competitive advantage and long-term success in its chosen areas or industries. Alternatively, according to W. Chan Kim and Renée Mauborgne, an organization can achieve high growth and profits by creating a Blue Ocean Strategy that breaks the previous value-cost tradeoff by simultaneously pursuing both differentiation and low cost.

Functional strategies include marketing strategies, new product development strategies, human resource strategies, financial strategies, legal strategies, supply-chain strategies, and information technology management strategies. The emphasis is on short and medium term plans and is limited to the domain of each department's functional responsibility. Each functional department attempts to do its part in meeting overall corporate objectives, and hence to some extent their strategies are derived from broader corporate strategies.

Many companies feel that a functional organizational structure is not an efficient way to organize activities so they have reengineered according to processes or SBUs. A strategic business unit is a semi-autonomous unit that is usually responsible for its own budgeting, new product decisions, hiring decisions, and price setting. An SBU is treated as an internal profit centre by corporate headquarters. A technology strategy, for example, although it is focused on technology as a means of achieving an organization's overall objective(s), may include dimensions that are beyond the scope of a single business unit, engineering organization or IT department.

An additional level of strategy called operational strategy was encouraged by Peter Drucker in his theory of management by objectives (MBO). It is very narrow in focus and deals with day-to-day operational activities such as scheduling criteria. It must operate within a budget but is not at liberty to adjust or create that budget. Operational level strategies are informed by business level strategies which, in turn, are informed by corporate level strategies.

Since the turn of the millennium, some firms have reverted to a simpler strategic structure driven by advances in information technology. It is felt that knowledge management systems should be used to share information and create common goals. Strategic divisions are thought to hamper this process. This notion of strategy has been captured under the rubric of dynamic strategy, popularized by Carpenter and Sanders's textbook. This work builds on that of Brown and Eisenhart as well as Christensen and portrays firm strategy, both business and corporate, as necessarily embracing ongoing strategic change, and the seamless integration of strategy formulation and implementation. Such change and implementation are usually built into the strategy through the staging and pacing facets.

Historical Development of Strategic Management

Birth of Strategic Management

Strategic management as a discipline originated in the 1950s and 60s. Although there were numerous early contributors to the literature, the most influential pioneers were Alfred D. Chandler, Philip Selznick, Igor Ansoff, and Peter Drucker.

Alfred Chandler recognized the importance of coordinating the various aspects of management under one all-encompassing strategy. Prior to this time the various functions of management were separate with little overall coordination or strategy. Interactions between functions or between departments were typically handled by a boundary position, that is, there were one or two managers that relayed information back and forth between two departments.

Chandler also stressed the importance of taking a long term perspective when looking to the future. In his 1962 groundbreaking work *Strategy and Structure*, Chandler showed that a long-term coordinated strategy was necessary to give a company structure, direction, and focus. He says it concisely, "structure follows strategy."

In 1957, Philip Selznick introduced the idea of matching the organization's internal factors with external environmental circumstances. This core idea was developed into what we now call SWOT analysis by Learned, Andrews, and others at the Harvard Business School General Management Group. Strengths and weaknesses of the firm are assessed in light of the opportunities and threats from the business environment.

Igor Ansoff built on Chandler's work by adding a range of strategic concepts and inventing a whole new vocabulary. He developed a strategy grid that compared market penetration strategies, product development strategies, market development strategies and horizontal and vertical integration and diversification strategies. He felt that management could use these strategies to systematically prepare for future opportunities and challenges. In his 1965 classic *Corporate Strategy*, he developed the gap analysis still used today in which we must understand the gap between where we are currently and where we would like to be, then develop what he called "gap reducing actions".

Peter Drucker was a prolific strategy theorist, author of dozens of management books, with a career spanning five decades. His contributions to strategic management were many but two are most important.

Firstly, he stressed the importance of objectives. An organization without clear objectives is like a ship without a rudder. As early as 1954 he was developing a theory of management based on objectives. This evolved into his theory of management by objectives (MBO). According to Drucker, the procedure of setting objectives and monitoring your progress towards them should permeate the entire organization, top to bottom. His other seminal contribution was in predicting the importance of what today we would call intellectual capital. He predicted the rise of what he called the "knowledge worker" and explained the consequences of this for management. He said that knowledge work is non-hierarchical. Work would be carried out in teams with the person most knowledgeable in the task at hand being the temporary leader.

In 1985, Ellen-Earle Chaffee summarized what she thought were the main elements of strategic management theory by the 1970s:

- Strategic management involves adapting the organization to its business environment.
- Strategic management is fluid and complex. Change creates novel combinations of circumstances requiring unstructured non-repetitive responses.
- Strategic management affects the entire organization by providing direction.
- Strategic management involves both strategy formation (she called it content) and also strategy implementation (she called it process).
- Strategic management is partially planned and partially unplanned.
- Strategic management is done at several levels: overall corporate strategy, and individual business strategies.
- Strategic management involves both conceptual and analytical thought processes.

Growth and Portfolio Theory

In the 1970s much of strategic management dealt with size, growth, and portfolio theory.

The PIMS study was a long term study, started in the 1960s and lasted for 19 years, that attempted to understand the Profit Impact of Marketing Strategies (PIMS), particularly the effect of market share. Started at General Electric, moved to Harvard in the early 1970s, and then moved to the Strategic Planning Institute in the late 1970s, it now contains decades of information on the relationship between profitability and strategy.

Their initial conclusion was unambiguous: The greater a company's market share, the greater will be their rate of profit. The high market share provides volume and economies of scale. It also provides experience and learning curve advantages. The combined effect is increased profits. The studies conclusions continue to be drawn on by academics and companies today: "PIMS provides compelling quantitative evidence as to which business strategies work and don't work"-Tom Peters.

The benefits of high market share naturally lead to an interest in growth strategies. The relative advantages of horizontal integration, vertical integration, diversification, franchises, mergers and acquisitions, joint ventures, and organic growth were discussed. The most appropriate market dominance strategies were assessed given the competitive and regulatory environment.

There was also research that indicated that a low market share strategy could also be very profitable. Schumacher (1973), Woo and Cooper (1982), Levenson (1984), and later Traverso (2002) showed how smaller niche players obtained very high returns.

By the early 1980s the paradoxical conclusion was that high market share and low market share companies were often very profitable but most of the companies in between were not. This was sometimes called the "hole in the middle" problem. This anomaly would be explained by Michael Porter in the 1980s.

The management of diversified organizations required new techniques and new ways of thinking. The first CEO to address the problem of a multi-divisional company was Alfred Sloan at General Motors. GM was decentralized into semi-autonomous "strategic business units" (SBU's), but with centralized support functions.

One of the most valuable concepts in the strategic management of multi-divisional companies was portfolio theory. In the previous decade Harry Markowitz and other financial theorists developed the theory of portfolio analysis. It was concluded that a broad portfolio of financial assets could reduce specific risk. In the 1970s marketers extended the theory to product portfolio decisions and managerial strategists extended it to operating division portfolios. Each of a company's operating divisions were seen as an element in the corporate portfolio. Each operating division (also called strategic business units) was treated as a semi-independent profit centre with its own revenues, costs, objectives, and strategies. Several techniques were developed to analyse the relationships between elements in a portfolio. B.C.G. Analysis, for example, was developed by the Boston Consulting Group in the early 1970s. This was the theory that gave us the wonderful image of a CEO sitting on a stool milking a cash cow. Shortly after that the G.E. multi factoral model was developed by General Electric. Companies continued to diversify until the 1980s when it was realized that in many cases a portfolio of operating divisions was worth more as separate completely independent companies.

The Marketing Revolution

The 1970s also saw the rise of the marketing oriented firm. From the beginnings of capitalism it was assumed that the key requirement of business success was a product of high technical quality. If you produced a product that worked well and was durable, it was assumed you would have no difficulty selling them at a profit. This was called the production orientation and it was generally true that good products could be sold without effort, encapsulated in the saying "Build a better mousetrap and the world will beat a path to your door." This was largely due to the growing numbers of affluent and middle class people that capitalism had created. But after the untapped demand caused by the second world war was saturated in the 1950s it became obvious that products were not selling as easily as they had been. The answer was to concentrate on selling.

The 1950s and 1960s is known as the sales era and the guiding philosophy of business of the time is today called the sales orientation. In the early 1970s Theodore Levitt and others at Harvard argued that the sales orientation had things backward.

They claimed that instead of producing products then trying to sell them to the customer, businesses should start with the customer, find out what they wanted, and then produce it for them. The customer became the driving force behind all strategic business decisions. This marketing orientation, in the decades since its introduction, has been reformulated and repackaged under numerous names including customer orientation, marketing philosophy, customer intimacy, customer focus, customer driven, and market focused.

The Japanese Challenge

By the late 70s, Americans had started to notice how successful Japanese industry had become. In industry after industry, including steel, watches, ship building, cameras, autos, and electronics, the Japanese were surpassing American and European companies. Westerners wanted to know why. Numerous theories purported to explain the Japanese success including:

- Higher employee morale, dedication, and loyalty;
- Lower cost structure, including wages;
- Effective government industrial policy;
- Modernization after WWII leading to high capital intensity and productivity;
- Economies of scale associated with increased exporting;
- Relatively low value of the Yen leading to low interest rates and capital costs, low dividend expectations, and inexpensive exports;
- Superior quality control techniques such as Total Quality Management and other systems introduced by W. Edwards Deming in the 1950s and 60s.

Although there was some truth to all these potential explanations, there was clearly something missing. In fact by 1980 the Japanese cost structure was higher than the American. And post WWII reconstruction was nearly 40 years in the past. The first management theorist to suggest an explanation was Richard Pascale.

In 1981, Richard Pascale and Anthony Athos in *The Art of Japanese Management* claimed that the main reason for Japanese success was their superior management techniques. They divided management into 7 aspects (which are also known as McKinsey 7S Framework): Strategy, Structure, Systems, Skills, Staff, Style, and Supraordinate goals (which we would now call shared values). The first three of the 7 S's were called hard factors and this is where American companies excelled. The remaining four factors (skills, staff, style, and shared values) were called soft factors and were not well understood by American businesses of the time. Americans did not yet place great value on corporate culture, shared values and beliefs, and social cohesion in the workplace. In Japan the task of management was seen as managing the whole complex of human needs, economic, social, psychological, and spiritual. In America work was seen as something that was separate from the rest of one's life. It was quite common for Americans to exhibit a very different personality at work compared to the rest of their lives. Pascale also highlighted the difference between decision making styles; hierarchical in America, and consensus in Japan. He also claimed that American business lacked long term vision, preferring instead to apply management fads and theories in a piecemeal fashion.

One year later, *The Mind of the Strategist* was released in America by Kenichi Ohmae, the head of McKinsey & Co.'s Tokyo office. (It was originally published in Japan in 1975.) He claimed that strategy in America was too analytical. Strategy should be a creative art: It is a frame of mind that requires intuition and intellectual flexibility. He claimed that Americans constrained their strategic options by thinking in terms of analytical techniques, rote formula, and step-by-step processes. He compared the culture of Japan in which vagueness, ambiguity, and tentative decisions were acceptable, to American culture that valued fast decisions.

Also in 1982, Tom Peters and Robert Waterman released a study that would respond to the Japanese challenge head on. Peters and Waterman, who had several years earlier collaborated with Pascale and Athos at McKinsey & Co. asked "What makes an excellent company?". They looked at 62 companies that they thought were fairly successful. Each was subject to six performance criteria. To be classified as an excellent company, it had to be above the 50th percentile in 4 of the 6 performance metrics for 20 consecutive years. Forty-three companies passed the test. They then studied these successful companies and interviewed key executives. They concluded in *In Search of Excellence* that there

Peters and Nancy Austin. Japanese managers employ a similar system, which originated at Honda, and is sometimes called the 3 G's (Genba, Genbutsu, and Genjitsu, which translate into "actual place", "actual thing", and "actual situation").

Probably the most influential strategist of the decade was Michael Porter. He introduced many new concepts including; 5 forces analysis, generic strategies, the value chain, strategic groups, and clusters. In 5 forces analysis he identifies the forces that shape a firm's strategic environment. It is like a SWOT analysis with structure and purpose. It shows how a firm can use these forces to obtain a sustainable competitive advantage. Porter modifies Chandler's dictum about structure following strategy by introducing a second level of structure: Organizational structure follows strategy, which in turn follows industry structure.

Porter's generic strategies detail the interaction between cost minimization strategies, product differentiation strategies, and market focus strategies. Although he did not introduce these terms, he showed the importance of choosing one of them rather than trying to position your company between them. He also challenged managers to see their industry in terms of a value chain. A firm will be successful only to the extent that it contributes to the industry's value chain. This forced management to look at its operations from the customer's point of view. Every operation should be examined in terms of what value it adds in the eyes of the final customer.

In 1993, John Kay took the idea of the value chain to a financial level claiming " Adding value is the central purpose of business activity", where adding value is defined as the difference between the market value of outputs and the cost of inputs including capital, all divided by the firm's net output. Borrowing from Gary Hamel and Michael Porter, Kay claims that the role of strategic management is to identify your core competencies, and then assemble a collection of assets that will increase value added and provide a competitive advantage. He claims that there are 3 types of capabilities that can do this; innovation, reputation, and organizational structure.

The 1980s also saw the widespread acceptance of positioning theory. Although the theory originated with Jack Trout in 1969, it didn't gain wide acceptance until Al Ries and Jack Trout wrote their classic book "Positioning: The Battle For Your Mind" (1979). The basic premise is that a strategy should not be judged by internal company factors but by the way customers see it relative to the competition. Crafting and implementing a strategy involves creating a position in the mind of the collective consumer. Several techniques were applied to positioning theory, some newly invented but most borrowed from other disciplines. Perceptual mapping for example, creates visual displays of the relationships between positions. Multidimensional scaling, discriminant analysis, factor analysis, and conjoint analysis are mathematical techniques used to determine the most relevant characteristics (called dimensions or factors) upon which positions should be based.

Preference regression can be used to determine vectors of ideal positions and cluster analysis can identify clusters of positions. Others felt that internal company resources were the key. In 1992, Jay Barney, for example, saw strategy as assembling the optimum mix of resources, including human, technology, and suppliers, and then configure them in unique and sustainable ways.

Michael Hammer and James Champy felt that these resources needed to be restructured. This process, that they labeled reengineering, involved organizing a firm's assets around whole processes rather than tasks. In this way a team of people saw a project through, from inception to completion. This avoided functional silos where isolated departments seldom talked to each other. It also eliminated waste due to functional overlap and interdepartmental communications.

In 1989 Richard Lester and the researchers at the MIT Industrial Performance Centre identified seven best practices and concluded that firms must accelerate the shift away from the mass production of low cost standardized products. The seven areas of best practice were:

- Simultaneous continuous improvement in cost, quality, service, and product innovation
- Breaking down organizational barriers between departments
- Eliminating layers of management creating flatter organizational hierarchies.
- Closer relationships with customers and suppliers

accelerating rates of change. He illustrated how social and technological norms had shorter lifespans with each generation, and he questioned society's ability to cope with the resulting turmoil and anxiety. In past generations periods of change were always punctuated with times of stability. This allowed society to assimilate the change and deal with it before the next change arrived. But these periods of stability are getting shorter and by the late 20th century had all but disappeared.

In 1980 in *The Third Wave,* Toffler characterized this shift to relentless change as the defining feature of the third phase of civilization (the first two phases being the agricultural and industrial waves). He claimed that the dawn of this new phase will cause great anxiety for those that grew up in the previous phases, and will cause much conflict and opportunity in the business world. Hundreds of authors, particularly since the early 1990s, have attempted to explain what this means for business strategy. In 1997, Watts Wacker and Jim Taylor called this upheaval a "500 year delta." They claimed these major upheavals occur every 5 centuries. They said we are currently making the transition from the "Age of Reason" to a new chaotic Age of Access. Jeremy Rifkin (2000) popularized and expanded this term, "age of access" three years later in his book of the same name.

In 1968, Peter Drucker (1969) coined the phrase Age of Discontinuity to describe the way change forces disruptions into the continuity of our lives. In an age of continuity attempts to predict the future by extrapolating from the past can be somewhat accurate. But according to Drucker, we are now in an age of discontinuity and extrapolating from the past is hopelessly ineffective. We cannot assume that trends that exist today will continue into the future. He identifies four sources of discontinuity: new technologies, globalization, cultural pluralism, and knowledge capital.

In 2000, Gary Hamel discussed strategic decay, the notion that the value of all strategies, no matter how brilliant, decays over time.

In 1978, Dereck Abell (Abell, D. 1978) described strategic windows and stressed the importance of the timing (both entrance and exit) of any given strategy. This has led some strategic planners to build planned obsolescence into their strategies.

In 1989, Charles Handy identified two types of change. Strategic drift is a gradual change that occurs so subtly that it is not noticed until it is too late. By contrast, transformational change is sudden and radical. It is typically caused by discontinuities (or exogenous shocks) in the business environment. The point where a new trend is initiated is called a strategic inflection point by Andy Grove. Inflection points can be subtle or radical.

In 2000, Malcolm Gladwell discussed the importance of the tipping point, that point where a trend or fad acquires critical mass and takes off. In 1983, Noel Tichy wrote that because we are all beings of habit we tend to repeat what we are comfortable with. He wrote that this is a trap that constrains our creativity, prevents us from exploring new ideas, and hampers our dealing with the full complexity of new issues. He developed a systematic method of dealing with change that involved looking at any new issue from three angles: technical and production, political and resource allocation, and corporate culture.

In 1990, Richard Pascale (Pascale, R. 1990) wrote that relentless change requires that businesses continuously reinvent themselves. His famous maxim is "Nothing fails like success" by which he means that what was a strength yesterday becomes the root of weakness today, We tend to depend on what worked yesterday and refuse to let go of what worked so well for us in the past. Prevailing strategies become self-confirming. In order to avoid this trap, businesses must stimulate a spirit of inquiry and healthy debate. They must encourage a creative process of self renewal based on constructive conflict.

In 1996, Art Kleiner (1996) claimed that to foster a corporate culture that embraces change, you have to hire the right people; heretics, heroes, outlaws, and visionaries. The conservative bureaucrat that made such a good middle manager in yesterday's hierarchical organizations is of little use today. A decade earlier Peters and Austin (1985) had stressed the importance of nurturing champions and heroes. They said we have a tendency to dismiss new ideas, so to overcome this, we should support those few people in the organization that have the courage to put their career and reputation on the line for an unproven idea.

In 1996, Adrian Slywotzky showed how changes in the business environment are reflected in value migrations between industries, between companies, and within companies. He claimed that recognizing the patterns behind these value migrations is necessary if we wish to understand the world of chaotic change. In "Profit Patterns" (1999) he described businesses as being in a state of strategic anticipation as they try to spot emerging patterns. Slywotsky and his team identified 30 patterns that have transformed industry after industry.

In 1997, Clayton Christensen (1997) took the position that great companies can fail precisely because they do everything right since the capabilities of the organization also defines its disabilities. Christensen's thesis is that outstanding companies lose their market leadership when confronted with disruptive technology. He called the approach to discovering the emerging markets for disruptive technologies agnostic marketing, i.e., marketing under the implicit assumption that no one-not the company, not the customers-can know how or in what quantities a disruptive product can or will be used before they have experience using it.

A number of strategists use scenario planning techniques to deal with change. Kees van der Heijden (1996), for example, says that change and uncertainty make "optimum strategy" determination impossible. We have neither the time nor the information required for such a calculation. The best we can hope for is what he calls "the most skillful process". The way Peter Schwartz put it in 1991 is that strategic outcomes cannot be known in advance so the sources of competitive advantage cannot be predetermined.

The fast changing business environment is too uncertain for us to find sustainable value in formulas of excellence or competitive advantage. Instead, scenario planning is a technique in which multiple outcomes can be developed, their implications assessed, and their likeliness of occurrence evaluated. According to Pierre Wack, scenario planning is about insight, complexity, and subtlety, not about formal analysis and numbers.

In 1988, Henry Mintzberg looked at the changing world around him and decided it was time to reexamine how strategic management was done. He examined the strategic process and concluded it was much more fluid and unpredictable than people had thought. Because of this, he could not point to one process that could be called strategic planning. Instead he concludes that there are five types of strategies. They are:

- Strategy as plan-a direction, guide, course of action-intention rather than actual
- Strategy as ploy-a maneuver intended to outwit a competitor
- Strategy as pattern-a consistent pattern of past behaviour-realized rather than intended
- Strategy as position-locating of brands, products, or companies within the conceptual framework of consumers or other stakeholders-strategy determined primarily by factors outside the firm
- Strategy as perspective-strategy determined primarily by a master strategist

In 1998, Mintzberg developed these five types of management strategy into 10 "schools of thought". These 10 schools are grouped into three categories. The first group is prescriptive or normative. It consists of the informal design and conception school, the formal planning school, and the analytical positioning school. The second group, consisting of six schools, is more concerned with how strategic management is actually done, rather than prescribing optimal plans or positions.

The six schools are the entrepreneurial, visionary, or great leader school, the cognitive or mental process school, the learning, adaptive, or emergent process school, the power or negotiation school, the corporate culture or collective process school, and the business environment or reactive school. The third and final group consists of one school, the configuration or transformation school, an hybrid of the other schools organized into stages, organizational life cycles, or "episodes".

In 1999, Constantinos Markides also wanted to reexamine the nature of strategic planning itself. He describes strategy formation and implementation as an on-going, never-ending, integrated process requiring continuous reassessment and reformation. Strategic management is planned and emergent, dynamic, and interactive. J. Moncrieff (1999) also stresses strategy dynamics. He recognized that strategy is partially deliberate and partially unplanned. The unplanned element comes from two sources:

emergent strategies (result from the emergence of opportunities and threats in the environment) and Strategies in action (ad hoc actions by many people from all parts of the organization).

Some business planners are starting to use a complexity theory approach to strategy. Complexity can be thought of as chaos with a dash of order. Chaos theory deals with turbulent systems that rapidly become disordered. Complexity is not quite so unpredictable. It involves multiple agents interacting in such a way that a glimpse of structure may appear. Axelrod, R., Holland, J., and Kelly, S. and Allison, M.A., call these systems of multiple actions and reactions complex adaptive systems. Axelrod asserts that rather than fear complexity, business should harness it. He says this can best be done when "there are many participants, numerous interactions, much trial and error learning, and abundant attempts to imitate each others' successes". In 2000, E. Dudik wrote that an organization must develop a mechanism for understanding the source and level of complexity it will face in the future and then transform itself into a complex adaptive system in order to deal with it.

Information-and Technology-driven Strategy

Peter Drucker had theorized the rise of the "knowledge worker" back in the 1950s. He described how fewer workers would be doing physical labour, and more would be applying their minds. In 1984, John Nesbitt theorized that the future would be driven largely by information: companies that managed information well could obtain an advantage, however the profitability of what he calls the "information float" (information that the company had and others desired) would all but disappear as inexpensive computers made information more accessible. Daniel Bell (1985) examined the sociological consequences of information technology, while Gloria Schuck and Shoshana Zuboff looked at psychological factors. Zuboff, in her five year study of eight pioneering corporations made the important distinction between "automating technologies" and "infomating technologies". She studied the effect that both had on individual workers, managers, and organizational structures.

She largely confirmed Peter Drucker's predictions three decades earlier, about the importance of flexible decentralized structure, work teams, knowledge sharing, and the central role of the knowledge worker. Zuboff also detected a new basis for managerial authority, based not on position or hierarchy, but on knowledge (also predicted by Drucker) which she called "participative management".

In 1990, Peter Senge, who had collaborated with Arie de Geus at Dutch Shell, borrowed de Geus' notion of the learning organization, expanded it, and popularized it. The underlying theory is that a company's ability to gather, analyse, and use information is a necessary requirement for business success in the information age. In order to do this, Senge claimed that an organization would need to be structured such that:

- People can continuously expand their capacity to learn and be productive,
- New patterns of thinking are nurtured,
- Collective aspirations are encouraged, and
- People are encouraged to see the "whole picture" together.

Senge identified five disciplines of a learning organization. They are:

- Personal responsibility, self reliance, and mastery – We accept that we are the masters of our own destiny. We make decisions and live with the consequences of them. When a problem needs to be fixed, or an opportunity exploited, we take the initiative to learn the required skills to get it done.
- Mental models – We need to explore our personal mental models to understand the subtle effect they have on our behaviour.
- Shared vision – The vision of where we want to be in the future is discussed and communicated to all. It provides guidance and energy for the journey ahead.
- Team learning – We learn together in teams. This involves a shift from "a spirit of advocacy to a spirit of enquiry".
- Systems thinking – We look at the whole rather than the parts. This is what Senge calls the "Fifth discipline". It is the glue that integrates the other four into a coherent strategy. For an alternative approach to the "learning organization".

customer loyalty is far less important and difficult to maintain as new brands and products emerge all the time.

In such a world, differentiation, as elicudated by Michael Porter, Botten and McManus is the only way to maintain economic or market superiority (i.e., comparative advantage) over competitors. A company must OWN the thing that differentiates it from competitors. Without IP ownership and protection, any product, process or scale advantage can be compromised or entirely lost. Competitors can copy them without fear of economic or legal consequences, thereby eliminating the advantage.

Strategic Decision Making Processes

Will Mulcaster argues that whilst much research and creative thought has been devoted to generating alternative strategies, too little work has been done on what influences the quality of strategic decision making and the effectiveness with which strategies are implemented. For instance, in retrospect it can be seen that the financial crisis of 2008/9 could have been avoided if the banks had paid more attention to the risks associated with their investments, but how should banks change the way in which they make decisions in order to improve the quality of their decisions in the future? Mulcaster's Managing Forces framework addresses this issue by identifying 11 forces that should be incorporated into the processes of decision making and strategic implementation. The 11 forces are:-Time; Opposing forces; Politics; Perception; Holistic effects; Adding value; Incentives; Learning capabilities; Opportunity cost; Risk; Style. The mnemonic "TOPHAILORS" is used to assist in the memory of these forces.

The Psychology of Strategic Management

Several psychologists have conducted studies to determine the psychological patterns involved in strategic management. Typically senior managers have been asked how they go about making strategic decisions. A 1938 treatise by Chester Barnard, that was based on his own experience as a business executive, sees the process as informal, intuitive, non-routinized, and involving primarily oral, 2-way communications. Bernard says "The process is the sensing of the organization as a whole and the total situation relevant to it. It transcends the capacity of merely intellectual methods, and the techniques of discriminating the factors of the situation. The terms pertinent to it are "feeling", "judgement", "sense", "proportion", "balance", "appropriateness". It is a matter of art rather than science." In 1973, Henry Mintzberg found that senior managers typically deal with unpredictable situations so they strategize in *ad hoc,* flexible, dynamic, and implicit ways.. He says, "The job breeds adaptive information-manipulators who prefer the live concrete situation. The manager works in an environment of stimulous-response, and he develops in his work a clear preference for live action." In 1982, John Kotter studied the daily activities of 15 executives and concluded that they spent most of their time developing and working a network of relationships from which they gained general insights and specific details to be used in making strategic decisions. They tended to use "mental road maps" rather than systematic planning techniques.

Daniel Isenberg's 1984 study of senior managers found that their decisions were highly intuitive. Executives often sensed what they were going to do before they could explain why. He claimed in 1986 that one of the reasons for this is the complexity of strategic decisions and the resultant information uncertainty. Shoshana Zuboff (1988) claims that information technology is widening the divide between senior managers (who typically make strategic decisions) and operational level managers (who typically make routine decisions). She claims that prior to the widespread use of computer systems, managers, even at the most senior level, engaged in both strategic decisions and routine administration, but as computers facilitated (She called it "deskilled") routine processes, these activities were moved further down the hierarchy, leaving senior management free for strategic decions making.

In 1977, Abraham Zaleznik identified a difference between leaders and managers. He describes leadershipleaders as visionaries who inspire. They care about substance. Whereas managers are claimed to care about process, plans, and form. He also claimed in 1989 that the rise of the manager was the main factor that caused the decline of American business in the 1970s and 80s.The main difference between leader and manager is that, leader has followers and manager has subordinates. In capitalistic society leaders make decisions and manager usually follow or execute. Lack of leadership is most damaging at the level of strategic management where it can paralyze an entire organization.

According to Corner, Kinichi, and Keats, strategic decision making in organizations occurs at two levels: individual and aggregate. They have developed a model of parallel strategic decision making.

The model identifies two parallel processes both of which involve getting attention, encoding information, storage and retrieval of information, strategic choice, strategic outcome, and feedback. The individual and organizational processes are not independent however. They interact at each stage of the process.

Reasons why strategic plans fail

There are many reasons why strategic plans fail, especially:

- Failure to execute by overcoming the four key organizational hurdles:
  - o Cognitive hurdle
  - o Motivational hurdle
  - o Resource hurdle
  - o Political hurdle.
- Failure to understand the customer:
  - o Why do they buy
  - o Is there a real need for the product
  - o inadequate or incorrect marketing research.
- Inability to predict environmental reaction:
  - o What will competitors do:
    - Fighting brands
    - Price wars.
  - o Will government intervene.
- Over-estimation of resource competence:
  - o Can the staff, equipment, and processes handle the new strategy
  - o Failure to develop new employee and management skills.
- Failure to coordinate:
  - o Reporting and control relationships not adequate
  - o Organizational structure not flexible enough.

- Failure to obtain senior management commitment:
  - o Failure to get management involved right from the start
  - o Failure to obtain sufficient company resources to accomplish task.
- Failure to obtain employee commitment:
  - o New strategy not well explained to employees
  - o No incentives given to workers to embrace the new strategy.
- Under-estimation of time requirements:
  - o No critical path analysis done.
- Failure to follow the plan:
  - o No follow through after initial planning
  - o No tracking of progress against plan
  - o No consequences for above.
- Failure to manage change:
  - o Inadequate understanding of the internal resistance to change
  - o Lack of vision on the relationships between processes, technology and organization.
- Poor communications:
  - o Insufficient information sharing among stakeholders
  - o Exclusion of stakeholders and delegates.

Limitations of Strategic Management

Although a sense of direction is important, it can also stifle creativity, especially if it is rigidly enforced. In an uncertain and ambiguous world, fluidity can be more important than a finely tuned strategic compass. When a strategy becomes internalized into a corporate culture, it can lead to group think. It can also cause an organization to define itself too narrowly. An example of this is marketing myopia.

Many theories of strategic management tend to undergo only brief periods of popularity. A summary of these theories thus inevitably exhibits survivorship bias (itself an area of research in strategic management). Many theories tend either to be too narrow in focus to build a complete corporate strategy on, or too general and abstract to be applicable to specific situations. Populism or faddishness can have an impact on a particular theory's life cycle and may see application in inappropriate circumstances. In 2000, Gary Hamel coined the term strategic convergence to explain the limited scope of the strategies being used by rivals in greatly differing circumstances. He lamented that strategies converge more than they should, because the more successful ones are imitated by firms that do not understand that the strategic process involves designing a custom strategy for the specifics of each situation.

Ram Charan, aligning with a popular marketing tagline, believes that strategic planning must not dominate action. "Just do it!", while not quite what he meant, is a phrase that nevertheless comes to mind when combatting analysis paralysis.

The Linearity Trap

It is tempting to think that the elements of strategic management – (i) reaching consensus on corporate objectives; (ii) developing a plan for achieving the objectives; and (iii) marshalling and allocating the resources required to implement the plan – can be approached sequentially. It would be convenient, in other words, if one could deal first with the noble question of ends, and then address the mundane question of means.

But in the world in which strategies have to be implemented, the three elements are interdependent. Means are as likely to determine ends as ends are to determine means. The objectives that an organization might wish to pursue are limited by the range of feasible approaches to implementation. (There will usually be only a small number of approaches that will not only be technically and administratively possible, but also satisfactory to the full range of organizational stakeholders.) In turn, the range of feasible implementation approaches is determined by the availability of resources.

And so, although participants in a typical "strategy session" may be asked to do "blue sky" thinking where they pretend that the usual constraints – resources, acceptability to stakeholders, administrative feasibility – have been lifted, the fact is that it rarely makes sense to divorce oneself from the environment in which a strategy will have to be implemented. It's probably impossible to think in any meaningful way about strategy in an unconstrained environment. Our brains can't process "boundless possibilities", and the very idea of strategy only has meaning in the context of challenges or obstacles to be overcome. It's at least as plausible to argue that acute awareness of constraints is the very thing that stimulates creativity by forcing us to constantly reassess both means and ends in light of circumstances.

The key question, then, is, "How can individuals, organizations and societies cope as well as possible with... issues too complex to be fully understood, given the fact that actions initiated on the basis of inadequate understanding may lead to significant regret?"

The answer is that the process of developing organizational strategy must be iterative. It involves toggling back and forth between questions about objectives, implementation planning and resources. An initial idea about corporate objectives may have to be altered if there is no feasible implementation plan that will meet with a sufficient level of acceptance among the full range of stakeholders, or because the necessary resources are not available, or both.

Even the most talented manager would no doubt agree that "comprehensive analysis is impossible" for complex problems. Formulation and implementation of strategy must thus occur side-by-side rather than sequentially, because strategies are built on assumptions which, in the absence of perfect knowledge, will never be perfectly correct. Strategic management is necessarily a "repetitive learning cycle [rather than] a linear progression towards a clearly defined final destination." While assumptions can and should be tested in advance, the ultimate test is implementation. You will inevitably need to adjust corporate objectives and/or your approach to pursuing outcomes and/or assumptions about required resources. Thus a strategy will get remade during implementation because "humans rarely can proceed satisfactorily except by learning from experience; and modest probes, serially modified on the basis of feedback, usually are the best method for such learning."

It serves little purpose (other than to provide a false aura of certainty sometimes demanded by corporate strategists and planners) to pretend to anticipate every possible consequence of a corporate decision, every possible constraining or enabling factor, and every possible point of view.

At the end of the day, what matters for the purposes of strategic management is having a clear view – based on the best available evidence and on defensible assumptions – of what it seems possible to accomplish within the constraints of a given set of circumstances.

As the situation changes, some opportunities for pursuing objectives will disappear and others arise. Some implementation approaches will become impossible, while others, previously impossible or unimagined, will become viable.

The essence of being "strategic" thus lies in a capacity for "intelligent trial-and error" rather than linear adherence to finally honed and detailed strategic plans. Strategic management will add little value — indeed, it may well do harm — if organizational strategies are designed to be used as a detailed blueprints for managers. Strategy should be seen, rather, as laying out the general path-but not the precise steps-by which an organization intends to create value.

Strategic management is a question of interpreting, and continuously reinterpreting, the possibilities presented by shifting circumstances for advancing an organization's objectives. Doing so requires strategists to think *simultaneously* about desired objectives, the best approach for achieving them, and the resources implied by the chosen approach. It requires a frame of mind that admits of no boundary between means and ends.

Bibliography

Bhatia, A.K. : *Tourism Development: Principles and Practices,* New Delhi, 1982.

Brown, L.A. : *Innovation Diffusion: A New Perspective,* London and New York, 1981.

Brunt, Paul: *Market Research in Travel and Tourism,* Oxford, Butterworth Heinemann, 1997.

Chakravarti B.K. : *Hotel and Hospitality Management,* A.P.H., Delhi, 2011.

David L: *International Tourism Policy, New York,* Van Nostrand and Reinhold, 1990.

Donald E. : *Public Personnel Management: Contexts and Strategies,* Upper Saddle River, NJ: Prentice Hall, 1998.

Donald M.: *Customer Service in the Hospitality and Tourism Industry,* Englewood Cliffs, Prentice Hall, 1994.

Fesenmaier D., Klein, S. : *Information & Communication Technologies in Tourism,* Springer-Verlag, Wien-New York, 2000.

Frechtling, Douglas C: *Practical Tourism Forecasting,* Oxford, Butterworth Heinemann, 1996.

Getz, D.P. : *Effects of Tourism on the Host Population, A Case Study of Tourism and Regional Development in the Badenoch-Strathspey District of the Scottish Highlands,* Edinburgh: University of Edinburgh, 1980.

Horner, S. and Swarbrooke, J.: *Marketing Tourism, Hospitality and Leisure in Europe,* London, International Thomson Business Press, 1996.

Judi Radice: *Restaurant & Food Graphics,* Glen Cove, PBC International, 1994.

Kaae, B.C. : *The Perceptions of Tourists and Residents of Sustainable Tourism Principles and Environmental Initiatives*, Tourism, Recreation and Sustainability, New York, 2001.

Kotler, Philip: *Marketing for Hospitality and Tourism*: New Jersey, Prentice-Hall, 1998.

Larkham, P J: *Building a New Heritage: Tourism, Culture & Identity in the New Europe*, London, Routledge,1994.

Leivadi, S: *Sociology of Tourism, The: Theoretical And Empirical Investigations*, London, Retailed, 1996.

Lewis, Robert C.: *Cases in Hospitality Marketing and Management*, New York, John Wiley, 1997.

Lucas, Rosemary E.: *Managing Employee Relations in the Hotel and Catering Industry*, London, Cassell, 1995.

Madhukar Manoj : *Hospitality Industries in Next Millennium*, Rajat, Delhi, 2001.

Marcussen, Carl H. : *Internet Distribution of European Travel and Tourism Services*, Research Centre of Bornholm, Denmark, 1999.

Martin, B.S. : *The Efficacy of Growth Machine Theory in Explaining Resident Perceptions of Community Tourism Development*, Clemson University, 1996.

McNicol, B.J. : *Views of Residents, Developers and Government Planners About Tourists and Tourism Resort Developments in Canmore, Alberta*, The University of Galgary, Alberta, 1996.

Moscardo, G. : *Tourism Community Analysis*, London and New York: Routledge, 1999.

Murphy, P.E. : *Tourism: A Community Approach*, London: Methuen, 1985.

Nijkamp, Peter: *Sustainable Tourism Development*, Aldershot, Avebury, 1995.

Norman G.: *Hotel, Restaurant, and Travel Law: A Preventive Approach*, Albany, Delmar Publishers, 1993.

Peter J.: *College & University Foodservice Management Standards*, Westport, AVI Pub. Company, 1985.

Prentice, R: *Conceptualising The Experiences of Heritage Tourists*, 1997.

Ratti Manish : *Hospitality Management : Theories and Practices,* Rajat Pub, Delhi, 2007.

Richards, G. : *Culture, Crafts and Tourism: A Vital Relationship,* Tilburg: Atlas, 1999.

Robert, C.: *Cases in Hospitality Marketing and Management,* New York, John Wiley, 1997.

Sabharwal Rajiv : *Tourism and Hospitality Management in Liberalised Era,* Pacific, Delhi, 2011.

Sharma Sunil : *Planning and Development of Tourism and Hospitality,* Rajat Pub, Delhi, 2007.

Shrivastava Atul : *Modern Hospitality and Tourism Management,* Centrum Press, Delhi, 2010.

Simmons, D. : *Community Adaptation to Tourism: Comparisons between Rotorua and Kaikoura,* New Zealand. Tourism Management, 2002.

Slinn, Judy A: *Tourism: Management of Facilities,* London, Pitman: M & E, 1993.

Smith, V.L. : *Hosts and Guests: The Anthropology of Tourism,* Oxford: Blackwell, 1978.

Swarbrooke, J.: *Marketing Tourism, Hospitality and Leisure in Europe,* London, International Thomson Business Press, 1996.

Tribe, John *Corporate Strategy for Tourism, London,* International Thomson Business Press, 1997.

Var, Turgut: *Tourism Planning,* London, Retailed, 2002.

Vaughan, D.R. : *Segmentation of Cretan Residents According to their Perceptions of Tourism Development,* London: University of Westminster, 1999.

Index

❑❑❑